Survivors of Atlantis

Their Impact on the World

FRANK JOSEPH

Bear & Company
Rochester, Vermont

Bear & Company
One Park Street
Rochester, Vermont 05767
www.InnerTraditions.com

LIBRARY OF CONGRESS CATALOGING-IN-PUBLICATION DATA
Joseph, Frank.
Survivors of Atlantis : their impact on the world / Frank Joseph.
p. cm.
Includes bibliographical references.
ISBN 1-59143-040-2 (pbk.)
1. Atlantis. I. Title.

GN751.J694 2004
001.94—dc22
2004008576

Printed and bound in Canada at Transcontinental

10   9   8   7   6   5   4   3   2

Text design and layout by Virginia Scott Bowman
This book was typeset in Sabon and Avenir with Fascinate as the display typeface

Survivors
of
Atlantis

*To N. Thomas Miller, in whose art the
spirit of Atlantis lives*

CONTENTS

A MILLION TONS OF COPPER

*There have been and will be many different calamities to
destroy mankind, the greatest of them by fire and water.*

PLATO, *TIMAEUS*

Atlantis. No name is so evocative for millions of people around the
world after thousands of years. It has lent its identity to a space
shuttle and is featured in major motion pictures and television pro-
grams. It figures into the titles of more new books published about the
sunken realm than ever before, adding to an estimated 2,500 volumes
and magazine articles already in print on the subject. Mere allusion to
it among conventional scholars is enough to elicit their emphatic con-
demnation of any "mythomaniac" who suggests some basis in fact for
the lost city. But despite more than one hundred years of official oppo-
sition, popular fascination with Atlantis, as well as intense interest on
the part of an international circle of mostly independent researchers,
demonstrates the durability of general belief that it was once a reality.
At the beginning of the twenty-first century that circle has grown to an
unprecedented magnitude as an accumulating body of hard scientific
evidence is rapidly transforming theory into fact.

For all the fame of Atlantis, most people know very little about it.
They presume it was an oceanic kingdom that long ago dominated
much of the globe before a natural catastrophe sank it beneath the sea,
followed by the escape of some survivors to various parts of the planet.
Many Atlantologists believe civilization first arose on the "continent"
of Atlantis at least a dozen millennia ago and was destroyed around

1

9500 B.C.E. by a great flood. Both skeptics and true believers, however, are in danger of being outdated by this book. It is not a rehash of my earlier investigation, *The Destruction of Atlantis,* but a presentation of entirely new material on the same subject. The Atlantean war, four global cataclysms, and the fate of survivors in various parts of the world are described here for the first time.

Survivors of Atlantis takes its cue from a conference of leading scientific authorities that met in Cambridge, England. During the summer of 1997 experts in a variety of academic disciplines, from geology and astrophysics to archaeoastronomy and oceanography, combined their independent findings to paint a picture of the past radically different from the familiar image taught by generations of mainstream educators. The new evidence they presented was as startling as it was convincing. They demonstrated that close passes made by a series of several comets inflicted four different cataclysms on our planet during the first epoch of human history. These celestial events and the disasters they generated are not merely the conjectures of theorists. A wealth of material proof confirms that the worldwide calamities did indeed take place, and that the last one pushed civilization to the brink of extinction.

Studying dozens of presentations from the Cambridge conference, I was forcibly reminded that numerous cultures around the world remembered four major floods followed by mass migrations. This tradition was shared by such diverse peoples as the Incas of Peru, the Celtic Irish, the classical Greeks, the Aztecs of Mexico, and many others. Moreover, there is a close fit between their folk memories and what science now recognizes as a quartet of natural catastrophes that ravaged the earth beginning more than five thousand years ago. But when the evidence of physical archaeology is added to myth, astronomy, and geology, a new light on the ancient past suddenly winks on. Its brightness has illuminated the hitherto unseen causes that brought history into existence. Clearly exposed is a common theme that over and over again threads together and makes sense of all the diverse twists and turns in a vast human drama: Atlantis. The name is as inescapable as it is powerfully revealing.

Connecting that sunken realm to four separate global calamities that we now know occurred explains the beginning and development of civilization, while simultaneously defining Atlantis within the credible parameters of real history, not speculative fantasy. It suffered not one but several different catastrophes, each one separated by many centuries, until a fourth destruction finally obliterated the kingdom. *Survivors of Atlantis* describes these individual events for the first time, elucidating them via traditions from Egypt, Mesopotamia, Morocco, the Canary Islands, Ireland, Wales, Scandinavia, pre-Columbian North America, Mesoamerica, and preconquest South America. Many of their Atlantean flood myths about the sunken realm have never before been made available to a general audience, but are presented here to humanize the scientific evidence. After all, the men and women of preclassical times were eyewitnesses to cataclysms that repeatedly devastated their world, disasters they chronicled in an imperishable medium. Papyri burn; words carved in stone erode; clay tablets crumble. But a vitally important message wrapped in myth endures over time like the body of an insect preserved in amber.

Survivors of Atlantis relates another story that has not yet been told, that of the war Plato said the Atlanteans launched in a bold bid to conquer the world. Their military adventure, previously neglected by historians, was intimately connected with and actually determined by the natural calamities that eventually overwhelmed them. The chaos humankind brought about on Earth was mirrored in the angry heavens. In this regard *Survivors of Atlantis* is a companion volume to my first investigation of the subject, which touched on the war but did not detail it.

The Destruction of Atlantis focused on the last moments of that doomed civilization, because those moments were nearest to us in time and therefore more easily documented. Readers who assumed Atlantis was already many millennia old at the time of its demise around 10,000 B.C.E. were surprised to learn that the city met its ultimate fate just 3,200 years ago. The book's purpose, however, was not to discuss Atlantean origins or age, but to explain a final annihilating event in the context of the Bronze Age. With its sudden end around 1200 B.C.E., preclassical civilization everywhere collapsed or went into irreversible decline, from pharaonic Egypt and Homeric Greece to the Hittite empire and China's Shang dynasty. Atlantis was one more victim of the worldwide catastrophe. Like the others, it was an identifiably Bronze Age city, according to Plato's description.

His dialogues *Timaeus* and *Critias*, composed around 340 B.C.E., contain the earliest surviving narratives of their kind. They portray the

Atlanteans as preeminent mariners and metalsmiths who sailed great distances and manufactured *orichalcum,* an exceptionally high-grade copper that Plato reported was no longer available in his day. Through their export of orichalcum, he said, the Atlanteans became fabulously wealthy and powerful. His characterization of them as prosperous seafaring miners is the piece of evidence connecting two great historical enigmas.

For more than ten thousand years the North American continent was sparsely inhabited by Paleo-Indian tribes of nomadic hunter-gatherers who followed migrating animal herds and possessed little in the way of material culture. In the Upper Great Lakes region they occasionally picked up pieces of "float copper" left behind by retreating glaciers and then annealed, or cold-hammered, the chunks into trinkets with which to adorn themselves. Then, around 3000 B.C.E., an ambitious mining enterprise opened with great suddenness along the Lake Superior shores of the Michigan Peninsula and on Isle Royale in Lake Superior. Over the next twenty-two centuries, a minimum of half a billion pounds of the world's highest-grade copper were excavated from five thousand pit mines, some of them sunk sixty feet down through solid rock.

As recounted in my 1995 book *Atlantis in Wisconsin,* an average of 1,000 to 1,200 tons of ore per pit were removed, each yielding about 100,000 pounds of copper. To achieve such prodigious yields the ancient miners employed simple techniques that enabled them to work with speed and efficiency. They created intense fires atop a copper-bearing vein, heated the rock to very high temperatures, and then doused it with water. The rock fractured, after which stone tools were employed to extract the copper. Deep in the pits a vinegar mixture was used to speed spalling (breaking the rock in layers) and reduce smoke. How such temperatures were applied is part of the enigma. The bottom of a fire sitting on a rock face is its coolest area. Even especially hot cane fires would take a long time to sufficiently heat the vein for spalling, if they succeeded at all. How the prehistoric miners directed concentrated acetylene temperatures to the ground is a disturbing question modern technology is unable to answer.

Much of their high technology still survives, however. Masses of copper rock weighing 6,000 pounds and more were excavated and

Identified by his full-length garment, a member of the Sea People carries an "oxhide" copper ingot in this representation from a stand for a Cypriot incense burner, circa 1200 B.C.E. According to Plato, the Atlanteans were the foremost copper barons of the Bronze Age. (Bodrum Archaeology Museum, Turkey)

raised on well-made crib work, stone and timber platforms used to lift ponderous material to the surface. These cribs were usually built of shaped boughs and structured like a log cabin that could be raised by a series of levers and wedges. An example of the massive proportions of the rock mined in ancient Michigan is the Ontonagon Boulder. Removed to the Smithsonian Institution around the turn of the nineteenth century, it weighs 5 tons. A 6-ton copper mass was discovered *in situ* on one of the raised cribs, where it appears to have been abandoned. Partially trimmed of its spurs and projecting points, it is 10 feet long, 3 feet wide, and 2 feet thick. Could the miners who manipulated tons of raw copper on Michigan's Upper Peninsula have been the same people who similarly lifted the stone blocks of the Great Pyramid?

Incredibly, thousands of tools used by the ancient miners have been found. As long ago as 1840 ten wagonloads of their stone hammers were taken from a single location near Rockland, Michigan. Those in McCargo Cove, on the north shore of Isle Royale, amounted to 1,000 tons. Nor were these hammers crudely manufactured. According to Roy W. Drier, a mid-twentieth-century expert on the ancient copper mines:

> In examining the tools that have been recovered, one is involuntarily amazed at the perfection of workmanship and at their identity of form with the tools made for like purposes and used in the present day, the prototypes of the implements of our present civilization. The sockets of the spears, chisels, arrowheads, knives and fleshers are, in nearly all instances, formed as symmetrically and perfectly as could be done by the best smith of the present day, with all the improved aids of his art (DuTemple 1962, 27).

The mines themselves were not simple pits but were outfitted with modernlike irrigation systems to flush out debris and fill via substantial trenches, some as long as 500 feet. To William P. F. Ferguson, an early and still-respected authority on North America's ancient mining, "The work is of a colossal nature, and amounted to the turning over of the whole formation to its depth and moving many cubic acres—it would not be seriously extravagant to say *cubic miles*—of rock."

The diggings extended over 150 miles on the Lake Superior coast through three Michigan counties, and ran for 40 miles at Isle Royale. If all the prehistoric pit mines were combined, they would form a trench more than 5 miles long, 20 feet wide, and 30 feet deep. Then, just as abruptly as the mines opened, they closed around 1200 B.C.E. Octave DuTemple, the leading authority on these pits, wonders,

> Why did these miners leave their operations and implements as though planning on taking up their labors the next day, and yet mysteriously never returned? Indian legends make no mention of these mining operations, which were of a magnificence and a magnitude worthy of being included in the history of any race. The legends do mention that a white race was driven out far back in the Indians' history (1962, 59).

The Indians DuTemple refers to are the Menominee, with ancestral roots in Michigan's Upper Peninsula. Their folk traditions speak of the

Marine Men, fair-skinned sailors who arrived over the sea in large numbers to "wound Earth Mother by digging out her shiny bones," a poetic allusion to copper. The enigma of prehistoric mining in North America expands when we realize that a half-billion or more pounds of copper vanished. "Where this copper went is still a mystery," according to DuTemple. In the words of Dr. James P. Scherz, professor emeritus at the University of Wisconsin in Madison,

> One of the basic questions that hasn't been answered yet is, where did the copper from Lake Superior go? All of the copper found in the mounds, although of a large amount, is but a small percentage of that mined. The Europeans have a comparable problem. Where did all their copper come from? The Europeans were in a copper trading frenzy from 3000 to 1000 B.C.E., like we are now about oil, because copper drove their economy (Joseph 1995, 54).

Scherz has introduced the other side of the enigma. The Bronze Age began in Europe and the Near East because bronze made weapons and tools superior to those of copper or stone because it is harder, more resilient, and better able to hold a sharp edge than copper, and lighter than stone. To manufacture bronze, copper must be combined with tin and zinc. The higher the grade of copper, the better the weapon or tool. The ancient Old World never possessed sufficient sources of high-grade copper to sustain the mass production of good-quality bronzework engaged in by every kingdom throughout the civilized world. Where did their metalsmiths find enough high-grade copper for the millions of spears, swords, rams, chisels, drills, statues, cauldrons, altars, temple doors, and all the other innumerable objects they made? Evidence that is more than circumstantial points to the Upper Peninsula of Michigan. It was there that the Marine Men not only excavated the world's largest supplies of high-grade copper, but also mined tin, that other essential component of bronze production.

Strategically located midway between North America's massive copper-mining enterprise and the ancient Old World's hunger for copper lay Atlantis, famed for its sailors and miners. The coincidence of copper mining and Old World copper use becomes even clearer when their time parameters are compared: Copper and tin mining began on

Michigan's Upper Peninsula right before 3000 B.C.E., just as the Bronze Age was beginning in Europe and the Near East. Both North American mining and the ancient Old World Bronze Age ended simultaneously around 1200 B.C.E., the original lunar date, as described below, for the final destruction of Atlantis.

Plato states that the destruction of Atlantis occurred 8,300 years earlier. But what makes us imagine that his conception of time back in the fourth century B.C.E. was the same as ours? Indeed, it was very different! No one knows for certain what he meant when he reported that Atlantis was destroyed 11,500 years ago. What were those "years" to him? Solar, lunar, sidereal, astrological, generational? All these measurements and more were used throughout classical times, and scholars have long argued about which system Plato used. I suggest four primary reasons that he referred to the lunar calendar: (1) It places Atlantis in the Late Bronze Age, when its citadel, as described by Plato, typified the monumental construction taking place in the Mediterranean area at that time. The same citadel could not have been built before 3000 B.C.E. and would have been as out of place at the end of the last Ice Age as a skyscraper in the middle of the Bronze Age. (2) The final destruction of Atlantis coincided with the simultaneous collapse of the ancient Old World's Bronze Age and North America's copper mining. (3) The Egyptian priests from whom the story of Atlantis was originally obtained used a lunar system. (4) Science now recognizes that our planet had a very close brush with a debris-ridden comet around 1200 B.C.E. The earth was subjected to a global catastrophe that annihilated other contemporary civilizations, including that of Atlantis.

Fresh evidence compels us to abandon preconceived notions of the lost civilization as an identifiably Bronze Age phenomenon flourishing incongruously during the last Ice Age. Conditions then were hardly typified by the balmy climate Plato described. We are now able to determine when Atlantis was finally destroyed as well as something of its history for nearly two thousand years before this final event. *Survivors of Atlantis* combines science and folk tradition to tell us what became of those who escaped disaster.

Just when Atlantis was founded, however, and how long it flourished are uncertain; we cannot see events prior to the first cataclysm of 3100 B.C.E. By then Atlantis, from all indications, had already grown into a highly developed society with a sophisticated material culture whose growth from its Stone Age origins must have required many centuries. We may, however, look to contemporary prehistory in western Europe for answers. Paleolithic and Neolithic epochs evolved throughout the fourth millennium B.C.E. Humans were more proficient mariners then—and long before then, modern scholars now know. The Red Paint People of North America and Red Ochre People of northern Europe were almost certainly the same proto-Atlanteans who navigated transatlantic voyages on a regular basis as long ago as seven thousand years. These early sailors and their descendants probably brought their megalithic skills to the island later known as Atlas, after its chief volcano. The fertile soil for which the volcano was responsible and the island's temperate climate facilitated agriculture and settled growth, the basis for civilization. Around 3500 B.C.E. a community that had developed between the south coast and the mountain reached population density sufficient to blossom into a city—the "daughter of Atlas," Atlantis. In Sanskrit Atlas means "the up-holder." Six thousand or more years ago it may have simply been synonymous with "mountain," leading some researchers to wonder if the *A* in our modern alphabet is actually a surviving ideogram from Atlantean times which signified a mountain standing in the sea. In any case, Atlantis could have reached high levels of culture comparable to if not more advanced than those achieved in its contemporary Mesopotamia during the mid-fourth millennium B.C.E.

But all this is speculation based on inference. *Survivors of Atlantis* focuses instead on each of four global cataclysms as uncovered by science and graphically related in the folk memories of peoples whose shores were washed by the Atlantic Ocean. In the course of these accounts, the lost empire comes into clearer focus than ever before. The legacy of its enduring influence on our current civilization stands out for the first time in bold relief—and we come to realize that the story of Atlantis is the story of the world.

1

ATLANTIS AT WAR

*When luxury prevails, fire consumes the world and water
washes it away.*

BURMESE PROVERB

The First World War did not begin on July 21, 1914, in Serbia. It began more than three thousand years earlier on the northwestern shores of what is now Turkey. Like its twentieth-century counterpart, that ancient conflict involved virtually all the peoples of the civilized world in mutual slaughter. Their mighty navies spread a wake of blood from the Atlantic Ocean to the eastern Mediterranean Sea. Battlefields across North Africa and the Near East were heaped with mounds of dead soldiers and civilians. The capital cities of rival empires went up in flames while millions of uprooted people migrated for their lives. Never before had there been a military confrontation of this magnitude or ferocity. Whole civilizations disappeared and human races were exterminated. No one was spared. An entire era collapsed, wiping out millennia of cultural achievement. In its aftermath a dark age descended over the smoldering ruins of humankind, obscuring even its memory for the next five hundred years.

Although this enormous tragedy is largely forgotten, it was recorded by four of the leading personalities of their time—two Egyptians and two Greeks. Each one documented a particular phase of the immense struggle as they knew or experienced it. Combined, their separate but complementary accounts reveal the conflict in its panoramic entirety.

The earliest version is found among the royal records of Merenptah, a Nineteenth Dynasty king who defended Egypt against the Hanebu, or Sea People. He defeated their invasion of the Nile Delta in 1229 B.C.E., but they returned in greater force forty years later. Again the Hanebu were vanquished, this time by Merenptah's successor, Ramses III, who raised a victory temple to his triumph. The sprawling complex, known today as Medinet Habu (figs. 1.1 and 1.2), was built around 1187 B.C.E. at West Thebes in the Upper Nile Valley and followed the finest tradition of New Kingdom monumentality. On its walls was inscribed a vivid eyewitness account of the pharaoh's military success, including testimony from captured Sea People as well as illustrations of uniforms, weapons, and ships.

Their confrontations in Egypt were contemporary with and part of the Trojan War described by Homer. His *Iliad*, written some five centuries after the events it depicts, is the poetic transcription of oral accounts that had already been known for generations. Long regarded as fantasy, Ilios, the Trojan capital, was discovered in 1871, together with physical evidence of the war associated with its name.

Fig. 1.1. Medinet Habu, the victory temple of Ramses III, where his account of Egypt's war with Atlantis is still preserved in stone.

Fig. 1.2. A scale model reconstruction of Medinet Habu depicts the temple as it nears the end of its construction around 1185 B.C.E. On the far wall a gigantic Ramses III is portrayed as he leads defeated Atlantean Sea People into captivity, their hands bound over their heads. (Milwaukee Public Museum)

Around 355 B.C.E. the Athenian philosopher Plato composed two dialogues, *Timaeus* and *Critias*, which relate the story of outside aggression against the Mediterranean world. He tells how Atlantean naval and land forces conquered western Italy and most of North Africa. They went on to menace Egypt but were finally overcome by a Greek coalition. In the midst of this debacle, the imperial city of Atlantis was destroyed by a natural disaster.

Merenptah, Ramses III, Homer, and Plato each described the same war from different perspectives. Nor were they its only historians. Native Americans from New England to the Yucatán Peninsula and Andes Mountains told of a great flood from which their forefathers escaped after a terrific war. A synthesis of these scattered sources from both sides of the Atlantic Ocean provides a complete picture of the conflict for the first time. It is revealed as a seminal clash of arms that not only brought an entire age to a fiery close, but laid the early foundations upon which our modern world still stands.

The origins of that gigantic contest foreshadowed it by nearly twenty centuries. Near the close of the fourth millennium B.C.E. civilization on the island of Atlas had risen to unprecedented levels of sophistication. The cultural and technological achievements of its inhabitants were far in advance of anything elsewhere in the world. Every people has a national ethic that defines its identity, and the Atlanteans were no different. They were peace loving and virtuous, proud of their singular accomplishments as architects, irrigationists, medical practitioners, astronomers, and sailors. But their roots went back to the Old Stone Age and the subterranean mysticism of its painted caves. They preserved and nurtured deeply ancestral beliefs that emphasized the recurring cycles of a fundamentally just natural order. Humans, like all living things, belonged to this eternal repetition of birth, maturity, decline, death, and rebirth. Behaving in concert with the perceived patterns of life created a balanced society wherein outward material greatness reflected an inner spiritual accord.

But that harmony and its primordial worldview were shattered in 3100 B.C.E. A passing comet or series of comets rained down a barrage of meteoric debris on the world, igniting widespread geologic upheavals. Beset by fire from the heavens and seismic violence beneath their feet, the Atlanteans witnessed the breakup and partial inundation of their sacred homeland. With the convulsions of sky, sea, and earth, thousands perished as civilization crashed about them in ruins. When the violence passed survivors beheld a landscape transfigured by disaster. Many despaired of ever reconstructing their homeland and fled to distant parts of the world, away from a place obviously cursed by the gods. Atlantean society suffered a brain drain as most of its leading thinkers joined mass migrations to the Nile Valley and Mesopotamia. In these regions they cooperated with local inhabitants, sharing their technology and spirituality to spark new dynasties and cities. In the process their identity merged with that of the native populations, giving birth to the hybrid peoples and cultures of pharaonic Egypt and metropolitan Sumer. Over time the Atlanteans were only dimly remembered in foundation legends of the Followers of Horus or in *The Epic of Gilgamesh*.

Other survivors chose to stay, clear away the rubble, and build a new civilization on the broken remains of the old. In the midst of their restoration work, however, they were vulnerable to outside aggression. Foreign militarists took advantage of the traditionally amicable islanders' distress, even going so far as to conquer them, if only temporarily. These humiliations helped bring about a primal alteration in the Atlantean psyche. The harsh realities of foreign intimidation and occupation in addition to the trauma of a natural catastrophe gradually persuaded the islanders to abandon the peaceful doctrines of harmony and humanity they inherited from their ancestors.

Another influential factor contributed to their change of attitude: wealth. Some survivors of the cataclysm sailed across the open sea to build new lives for themselves in distant lands. Their transatlantic flight took them to the shores of North America. There they were met by native inhabitants wearing the most extraordinary copper ornaments the Atlanteans had ever seen. When questioned about the source of the metal, the Indians took them a thousand miles inland to the Great Lakes region of Michigan's Upper Peninsula. The world's highest-grade specimens littered the ground in the form of float copper left behind millennia before by retreating glaciers and since picked up by tribal peoples as trinkets. The foreigners, however, valued the enormous copper veins along the shores of Lake Superior far more highly. Already experienced prospectors, they knew that such remnants indicated subterranean riches.

They hurried back to the island of Atlas, which was still recovering from the disaster of 3100 B.C.E., and told their countrymen about the mineral abundance across the sea. Returning to the Upper Peninsula as miners, not refugees, they began mining on a truly Atlantean scale. Millions of tons of earth were excavated to dig out tons of copper. Hundreds of thousands of copper chunks and boulders were smelted into ingots for shipment to the island of Atlas, where they were combined with zinc and tin. Thus the Bronze Age was born.

The Atlanteans cornered the market on what Plato called orichalcum—the highest-grade copper on earth—the irreplaceable element in bronze production. Every ruler in the civilized world became a customer of these oceanic metal barons. No king could defend his realm against the bronze weapons of an opponent if his own armed forces were not so outfitted. Bronze made superior tools as well, and proclaimed the wealth and power of a monarch who sheeted his walls or city gates with it. Bronze was the nuclear fission of its day: Not to possess it disqualified a people from the league of civilized societies—and the Atlanteans were its sole brokers. As a consequence, the riches of the world flowed into their island, altering it and its people forever.

Already skilled mariners, they built a strong navy in defense of the secret sea lanes to North America's copper country. Mighty ships not only carried cargoes of the mineral but fought piracy and competition, for the Atlanteans' prosperity depended on their monopoly on orichalcum. They established colonies from Yucatán and Colombia to the British Isles, Iberia, and North Africa—including other Atlantic islands such as the Azores and Canaries—to further exploit local resources of food, exotic materials, precious woods, luxury items, and other trade goods.

Long after the Atlantean land had recovered from its first brush with disaster, another cometary catastrophe struck in 2193 B.C.E. As before, large numbers of inhabitants fled the mother country, but this time they mostly migrated to its nine other affiliated kingdoms and various colonies spread out on both sides of the Atlantic Ocean, thereby strengthening the empire. The capital city was badly damaged, but restoration began at once—though significantly, some of the Atlantic lands collapsed beneath the sea amid spectacular vulcanism, causing new waves of immigration to wash over the shores of continents on both sides of the world. Nevertheless, the Atlanteans never lost their controlling grip on the Bronze Age they had created.

For the next six hundred years, the Michigan mines yielded millions of additional tons of copper for an insatiable market. While a new materialism may have overshadowed traditional spirituality in Atlantis, its people were commercially, not militarily, aggressive. Their fleets and armies stood guard over all colonial holdings and defended the homeland from any outside threat, but conquest was achieved through economics, not force of arms. For most of the first half of the second millennium B.C.E. the Atlanteans achieved unprecedented levels of prosperity and all the culture wealth could afford. This civilized idyll endured until the return of the "fire from heaven" in 1628 B.C.E. Yet again, the world was blasted by the worst effects of a killer comet raining down flaming boulders on a defenseless humanity. The Mid-Atlantic Ridge writhed under the celestial assault, sending seismic shock waves throughout the Atlantean lands.

As twice before in their long history, the Atlanteans became acquainted with devastation and migration. Their city suffered, but in the rebuilding of it this time there was a noticeable alteration. Long ago the city of Atlantis had risen upon the Neolithic ruins of a sacred site, but with each increase in population it continued to expand, eventually becoming an imperial metropolis. Now its military bearing was obvious in the circles of water that served as protective moats for artificial islands and in the high walls studded with watchtowers. The innermost ring of land, encircled by others, became the imperial residence, a busy headquarters of generals and admirals, together with parade grounds and barracks for sailors and marines. A new harbor, the largest, was built exclusively for warships. The capital's beefed-up defenses suggested concern for new potential dangers, perhaps even a different, more aggressive foreign policy. In fact, these changes reflected a shift in conditions on the other side of the world.

The cataclysm of 1628 B.C.E. had done its worst in the eastern Mediterranean Sea, where it triggered the volcanic island of Thera, modern Santorini, to explode with the force of a major nuclear event. Although civilization was not wiped out in the Aegean, it did totter, and there was a reshuffling of the political deck. Previously, Minoan Crete dominated this part of the world with its mercantile fleets, but now its sailors encountered serious competitors. The natural disaster had destabilized much of the region, generating a sharp rise in piracy from Cyprus, Rhodes, and the Cyclades Islands. Hardly less piratical, Mycenaeans from the Greek mainland eroded the fringes of the Minoans' commercial enterprise through growing coercion and plunder. Eventually their intimidation escalated into invasion, as indicated by the introduction of a new language, Linear B, in Crete.

The Greek takeover alarmed another people living near the shores of northwestern Asia Minor in today's Anatolia, or Turkey. The Trojans operated their own empire from a renowned city, Ilios, perched atop a hill that afforded superb views of all approaches, particularly those from the sea. The capital was a model of in-depth defense, its residents literally locked behind militarily engineered walls bristling with watchtowers and an array of antisiege weapons manned day and night. But the inhabitants of Ilios were not paranoid. They had good reason to fear the outside world. Their city had been sacked once before, and although that defeat occurred in the deep past, the Trojans were now richer than ever, primarily through their control of the Dardanelles, the straits that allowed sole access to lucrative markets for European trade around the Black Sea. Keenly aware of their strategic importance, the Trojans charged duty to merchants seeking a passage.

Resulting revenues filled the coffers of Ilios to overflowing, attracting allies who hoped to cash in on the city's prosperity and others who despised the high tariffs imposed on them for the privilege of sailing through the Dardanelles. The foremost of these competitors had just stepped forward with the seizure of Crete. Its takeover added immensely to the Mycenaeans' already far-flung acquisitions. As early as the sixteenth century B.C.E., their commercial reach extended through southwestern France across the Narbonne-Carcassone-Loire route to the Atlantic Ocean itself and into Cornwall. There they came into direct competition with the Atlanteans over a sensitive issue—the mining of tin, so essential to bronze production, which the kings of Atlantis considered their own monopoly.

The usurpation of Minoan trade, in which Ilios had been actively participating for centuries, by hostile Greek entrepreneurs threatened the Trojans, and they looked for helpful allies. Their mighty neighbor to the east, the Hittite emperor, was amicably disposed to Wilion, as he referred to the capital of Ilios, but was fixated on Egypt, his great rival in northern Syria, where serious trouble was brewing over spheres of influence between the two superpowers, the Egyptian and Hittite empires. The last thing he wanted was a diversion in the Aegean, where Hittite interests did not seem at issue.

Trojan emissaries had better luck in the west. Their foundation myth, after all, described them as descended from Dardanus, son of Electra, the daughter of Atlas, and, consequently, an Atlantis (meaning "daughter of Atlas"). True, but more recently, the Atlanteans were irritated by Mycenaean encroachment in Britain. Additionally, a pact with Troy would open up the Mediterranean to Atlantis. If it was granted favored-nation status, its merchants would have access to the Black Sea markets on the other side of the Dardanelles.

The Atlanto-Trojan agreement sent shock waves through the rest of the civilized world, especially after Libya, Egypt's perennial enemy, joined this pact. Pharaoh Ramses II hastily concluded his own alliance with the Hittites, who had just bested him during the epic battle at Kadesh, in northern Syria. The Hittites were no less appalled by the implications of Atlantean ambitions in the Mediterranean, especially if the Mycenaeans were either defeated or forced to join the Sea People, a name under which both Egyptians and Hittites grouped all participants of the growing confederation. During 1283 B.C.E., copies of their mutual-assistance pact were prominently displayed in their respective capitals at Thebes, in the Upper Nile Valley, and in Hattusas, in central Anatolia. After more than thirty-two centuries, visitors to the great temple at Luxor may still see its text incised into the city's monumental pylons, together with carved illustrations of the threatening Sea People specifically cited in the treaty.

The unexpected diplomatic turnabout between these erstwhile opponents, the Egyptians and the Hittites, alarmed the Atlanteans, and their military machine went into high gear. An entire section of the fourth part of Plato's *Critias* describes the armed forces of Atlantis at the zenith of its power. The land army was led by sixty thousand officers commanding "an unlimited supply of men in the mountains and other parts of the country." These foot soldiers were supplemented by ten thousand chariots, each carrying some variation of two hoplites (heavily armed foot soldiers), two archers, two slingers, three lightly armed stone throwers, three javelin men, or four marines. The navy was the largest on earth, with twelve hundred warships, supply vessels, and transports. These figures, however, pertain only to Atlantis itself and do not include the nine affiliated kingdoms that composed the rest of the empire. Altogether their forces were enough to frighten even the Egyptians and Hittites into a mutual-assistance pact.

But the Atlanteans, for all their fleets and armies, were still uncomfortable with the odds, stepping up the recruitment of confederates in Italy, Sardinia, Sicily, and Palestine. "They had not one speech and one language," Homer says of the Sea People, "but a confusion of tongues, since they were called from many lands." Lydia, Luvia, Kizzuwatna, and almost all the other coastal kingdoms of western Asia Minor joined the Trojan camp. One of Troy's favorite princes, Ilioneus, boasted, "Many nations and many races have sought alliance with us, and have wished to unite us with them." At this time the Atlantean empire, through its colonies, affiliated kingdoms, and allies, now stretched from the shores of Middle and South America in the west across the ocean, bearing its own name to the British Isles, Iberia, Italy, the whole of North Africa to the Egyptian frontier, and the west coast of Asia Minor. It embraced millions of people over many thousands of miles, a political network more vast than Rome's and unequaled for the next three thousand years, until the rise of British imperialism. As Ilioneus marveled, it was "an empire which was once the mightiest ever seen by the sun in all his journeying from the uttermost edge of the sky."

Meanwhile, Hittite Emperor Tudhaliyas IV tallied up allies for his royal client in the Amurri kingdom of Cyprus: "The kings who are of equal rank to me are the king of Egypt, the king of Babylon, the king of Assyria, and the king of Ahhiyawa [Homer's Achaea, Mycenaean Greece]." The combatants were being lined up for an international confrontation the like of which had never before amassed so many different armies and navies over such vast distances.

The Mycenaeans were having far less success in convincing their fellow Greeks that a universal alliance was necessary. But they had been assisted by acts of piracy (from which the Mycenaeans were themselves not immune) committed by Trojan privateers, whose depredations began to have a deleterious effect on the whole Peloponnese. There was, moreover, disconcerting news from Troy itself. King Priam had just initiated an intensive ship-building program. His people were the leading producers of sailcloth and pitch, and their country was uncommonly rich in forests for timber. The Mycenaeans concluded that an invasion fleet was being readied against them and that a naval arms race was on.

In the midst of this furious competition Trojan pirates may have gone too far, intentionally or not, when they captured a royal personage, perhaps someone named Helen. Her abduction would have been the propaganda act that rallied the fractious Greeks and forged their union. No less an authority on the events of these times than the renowned Lionel Casson suggests that Helen's "abduction" may indeed have been the spark that set off hostilities. She was at least a symbol of Mycenaean losses at the hands of Trojan pirates. Given the corsair nature of the age, it is by no means out of the question that a Greek princess was in fact taken in one of the numerous deeds of buccaneering that occurred throughout the Aegean at this time. Kidnapping a member of the royal house would certainly be sufficient cause for war between two peoples already poised on the razor's edge of international relations. Perhaps it was a deliberate act by the Trojans to provoke a decisive confrontation.

Whatever the motive, the Mycenaeans collected every available ship and warrior from Pylos to Phillipi for a single daring preemptive operation. Their resolve to get in the first strike was certainly a correct decision, because it not only cut off the Trojans from access to the sea, thereby nullifying their fleet, but also compelled them to fight on the defensive for the duration of the conflict. In 1237 B.C.E. Greek forces crossed the Ionian Sea *en masse* to stage landings at several key points along the western shores of Asia Minor, isolating Troy from all outside help, and immediately besieged the capital. From the first day of the war the advantage lay with the invaders. They defeated King Priam's Anatolian allies piecemeal, then prepared a major assault against Ilios. (See fig. 1.3.)

With the entire Greek navy in the north and the Egyptian navy poised for action in the south, the Atlantean admirals were not about to sail their fleet into so obvious a trap, no matter how desperate the

Fig. 1.3. The inclined defensive walls of Ilios, the capital of Troy. The Trojan War fought here was actually a local Aegean phase in the Atlantean invasion of the Mediterranean world described by Plato.

situation for their Anatolian cousins. They waited to see if a Trojan counteroffensive could break the enemy's encirclement and drive the Mycenaeans back into the sea, where they might be engaged to better advantage. On the other side of besieged Ilios the Hittites also waited. While fearing the Sea People and hoping for their destruction, they did not trust Egypt and knew that a final showdown with Pharaoh, treaty or no treaty, was inevitable. Moreover, relations with Troy had been cordial and profitable for generations and should be again. For their part, the Egyptians also kept their distance from the actual fighting, preferring to send grain and arms to their uncertain allies in Asia Minor. The Hittites decided to play all the combatants against each other until a favorable opportunity for intervention arose. If the Mycenaeans appeared to be winning, the Hittites would take Ilios to prevent it from falling to the Greeks. If the Trojans gained the upper hand, the Hittites would occupy Troy before the Sea People could gain a foothold in Asia Minor. Meanwhile, the Hittites concluded, the best strategy was to allow all sides to weaken themselves in mutual slaughter while they saved their own strength for the decisive moment.

It seemed to come just when Atlantean hopes for a Trojan strike were being fulfilled: A chariot sortie from Ilios broke through enemy lines and went after the Greeks' ships. Many vessels went up in flames. The Mycenaeans were pushed back into the sea, but they rallied and mounted a desperate counteroffensive from which the Trojans, after heavy losses, retreated behind the safety of their city walls.

While the goal of the operation—to cut off the enemy onshore without further possibility of supply—was not achieved, the Greeks were badly shaken by their hairbreadth escape from annihilation on the beaches in the Battle for the Ships. Taking advantage of their losses and exhaustion, the Atlantean fleet suddenly attacked, slicing at high speed through the lines of Mycenaean warships wherever they were most thinly spread. Vessels were held at bay or sunk, while troops of the Sea People made successful landings along the Anatolian coast. An entire army—ten thousand marines—went ashore to the wild acclaim of their Lydian allies.

They were led by Memnon, tall and robust like his fellow Atlanteans, so noted for their great stature that they were remembered in Greek myth as "Titans." In the *Posthomerica* Memnon is described as a king from Ethiopia, which was associated in early classical and pre-classical times with the Atlantic coasts of northwest Africa specifically and the Atlantean realm generally. Only centuries later was the name Ethiopia assigned to the land south of Egypt (see *The Destruction of Atlantis*, 115–17). In Ovid's *Metamorphoses* (Book 4), Princess Andromeda is described as having been fettered in Ethiopia to a high cliff overlooking the sea, a situation unlikely to have occurred in the Ethiopia we know today. Other elements of her myth not only define the country's oceanic border but contain discernible Atlantean themes. Andromeda was the great-granddaughter of Poseidon, the creator of Atlantis. He ravaged the seacoasts of Ethiopia with a monster described by Ovid as "volcanic," suggesting tsunamis generated by volcanic Mount Atlas. Another Roman scholar, Pliny the Elder, states that Ethiopia was originally known as Atlantia. Memnon says of his own early childhood, "The lily-like Hesperides raised me far away by the stream of Ocean." The Hesperides were Atlantises, daughters of Atlas, who attended the sacred golden apple tree at the center of his island kingdom. That Memnon was "raised" by them indicates that he was indeed a king, a member of the royal house of Atlantis. At his death he was mourned by another set of Atlantises, the Pleiades, daughters of the sea goddess Pleione by Atlas.

Politically and militarily Memnon was an ideal leader. His mother, Eos (Dawn), bore him in Atlantis, and his father, Tithonus, belonged to the royal house of Troy, a pedigree that ensured the cooperative spirit of both Atlantean and Trojan troops. United into a special army called the Memnonides, his soldiers wore distinctive chest armor emblazoned with the image of a black crow, the animal of Kronos, a Titan synonymous with the Atlantic Ocean. Even during the Roman era the Atlantic was known as Chronos Maris, the "Sea of Kronos." The crow insignia was an expression of the troops' proud origins, esprit de corps, and dedication to their chief.

Memnon marched them across the Lydian frontier, northward along the Anatolian coast, and on to the relief of Ilios. Standing in their way was an armed host of Solymi, Greek allies assigned to prevent siege-raising attempts such as his. The Memnonides attacked head-on with such lightning speed that the enemy's front lines split in two, followed almost instantly by the collapse of the entire center. Circling back in opposite directions on their stunned opponents, the Atlanteans executed a skillfully coordinated double-pincer movement, with Memnon himself amid the fighting. In Book I of *The Little Iliad,* Quintus of Smyrna tells "how he killed with his angry hands a great army of troublesome Solymi." Indeed, none survived to surrender. The rapidity and totality of their defeat shocked the other Greek allies, who scattered before the Memnonides' swift, now unopposed advance toward Ilios.

Memnon's troops arrived just in time. Hector, Troy's foremost general and leader of the nearly successful Battle for the Ships, had recently fallen in single combat to Achilles. Flaunting his triumph, the vengeful Greek bound the corpse of the general by its ankles to his chariot, which he then rode around the walls of Ilios in a macabre spectacle for all its mournful, helpless residents. At this low moment in the long siege the appearance of Memnon at the head of his army of Sea People had an uplifting effect on the war-weary Trojans. With his help, they might win after all. The Memnonides threw themselves into combat, suffering terrible losses but inflicting crippling blows on the enemy. In a quick series of hard-fought battles, the Mycenaeans were again beaten back to their ships. Nothing seemed to stop the Atlantean juggernaut. The tide of war was turning against the Greeks, and they talked of abandoning the field while they could. But just as the Memnonides were about to roll up the enemy camp, their commander died on the same sword that had been stained with Hector's blood.

2

THE PENALTY OF EMPIRE

A race of militarists had sailed out of the Atlantic and invaded all western Europe and North Africa, as far as Libya's deserts. They had a large navy and army. Paying no heed to any nations desiring, in that far-off day, to remain neutral, they overran every country between Gibraltar and the modern Levant.

HAROLD T. WILKINS, *MYSTERIES OF ANCIENT SOUTH AMERICA*

With Memnon's death, his followers lost heart for the fight. He had been Troy's last hope. After a ten-year siege, the capital fell in a firestorm as Homer's Achaeans looted the city of Ilios. Their ships, burdened with plunder and slaves, returned over the Ionian Sea to Greece, but the Atlantean fleet did not challenge them; instead it quietly turned away on a southerly heading. Any attempt to capture the Dardanelles now would have to pass between the victorious Mycenaeans and the poised Hittites, a situation to be avoided. Even if the straits could be taken, holding them was impossible.

Although the Atlanteans had lost a whole army, their ships, still largely intact, represented a potent if rootless sea power. Beating a retreat across the Mediterranean was a humiliation too great to consider—and dangerous, because authority would be undermined, something no imperialists can afford if they intend to keep their subjects in sufficient awe.

Atlantean strategists were not discouraged, however. Despite the debacle at Troy, their Libyan, Italian, Palestinian, and other allies were still standing by for action. Meanwhile, Greek unity was already backsliding into the contentious factions of prewar days, and their abandonment of smoldering Ilios after sacking it satisfied the Hittites, who snatched up the Troad (the Trojan sphere of influence in northwestern Asia Minor) without a fight. Although officially allied with Egypt, they were not about to defend it from outside attack, especially if the Sea People, in moving against the Nile Valley, left Asia Minor in peace. An Atlanto-Egyptian war would be sure to weaken both sides to Hittite advantage.

But Atlantean commanders were confident they could do better than stalemate the Egyptians. Shortly after the Trojan War began, the powerful Ramses II died at ninety-seven years of age, leaving behind another old man, his thirteenth son, in his place. About sixty years old at the time of his accession in 1236 B.C.E., Pharaoh Merenptah was generally regarded as weak and indecisive both at home and abroad. There were domestic labor strikes, unknown during his father's long reign, and Nubia showed signs of restlessness.

Encouraged by the general situation and unwilling to return home with little to show for almost ten years at sea, the Atlanteans developed a land-and-sea strategy aimed at nothing less than the armed subjugation of Egypt. Such a conquest would establish Atlantis as unquestionably the most powerful empire on earth and secure its position in the Near East. The chief military architect of this ambitious enterprise was Teucer, known to the Egyptians as Tjeker. He also appears in Homer's *Iliad* as the founder of Salamis, in Cyprus, one of the Sea People's major staging areas for the planned invasion.

Teucer's war plan called for a three-pronged attack on the Nile Delta by the Atlantean fleet, with its confederated squadrons descending from the north. Their task was to brush aside the Egyptian navy and put troops ashore in a single combined strike. The marines were to march inland, capturing the strategic cities of Damietta, Busiris, and Sais, while the main body of battle cruisers supported them by sailing down the Nile parallel to their advance. A main objective in this opening phase of the campaign was the leading administrative center at Memphis. If it could be taken, the Egyptians would have difficulty coordinating resistance.

In concert with the seaborne assault, Libyan forces led by King Meryey would invade the delta from the west. In the east, Atlantean transports were ordered to discharge an army of Paleste, one of the allies of the Sea People, for the occupation of Syria south of the Hittite lines. These troops would then march, probably with the Hittites' unofficial blessings, on the Nile Delta, already assailed from north and west.

In early spring of 1227 B.C.E., the night before these elaborate preparations were set in motion, their intended victim was in deep, if restless, sleep. Merenptah was having a vivid dream. The god after whom he was named appeared before him in gigantic form. Ptah, the divine artificer, wordlessly handed Pharaoh a sword, as though to indicate, "Defend my civilization!" Merenptah awoke with a start into full consciousness. Seizing a nearby mallet, he struck a bedside copper gong, and the king's chamber was instantly filled with armed guards. But no priest was needed to interpret his dream. He summoned all corps commanders and ordered that the delta defenses be put on full alert.

As they were readying their charges, two hundred miles away a freshening dawn breeze filled the two thousand sails of the Atlantean armada, carrying its ships away from their Aegean headquarters at Cyprus and Rhodes. The naval force they composed was the largest and best equipped on earth. Illustrations of the war vessels and mariners still survive on the walls of Medinet Habu in the Upper Nile Valley. (See fig. 2.1.) They were not the relatively flimsy coastbound rigs manned by the Egyptians, but, in the words of Lionel Casson, "truly sea-going ships" capable of extended open-water voyages. They did indeed constitute the navy of a Sea People, featuring such nautical advances for their time as brails, or heavy lines for controlling the area of sheet exposed to the wind, together with internally braced hulls to withstand heavy pounding by large waves.

These warships were not only much larger than anything the Egyptians commanded but physically distinct as well. Both prow and stern rose steeply to form figureheads of long-beaked birds of prey. The same ship design appears on a stirrup jar, dated to 1180 B.C.E., from Skyros, one of the Atlanteans' islands of refuge in the Aegean after the fall of Troy. The bird-headed maritime motif is found all through the Villanovan, or Archaic, period of Etruscan civilization, particularly at

Fig. 2.1. The profile of an Atlantean marine as it was portrayed on the illustrated walls of Medinet Habu in West Thebes, Upper Egypt

the old capital, Tarchon. Examples from the Monterozzi grave show that models of these peculiar ships were buried with Etruscan warriors of some stature, as is indicated by a splendid soldier's helmet and golden bracelets retrieved at the site.

Like Poseidon's trident, the invasion struck the Nile Delta simultaneously from three directions—north, west, and east. As dawn broke over the sea, Egyptian sentinels posted before the delta beheld an awesome spectacle: The northern horizon was blotted out by an armada of unfurled sail. Contributing to the frightening apparition were the grotesque carvings of monstrous birds' heads and other hellish beasts at the stemposts of oversized battleships. The outnumbered, outclassed Egyptian vessels maneuvered against them in a desperate confrontation. Their losses were appalling, and the Great Green, their name for the Mediterranean Sea, was stained with the defenders' blood. Heedlessly crashing through the drifting wreckage of broken ships, the mighty Atlantean fleet beached the prows of its triumphant ships on the sacred shores of Egypt to disgorge tens of thousands of Sea People warriors.

At the same moment thirty thousand Libyan troops stormed Egypt's western frontier, pushing its defenders behind their own border. King Meryey brought along royal family members and even personal luxuries, confident he would soon be setting up his throne in Memphis. Simultaneous Atlantean landings in the east went unopposed, allowing the Paleste allies an eminently successful occupation of Syria. They rolled over the Egyptian garrisons while the Hittites, as expected, looked on in nervous detachment. Flushed with early, easy victory, the Paleste drove at full speed toward the Nile Delta. Additional aid now came from the south, where the Nubians, taking advantage of events at the Lower Nile, unexpectedly staged a national revolt against their Egyptian overseers. Pharaoh Merenptah was being attacked from every quadrant.

The self-sacrifice of his navy had not been in vain, however. Their suicidal resistance held off the invasion just long enough for Merenptah's forces to fortify the port town of Prosopis. Unaware of its strategic location, the Sea People advanced within bowshot of several brigades of elite archers stationed there. The invaders were surprised and cut down by thick volleys of arrow fire directed at them from concealed positions. In the midst of their confusion, the main body of the Egyptian army fell on them in overwhelming numbers. Pinned between relentless flights of arrows and an entire infantry corps in the narrow terrain fronting the beaches, the Sea People marines were unable to break out of Prosopis. They fought a disciplined retreat to the ships, thereby cutting their losses to only a few thousand dead or captured.

The battle was dramatized by Homer in the *Odyssey*. After its hero returned to Ithaca, he concealed his identity by telling a local shepherd he was a Cretan who, following the Achaean success at Troy, had joined an armada of pirates for an expedition against Egypt. The adventure miscarried, he said, with most of the invaders killed and the remaining numbers enslaved. Describing the battle at Prosopis, Odysseus recounts:

> The whole place was filled with infantry and chariots and the glint
> of arms. Zeus, the Thunderer, struck abject panic into my party.

Not a man had fortitude to stand up to the enemy, for we were threatened on all sides. They ended by cutting down a large part of my force and carrying off the survivors to work for them as their slaves.

Back on board their ships, the Sea People waited offshore, watching for another opportunity to resume the invasion. But they were continually harassed by fresh Egyptian naval units, which, rather than engage the superior warships, staged hit-and-run sorties against transport and supply vessels to keep the enemy off balance.

Trusting his remnant fleet to keep the Sea People at bay, Merenptah evacuated most of his armies from Prosopis, leaving it virtually undefended, and sent them to hold Fortress Perite. It was the last important defensive position against King Meryey's advance, which had already reached the western delta. In the early morning of April 15, with the rising sun in their eyes, a larger contingent of Libyans attacked in expectation of a pitched battle. Instead, Pharaoh's redoubtable archers unleashed massed salvos of bowshot at the oncoming waves of foot soldiers. Despite the massacre of their comrades, the Libyans pushed on against the fusillade of arrows to engage the defenders in hand-to-hand combat under the fortress walls for six hours.

Coming to the Egyptians' aid was a chariot squadron and another brigade of spearmen. Libyan resistance weakened, then collapsed into a rout. As the tide of battle began to turn, so did King Meryey. He fled from the field, leaving his royal family to fall into enemy hands. His six sons were lost, all killed in combat. Together with the monarch's household furniture, the Egyptians captured 120,000 weapons and pieces of military equipment, in addition to 9,000 copper swords. They took heaps of Libyan booty, which, in its abundance and kind, was proof that the invasion had been a serious attempt at armed occupation. All trophies were dutifully handed over to army scribes, who inventoried everything down to the last article. Then the leather tents of the invaders were set ablaze. Nearly 10,000 Libyans lay dead near them. Another 9,111 were taken prisoner, but King Meryey was not among them. Returning to his palace in disgrace, he was deposed and executed by his own people. Even so, the Egyptians were not in a generous mood. As their price of surrender they severed the hands of 2,362 Libyan officers.

Merenptah could waste no time in victory celebrations, however. He wheeled his overworked army around in the opposite direction to confront the Paleste threatening the eastern delta. Learning of Atlantean and Libyan reverses, they were unsure if they should continue the invasion on their own. In the midst of indecision, the Egyptians hit them with a concerted frontal attack that sent them reeling all the way back to the Levant. There they laid down their arms and vowed never to take them up again. This time Pharaoh showed leniency to the defeated. He allowed them to settle permanently in the area, which henceforward took its name after the Paleste: Palestine. He was not disposed to grant the Nubians a similar forbearance, however, and speedily punished their ill-timed rebellion with an iron hand.

With failure on all fronts, the Sea People coalition disintegrated, and its ships sailed out of Egyptian waters. Merenptah had exceeded the expectations of friend and foe alike. The wily pharaoh was a tough old man who outthought, outmaneuvered, and outpunched his enemies, who outnumbered him. Licking their wounds, the Atlanteans retreated to their headquarters at Cyprus and Rhodes. Although the Dardanelles had been lost and Egypt remained unconquered, Italy, the Balearics, Sardinia, Sicily, and important islands in the Aegean were still in their hands. The Atlantis empire had its stake in the eastern Mediterranean, after all.

Merenptah's victory, spectacular as it seemed, also revealed Egyptian weakness. Battles at Prosopis and Fortress Perite had cost his forces dearly, so much so that they were unable to follow up on their defeat of the Libyans by pursuing King Meryey back to his palace. In addition, Pharaoh's apparent lenience toward the routed Paleste may have been based less on any high-minded magnanimity than on his inability to deal with them as he wanted. His overtly vigorous suppression of the materially unsophisticated Nubians was more likely intended to send out to the rest of the world a false signal of his army's unimpaired strength, thereby screening its real debility.

The losses of the Sea People, although severe, were confined to the landings. No ships had been sunk, in sharp contrast to the Egyptian navy, which was annihilated. Still, the Atlanteans could not risk a third debacle while so capable a leader was still in charge of their enemy.

While refitting the fleet at Rhodes and Cyprus they waited for Merenptah to die of old age. In the political chaos and uncertainty that invariably afflicted the Egyptians between the death of one pharaoh and the installment of another, they were at their most vulnerable to outside attack. The Atlanteans prepared for just such an opportune moment to strike again. But their wait was longer than they expected; Merenptah was almost as long-lived as his father.

Venting their impatience in a North African conquest, the Atlanteans invaded Tripoli, Libya's western neighbor, if only to keep their nervous allies in line. The Atlanteans were locally remembered a thousand years later as the ferocious Chariot People, who swiftly subdued native resistance with that innovative vehicle and weapon. Herodotus referred to them as Garamantes; their red-and-yellow rock art may still be seen at Tin-Abou Teka. They next attacked Corsica, where horned helmets, bronze swords, and Atlantean architecture in the form of great stone towers, known as *nuraghe*, still testify to occupation by the Sea People. They had become a real menace, prone to pillaging other islands and coastal cities all around the Mediterranean. Thanks to Greek disunity, Hittite reluctance, and Egyptian weakness at sea, they practiced piracy with impunity and on a grander scale of depredation than ever before.

In 1198 B.C.E. the day they had waited for so long finally arrived. Merenptah had died of old age and was followed in quick succession by no less than five rulers, including the clubfooted Siptah, and Tewosret, a queen whose reign was short. These prolonged political crises destabilized the Nineteenth Dynasty, and Atlantean strategists prepared to take advantage of the situation. The Egyptians were preoccupied with the accession of a new pharaoh and all the powerful implications, both good and evil, that a change of divine leadership inevitably brought. This time they had special cause for worry. A frightening omen appeared following the death of King Sethnahkt, who had just founded the Twentieth Dynasty. An immense dark cloud began to cover the sky at unnatural speed from the west. The sun turned blood-red, then disappeared. Broad daylight was reduced to twilight accompanied by a rain of black dust that fell for weeks over the entire land. "Men walk about like ravens," the Egyptian scribe records. "No one can keep their garments clean anymore."

These ominous conditions boded ill for the Atlanteans too. In the midst of organizing a renewed invasion of the Nile Delta, such signs and wonders in the heavens presaged disaster for someone. Having been born and raised on a geologically active island, they recognized the black dust as ashfall blown in on the prevailing westerlies from some major volcanic event beyond the Mediterranean. Naturally and anxiously, their thoughts turned to Mount Atlas, the ever-smoking mountain of their far-off homeland.

Their worst fears were confirmed when waves of human migration poured through the Pillars of Heracles. Panicked refugees streamed by the hundreds of thousands along North African shores or in ragged flotillas of boats and ships overcrowded with dispossessed families traumatized by disaster. Most of them were fellow Atlanteans, and they had a report to make. "You can't go home again," they said, "because home is no longer there." With hardly more than one day's warning consisting of extended seismic activity, the island of Atlantis had been torn by earthquake and sky fire before the angry sea swallowed it whole. The accompanying devastation was so pronounced and widespread that the entire region, including all foreign coastal areas, raked by a series of ruinous tsunami waves, had been rendered uninhabitable. The occupied areas of Italy, Tripoli, and the Mediterranean islands swelled with new populations of survivors, compromising living conditions everywhere.

But the exiles brought with them more than tales of woe. Important sections of the home fleet escaped the catastrophe and were able to carry warriors and supplies as well as crowds of displaced persons. The Sea People armada at Cyprus and Rhodes was appreciably reinforced by these new arrivals of warships and marines. The conquest of Egypt was needed now even more than before in order to provide a place to resettle the streams of refugees; their growing numbers made increasing demands on the limited resources of the occupied territories. Bolstered with fresh battle cruisers, munitions, and soldiers, the Atlantean commanders resolved to strike at once, while the Egyptians were still distracted by their royal interregnum and celestial portents. Nearly two thousand years earlier the Atlanteans had conquered Egypt for the first time as fugitives from a natural calamity. They would do so again. Let the fall of black dust be a sign of doom for the new pharaoh!

Fig. 2.2. A tomb portrait of Pharoah Ramses III, appropriately attired in the blue crown of supreme military commander. In the early twelfth century B.C.E. he confronted a massive invasion of the Nile Delta by Atlantean-led coalition forces.

He was Ramses III (see fig. 2.2), untried and unknown, but his ascent to the throne passed without priestly interference or political conflict, and his people were grateful at least for the smooth transition to power, despite the literal dark cloud under which his reign began. He was not unaware of the alien threat pointed directly at Egypt, and knew that the Hau-neb, or Hanebu—"Those Who Follow Their Ships"— would come again as soon as his predecessor was dead. Years before, Ramses had developed defensive measures that would go into effect as soon as invasion seemed imminent. Now the moment was swiftly approaching when his strategy and its most vital components—the skill, courage, and discipline of his warriors—would be put to the ultimate test.

The inevitability of attack was certified by a total lack of any diplomatic relations between Egypt and the Sea People's chief headquarters at Rhodes after the first battle of the Nile Delta. During the subsequent twenty-nine years Atlantean commanders came up with an invasion agenda based on their experience. Especially now that their armada had been strengthened by additional naval units and marine companies from drowned Atlantis, simultaneous landings in force would be able to support each other, unlike the single assault at Prosopis. As before, overpowering the defenders at sea was paramount. Between both Atlantean invasions the Egyptians had almost thirty years to rebuild their fleet arm, so a serious coastal confrontation preliminary to putting troops ashore was anticipated. Several squadrons of battleships held in reserve would participate only if the advance vessels needed assistance. In a replay of Teucer's tactics, the warships would provide support to the marines by moving down the Nile River parallel to their inland advance. Their chief objective was occupation of the entire delta, from which they could dominate the rest of the campaign and fight their way southward to Thebes, the enemy capital. Its capture would end the invasion.

New allies from Corsica and Tripoli joined old comrades. If the Libyans could penetrate deep enough inside the Egyptian frontier, Atlanteans landing in the north would endeavor to link up with them, thereby cutting the Nile Delta in two.

The Atlantean marines were the best outfitted of their time. Unlike their opponents, they wore metal vests and carried longer bronze swords of superior craftsmanship. Their helmets were precursors of Roman versions, with short-cropped horsehair crests dyed red. Body armor wrapped around the torso in a tied corset of leather pleated with bronze. Bronze-weighted leather greaves protected their shins. The foot soldiers were divided into companies of spear throwers, slingers, and swordsmen supported by squads of four-man chariots bigger and heavier than their Egyptian counterparts.

At first the operation seemed to duplicate the first invasion of nearly three decades before. Once again the smaller warships were scattered by the inexorable inertia of the Atlantean battle cruisers, and the expected sea battle with the Egyptian navy did not materialize. The landings were larger and more effective because their separate attacks were well coordinated. The Egyptian infantry did not know which way to turn. It was like trying to put out several fires at once; it could not be done. Avoiding Prosopis or any ground unfavorable to themselves, the invaders moved with ruthless speed, pushing the defenders out of one fortified position after another. Unlike the previous attempt against

Merenptah's Egypt, the Sea People juggernaut smashed through the early defenses. Its inertia carried the corps of marines and infantry across the face of the delta. One city and town after another fell before the onslaught until even the great administrative and religious centers at Memphis and Heliopolis were occupied.

This time the Atlantean warships actually entered the Nile. Long lines of the huge vessels began to infiltrate the sacred river. Their broad sails and monstrous bird-headed stemposts panicked the native inhabitants, who fled with their routed army toward the south. Meanwhile, Libyan forces overwhelmed enemy fortifications in the west, penetrating so deeply into Egyptian territory that they threatened to link up with the northern invaders. In a few days most primary objectives were taken by the Atlanteans, including important cities like Busiris. The whole delta was soon on the verge of falling into their hands.

Just above Sais, as the forces of the Sea People were assaulting the massive gates of that ancient city, the invading battle cruisers in the vanguard of the armada were challenged by a squadron of smaller warships. Given the sacrosanct reputation of Sais, the ferocity of the attacking Egyptians came as no surprise. But even their driven courage could not prevail against the much larger vessels, which crushed the defenders beneath their immense hulls. Remnants of the decimated squadron fled down river, their conquerors in murderous pursuit. Not far from the scene of their defeat the apparently routed captains left the Nile and entered one of its backwaters. Assuming the panicked enemy was making for its home port, the Atlanteans followed in anticipation of destroying the Egyptian naval headquarters.

The quarry veered off a branch of the Nile and filed through a long, narrow bay commanded on both sides by high ridges. Hard on their heels, the main body of the Atlantean vessels sailed inside, but no staff buildings, dockyards, port facilities, or anchored warships lined either shore. Only a few vessels of the recently beaten squadron hove into view. The oversized invaders regrouped for battle. Their bigger warships maneuvered for position. One by one, however, their deep keels ran aground on unseen shoals. Several more were held fast in disorderly array, but their sister ships were unable to come about in the narrow bay without avoiding collisions. A pileup of battle cruisers was under way, accompanied by orders and counterorders shouted to seamen who furiously struggled with hawsers and poles.

While endeavoring to disengage themselves from the growing confusion of shallow water and insufficient space in which to maneuver, fresh squadrons of Egyptian warships suddenly dashed into the bay from both ends. They joined their flotilla survivors from Sais in savaging the immobile enemy behemoths from every direction. Volleys of firepots were tossed on board. Huge sails emblazoned with the fearsome images of birds of prey erupted into sheets of flame, and decks ran awash with liquid fire. Great billows of black smoke rose to the skies in a spreading conflagration of ships. More Egyptian vessels, these loaded with regular troops, filled the overcrowded bay. Lines with grappling were shot over gunwales, followed by overwhelming boarding parties who engaged in hand-to-hand combat amid the fires of wounded vessels.

Word of the struggle was sent to the Sea People marines still battering Sais. They instantly abandoned their siege and marched at full speed to the rescue. An immense pall of burning pitch directed them from far off to the scene of the emergency. In their carts and chariots they carried innumerable folding rafts sufficient to carry armed men over the short stretch of water into the combat zone. Their prompt arrival on the shore nearest the fighting was met with loud cheers from their hard-pressed comrades aboard the Atlantean ships. But as the marines were hastily assembling their rafts, several companies of archers and slingers, personally led by Ramses himself, appeared as though by magic on the ridge behind and above them. They poured down a hailstorm of arrows and rock on the invaders, who fell by the thousands under the relentless barrage. (See fig. 2.3.) Perhaps a hundred men, mostly charioteers, escaped by driving away as fast as their wounded horses could carry them. Hardly many more survived to surrender.

With all hope gone for rescue by land, most of the Atlanteans aboard their beleaguered ships ran up the white flag. A few, with courage born of desperation, succeeded in breaking out from the bay of death, but their elation was short-lived. To their horror, hundreds more warships bristling with firepots and bowmen fairly choked the length of the Nile. Some battle cruisers were snared in a tangle of boarding lines and hauled into captivity, but the current was with those who persisted

Fig. 2.3. Atlantean invaders fall to Egyptian archers defending the Nile Delta in this battle scene portrayed on the walls of Medinet Habu.

and they pressed on at high speed, running a gauntlet of archers cross-firing at them from both sides of the river all the way to the Mediterranean. By the time these scorched, arrow-riddled vessels finally emerged into the freedom of the open sea to join the reserve fleet anchored on the delta's northern shore, nearly half the invasion armada had been lost.

The main body of Sea People troops—forty thousand of them—were nonetheless still bent on taking the controlling position of Sais. The Egyptians, however, now had the Nile on either side of the south-ernmost delta. Without their ships to support them, the invaders were hemmed in on two of three sides. Ramses landed virtually his entire armed forces, some fifty thousand warriors, above the city, then marched them double-quick straight across the territory from one branch of the river to the other, confining the enemy within the lower delta. As soon as the trap was sprung, he ordered the advance.

Just then Pharaoh learned that another thirty thousand Libyans were descending on him from their occupation of the western delta, coming to the aid of their cornered allies. He was now in danger of being caught by enemies from both sides. Without interrupting his southern offensive against the Sea People, he took the risk of withdrawing all his chariotry, rapidly formed them into a single company, and sent them, minus any infantry backup, to hold off the Libyans. The charioteers protested that they would be outnumbered by more than five to one, but Ramses assured them the operation was not as suicidal as it appeared. He gave them their orders, then rejoined the advance against the Atlanteans.

The Sea People's tenacious resistance was driven not only by the dire situation in which they found themselves, but also by the awareness that the Libyans were hurrying to relieve them. If the surrounded troops could only hold out until they arrived, the Egyptians would be crushed between two halves of the invasion. Ramses' offensive pushed steadily onward, the enemy reluctantly relinquishing every piece of ground. But losses on both sides were already high and progress was slow due to the forced absence of Pharaoh's chariots. The burden of combat rested entirely on the infantry. The foe in the west—the Libyans—would be making its appearance any moment, and the Egyptians were confronted by enemies on either hand.

The king's strategy, however, was being carried out to the letter. Although his charioteers found the marching Libyan host, they avoided contact entirely by skirting it all the way around to the rear. Their maneuver took so long to execute that the enemy was almost breathing down Ramses' neck when his chariots finally launched a coordinated surprise attack from three close directions—north, northeast, and northwest. The ferocity of this tridentlike assault utterly panicked the Libyans, who stumbled up against the spears of Pharaoh's own rear guard, surrendering before much more blood was spilled and the hopeful Atlanteans had time to react. The Sea People continued to defy the Egyptians, fighting at close quarters, until their backs were up against the Nile. They had fought well, but without hope.

Their invasion collapsed, but the war was not over. Atlanteans in the occupied areas of the northern delta were evacuated aboard their ships; hardly given much pause for despair, they were told that operations were being immediately resumed against Syria. The plan was to land troops among their old allies, the Paleste, who had settled there following the previous war with Merenptah. This renewed confederation would then march on Egypt from the east, surprising their

Egyptian foes, who had doubtless been enervated by too many battles.

The attenuated but still formidable armada approached the Syrian coast near the city of Amor, but no allies were there to greet them. Indifferent to their conquest, the Paleste were also intimidated by the presence of a huge army commanded in person by its pharaoh. Egyptian naval units shadowed the disengaged Atlantean ships, reporting to Ramses on their Syrian heading. Inferring the enemy's flanking intention, Ramses rode with his army to the Syrian coast near Amor. Once in position there, his alternating ranks of infantry and archers were backed up by chariot squads. Before the Atlanteans could begin landing troops, two fleets of Egyptian warships came up from north and south, simultaneously attacking the rear flanks, effectively pushing the battle cruisers toward shore and beaching them.

Then the carnage began. The invaders were stung from sea and land by flights of arrows from the bows of three thousand archers. Caught up in the excitement of the moment, Ramses drew his own great bow against the enemy. After covering the hapless foe with a torrent of missiles, his men pounced on the Atlanteans. "They were dragged, overturned, and laid low upon the beach," reports the Egyptian war scribe, "slain and made heaps from stern to bow of their galleys, while all their things were upon the waters."

The slaughter on the Syrian coast was the last act of war. Their capital sunk beneath a far-off sea, their empire shattered, and the last of their armed forces destroyed, those Atlanteans spared the cataclysms of nature or combat settled down with their dispossessed kinsmen in Italy, Iberia, Northwest Africa, even the British Isles and beyond to the distant former colonies of the Americas. In these remote lands they transmuted their energies from the art of war into the arts of peace, contributing their cultural and genetic heritage to other peoples with whom they lived. As a result of their impact, hybrid civilizations arose from the jungles of the Yucatán to the valleys of Ireland.

The fate of those Sea People captured as prisoners of war by the Egyptians was less happy. During a public parade through the capital at Thebes more than twenty thousand Atlanteans and their allies were marched in chains before Pharaoh seated upon his outdoor throne. (See fig. 2.4.)

The scene and highlights of the war were recorded in words and

Fig. 2.4 Reproduction and restoration of temple art at Medinet Habu depicts captured Sea People marines holding Ramses III's victory cup. The illustration offers some insight into attire and physical appearance of the Atlanteans. (Image by Virginia Hardyman)

illustrations (fig. 2.5) on the walls of Medinet Habu, Ramses' majestic victory temple over the Hanebu, erected west of the Nile.

They are all still there—the Atlantean battleships with their marines being massacred and toppled into the sea by archers; Pharaoh astride his chariot, mowing down the quailing enemies of Egypt; the long lines of Hau-neb (Atlanteans), Luka (Lydians), Scherdan (Sardinians), Drdny (Dardanians), Turisha (Trojans), Temeh (Libyans), Shekelesh (Sicilians), Tarshan (Etruscans of western Italy), and more. As Henry Brugsch-Bey, the renowned Egyptologist of the early twentieth century, observes:

> These names, handed down to us with all fidelity, bear upon them an unmistakable mark, namely that of a close connection founded on a political-geographic relation. They exhibit the military power of Western Asia in its chief representatives, just as we already have them enumerated by name in Homer, in the catalog of the allies of Troy (Ryan 1959).

The captured Atlanteans told their interrogators everything—how

Fig. 2.5. Atlantean prisoners of war from their invasion of Egypt, as depicted on the walls of the victory temple of Ramses III

their sacred island home had been destroyed, leaving them no choice but to invade. The prisoners were portrayed in lifelike detail, from their helmets and uniforms to the metal collars around their necks, which were employed to chain them together in groups. After their humiliating display before the crowds of Thebes, the soldiers were separated from their officers, who were castrated. A contemporary drawing incised on the walls of Medinet Habu shows a bureaucrat, computation pad and pen in hand, tallying up a mound of severed phalluses taller than himself. The survivors of this ordeal rejoined their comrades in the pit mines of the Tura limestone quarry, where they spent the rest of their lives cutting and hauling ponderous blocks for their captors' monumental public buildings, including Ramses' victory temple.

His triumph was one of the greatest successes in military history. It guaranteed that no one would invade Egypt for the next 625 years. Ramses was one of the outstanding strategists and field commanders of all time. Even so, there would be no more great Ramessid kings and only a few more memorable pharaohs after him. With his reign Egypt had entered a slow decline from which, with the exception of a revival now and then, it never recovered. Ramses himself would fall not on some heroic battlefield, but during an assassination attempt hatched in the palace harem. He lingered painfully while the trial of his conspirators dragged on, continuing even after he eventually died of the wounds they had inflicted on him.

His tomb in the Valley of the Kings has been excavated in modern times, revealing a profile portrait of the pharaoh, remarkably well preserved, that shows him wearing—appropriately—the Khepresh, or blue war crown. His victory temple is in better condition than any other major dynastic temple complex still standing in the Nile Valley; traces of original paint on the main portico may yet be seen. The so-called Harris Papyrus documenting his reign is likewise among the most complete and legible records of its kind. We are fortunate that Ramses III is one of the best-documented kings of ancient Egypt, because, as the pharaoh of the Atlantean War, these documents reveal so much of his time.

At the delta city of Sais, where he turned the tide of battle against the invaders, a great temple was erected to the war goddess, Neith. It was here, significantly, that a memorial pillar to the conflict was enshrined. Centuries later the hieroglyphic text was translated by the high priest for an important visitor, the man who gave Athens and the Western world its first code of law. Solon returned with this translation to Greece, where the story of Atlantis was thereafter handed down to Plato and the rest of the world. It describes a struggle not only between princes and kingdoms, but among whole peoples caught up in unprecedented self-destruction that brought an entire age of humankind to a close.

3

THE FOUR CATACLYSMS

Your own story of how Phaethon, child of the sun, harnessed his father's chariot, but was unable to guide it along his father's course, and so burnt up things on the Earth and was himself destroyed by a thunderbolt, is a mythical version of the truth that there is at long intervals a variation in the course of the heavenly bodies, and a consequent widespread destruction by fire of things upon the Earth.

PLATO, *TIMAEUS*

Two worlds were changed forever in 1994: Jupiter and Earth. When Jupiter was struck by a barrage of meteors from the comet Shoemaker-Levy during the summer of that year, its impact on the scientists of our planet was hardly less dramatic. Until then most of them believed, as stated in the *Larousse Encyclopedia of Astronomy*, that "the perfect timing and positioning required make the possibility of collision [between a meteor and a planet in our solar system] extremely slight." Nonetheless, when a comet six miles in diameter disintegrated in the Jovian gravitational field, its pieces broke free and began a final pass, in tandem, around the sun. During mid-July, stony remnants of the dead comet returned to Jupiter space. A line of twenty-one fragments, each about a mile and a half across, hit the planet at more than 306,850 miles per hour. Disbelieving observers watched as columns of flame shot several thousand miles high into the atmosphere. Ejected fireballs larger than the earth itself exploded in full view of the Hubble space telescope. Impact of the cometary debris generated energy ten thousand times more powerful than humankind's entire nuclear arsenal. For more than a year following these collisions Jupiter was still pockmarked by the resultant superheated gas bubbles, one of which was large enough to swallow our planet whole.

Centuries of calm assurance that the earth possessed some special immunity from outerspace threats had been dramatically replaced by a more sober appreciation of our precarious position in the solar system. But astronomers are not the only scientists who have been forced to reevaluate their theoretical positions. Long before the ravages of the comet Shoemaker-Levy archaeologists had been perplexed by the abrupt rise and fall of civilizations, particularly during the Bronze Age. This was a seminal era in the history of humankind: Tools and weapons of stone and copper were replaced by combining copper with zinc and tin, resulting in a hard, more resilient, altogether superior medium. The mass production of bronze characterized an entire age. It encompassed the rise of high cultures in the Nile Valley and Mesopotamia around the close of the fourth millennium B.C.E. and the sudden collapse of the civilized world less than two thousand years later.

But the invention of bronze could not have been the sole cause behind the birth of civilization. Nor was its alleged replacement by iron responsible for the extended dark ages that followed, because iron was used by Egyptians, Hittites, and others many centuries prior to their eclipse. In fact, the Bronze Age was itself punctuated by two major intervals, when all civilizations simultaneously went through periods of deep crisis that led them to the brink of extinction. What were the events that prompted these crises? War, famine, religious fervor, epidemics—nothing adequately explained how or why whole peoples similarly rose and fell on several occasions, and what might have brought about the total demise of their preclassical world.

From 3100 B.C.E., all the spiritual and material achievements associated with the sophisticated kingdoms of Asia Minor, the Aegean, and the Near East seemed to burst into existence and flourish for nearly two millennia. Then, around 1200 B.C.E., literature, the arts, monumental construction, city planning, medicine, organized religion, the mathematical sciences, manufacturing, physics, astronomy, commerce, and everything characteristic of high civilization vanished practically overnight. For the next four hundred years humans groped through a dark age so black that most of their ancestors' accomplishments were either forgotten or relegated to the realm of myth. Ever since, scholars have been unable to solve the great question of history: Where did civilization first come from, and what brought it to so sudden an end?

During the mid-1990s, university-trained scientists reconsidered this question in the light of Shoemaker-Levy's devastating effect on Jupiter. They began to seriously entertain the notion that similar cataclysms may have fundamentally determined the course of the early development of civilization here on Earth. In Europe, Asia, and the United States archaeologists reexamined their findings and were surprised to arrive at some common conclusions that promised to radically overturn long-held conceptions of the past, just as astronomers had been forced to revise their preconceived beliefs in an orderly solar system as a result of the surprising appearance of Shoemaker-Levy. Three years after the comet's encounter with Jupiter, many of the world's leading authorities in archaeology, archaeoastronomy, geology, paleobotany, climatology, and related sciences convened in a special conference aimed at pooling their new, disturbing data. They called their symposium "Natural Catastrophes During Bronze Age Civilizations: Archaeological, Geological, Astronomical, and Cultural Perspectives." From July 11 to 13, 1997, the Society for Interdisciplinary Studies hosted scientists from Sweden, Japan, Australia, and many other countries at England's Fitzwilliam College in Cambridge. Presenters included such academic luminaries as Mike Baillie, professor at the Paleoecology Centre at Queen's University, Belfast, Northern Ireland, where he is the leading expert in tree-ring dating. His fellow speakers included Duncan Steel, who worked on NASA's Pioneer Venus Orbiter Program, and Amos Nur, professor of geophysics at Stanford University. Altogether some one hundred of their colleagues participated in the conference.

Among the best-known presenters were Victor Clubbe and William N. Napier, astronomers at Ireland's Armagh Observatory. According to Florida researcher Kenneth Caroli,

> Their theory is that a giant comet was perturbed into a sub-Jovian orbit at some point between 30,000 and 70,000 years ago. Since

then, it has gradually fragmented into lesser, subsidiary comets or asteroids. The new comets created debris tubes which are still seen as annual meteor showers. But when they were younger, they were also denser, and could wreak havoc on our planet when Earth passed through their thickest portion. These meteor tubes swivel precessionally over several millennia, so that their periods of greatest danger are approximately 2,500 years apart. Since about 3150 B.C., Clubbe and Napier postulate a lesser subcycle of around 600 years (Palmer and Bailey 1998, 273).

Clubbe and Napier's theory attracted favorable attention from other Society scientists, who generally concurred that a primary set of Bronze Age cataclysms had been brought about by the close passage and/or actual impact of four different comets. These celestial confrontations fundamentally affected and traumatized civilization around 3100, 2200, 1628, and 1198 B.C.E. The Cambridge speakers provided abundant material evidence to argue convincingly that these Bronze Age catastrophes did indeed take place, determining only recently by independent scientific means something that human beings three thousand and more years ago already knew and had preserved in folk memories around the world. The same quartet of disasters was remembered by the Greeks, Irish, Egyptians, northern Europeans, Africans, and Native American Mesoamerican and Andean peoples.

Despite often vast separation from each other in time and distance, these oral traditions demonstrate a remarkable general consistency: They uniformly describe a former age of unparalleled civilized greatness centered on a large island in the Atlantic Ocean. Although initially virtuous, its people were corrupted by vice and greed. So the gods punished them with a "fire from heaven," followed by a terrible flood. Some refugees escaped to other parts of the world, where they founded new societies and sired original dynasties to rule them. Others remained in their decimated homeland to restore its former splendor. The cycle of power, cataclysm, migration, and rebirth were repeated thrice more until the offending empire, its leaders bent on military aggression, was utterly obliterated by a final deluge. The last survivors sailed to distant lands, which they dominated with their superior technology until they were absorbed by native populations.

Around 340 B.C.E. the Greek philosopher Plato gave a name to this fountainhead of civilization: Atlantis. To be sure, it was known under various names centuries before his time and among many other peoples, but these names were nothing more than individual cultural inflections on the same place. Scholars have long been aware of such traditions but dismissed them as nothing more than moral fables or royal allegories. With the recognition of our planet's cometary encounters during pre-classical times, however, and their restoration to their original context, these same myths take on an entirely fresh significance. In other words, they parallel and elucidate four natural calamities that delineated the entire Bronze Age. As a result, the origins and influences of early civilization as depicted in myth stand out for the first time in bold relief against the backdrop of scientific evidence. They tell the forgotten story of humankind, a drama brought back to life by a similar cataclysm in our own time on the planet Jupiter.

Investigators meeting at Fitzwilliam College in 1997 showed that a series of comets, some of them still known today, closely approached Earth's orbit at both the start and conclusion of the Bronze Age, with two additional encounters at its early and middle periods. Hale-Bopp and Halley are familiar comets, although they were many times more massive and closer to our planet five thousand years ago. Astronomers Clubbe and Napier believe another one, called Proto-Encke or Oljato, was part of the destructive band of marauders from space. Others are unknown, probably because they disappeared for reasons related to those that have rendered Hale-Bopp, Halley, and Encke far less dangerous than in the past.

With each pass near the
disintegrated as the matrix
has evaporated in the solar
they lost most of it in orbiti
able to determine that these
dominated the skies of Ear
clearly visible even during b
imity heralded fearsome cor
flaming boulders at a defens

The most obvious proo
mined number of impact cra

[handwritten marginal notes:]

4th comet:

Venus?

See Velikovsky

(?) Worlds in Collision.

Comet/fire 1600 + 1200 BCE

1600 BCE 3100, 2200,

Flood

Age—seemed inadequate. But Kenneth Caroli suggests that a majority of incoming debris left no trace on land because it struck the oceans, which cover most of the earth's surface. The chances of finding impact craters are further reduced because of an unknown but probably large percentage of air bursts, in which meteors, like the asteroid that detonated over Siberia in 1908, explode before colliding with the surface of Earth. The materials resulting from air bursts can be even more powerfully destructive because their radius of effect is broader, although they leave fewer obvious traces behind. These considerations are compounded by the natural forces of wind and rain, which, over the millennia, can erode impact craters beyond recognition or to the point of disappearance.

But an abundance of physical proof for worldwide destruction left by comets during the Bronze Age was offered by scientists meeting at Fitzwilliam College. They presented undeniable evidence in the form of annual growth rings of the vegetation in Irish bogs and oak forest; ashfall deposits from Greenland ice cores; impact lines made by colossal waves along the shores of Morocco; abrupt lake-level changes from western Europe to South America; and small, glassy spherules that result specifically from cometary collisions, which subject rock to intense heat. The same blast effect appears on seventy so-called vitrified forts in Scotland. Euan Mackie, former deputy director at Glasgow's Hunterian Museum, defines this unusual structure as "a ruined hilltop stronghold which has been affected by fire to such an extent that parts of the stone rubble ramparts have become fused together; temperatures up to 1000 degrees centigrade are indicated" (Palmer and Bailey 1998, 149). Since the late eighteenth century scholars have assumed that prehistoric peoples deliberately subjected the forts to intense heat to strengthen their walls. But as Mackie points out, "Excavation of these sites always shows that the burning and vitrification occurs at the *end* of their occupation, rendering them uninhabitable" (Palmer and Bailey 1998, 312). Encyclopedist William Corliss adds,

> The military utility of vitrified fort walls is not obvious. Many of the walls are only a few feet high and as easily scaled as an unvitrified wall. Vitrification adds little if anything to the military value of the walls. In fact, it is more reasonable to view the vitrified fort

walls as the torched remains of much *higher,* more forbidding, timberframed walls that were surmounted by wooden ramparts and sharp, wooden stakes pointed toward the advancing foe (Corliss 2001, 122).

Experiments carried out in the late 1980s by archaeologists from Oxford University demonstrated that early western Europeans lacked the capability to generate the temperatures needed to fuse walls of stone. Every tree in Britain would have had to have been burned to vitrify a single Scottish fort! While evidence of fire damage through war or accident is commonly found in archaeological digs, vitrification is rare because the required temperatures greatly exceed those of normal burning. Moreover, near structures that do show vitrification, boulders and other rock formations completely unrelated to the forts seem to have been simultaneously fused by abnormally intense heat. Further argument against vitrification as a deliberate military method is its presence in other parts of the world among diverse peoples. During 1982 Colorado construction workers digging a pipeline in the mountains northwest of Denver inadvertently unearthed the remains of a village of sixteen mud buildings fused by extreme heat more than four thousand years ago. "This site's antiquity along with its fiery demise," notes Corliss, "raises a red flag for anomalists" (Corliss 2001, 122).

American antiquarian Stephen Peet learned that prehistoric structures at Bourneville, Ohio, atop a hill twelve miles west of Chillicothe, had been subjected to extraordinarily high temperatures. "These stone mounds," he notes, "exhibit the marks of intense heat, which has vitrified the surfaces of the stones and fused them together. Strong traces of fire are visible at other places on the wall, the point commanding the broadest extent of country" (Corliss 2001, 123).

A traveler for the *American Journal of Science* who visited Iraq in 1839 inspected the ruins of Birs Nimroud, a collapsed ziggurat, or step pyramid, about fifty-five miles south of Baghdad and found that

> . . . the base of the structure was not altered, but the piles of fine bricks thrown down were vitrified with various colors, and they gave the ringing sound belonging to the vitrifications of glass in the manufactories; the lines of cement are visible and distinct, and are

vitrified. The consuming power appears to have acted from above, and the scattered ruins fell from a higher point than the summit of the present standing fragment. The heat of the fire which produced such amazing effects must have burned with the force of the strongest furnace; and from the general appearance of the cleft in the wall of these vitrified masses, I should be inclined to attribute the catastrophe to lightning from heaven (Corliss 2001, 179).

His impressions were seconded more than forty years later by a reporter for the Victoria Institute's *Journal of Transactions:* "At the foot of this tower-like structure lie great boulders of vitrified brickwork, which were evidently fused by fire from heaven or elsewhere, and hurled from the original summit of the building, which was no doubt 100 feet or 150 feet higher" (Corliss 2001, 178). A writer who described Birs Nimroud for *Antiquity* magazine in 1929 reported that the most curious of its fragments "are several misshapen masses of brickwork, quite black. These have certainly been subjected to some fierce heat, as they are completely molten" (Corliss 2001, 177).

In France there are a number of *forts vitrifiés* at Château-vieux, at Puy de Gaudy, and in the vicinity of Saint-Brieuc (Côtes-du-Nord). These French sites demonstrate no cultural relationship to their Scottish counterparts save the time frame in which they were vitrified: the Late Bronze Age. While present dating techniques indicate vitrification took place around 800 B.C.E. and after, Mackie believes "dating by thermoluminescence does, however, suggest a wider spread" (Palmer and Bailey 1998, 245). Appropriately, dates for vitrification in Colorado, Iraq, and India coincide with two previous comet strikes in 2200 and 1628 B.C.E. Indeed, nothing less than a fire from heaven could have generated sufficiently high temperatures to liquefy stone structures around the world.

There were four such planetwide catastrophes, and each one marked fundamental changes in human destiny. The first took place on August 12, 3113 B.C.E., a date preserved by the Maya in their sacred calendar as 4 Ahu 2 Cimhu. In the centuries prior to that terrible moment civilization grew and prospered in the midocean realm of Atlas. But before the close of the fourth millennium B.C.E., a comet or series of comets sortied against the earth, sowing devastation across its surface and sending monstrous waves to crash against humankind's first cities. Badly wounded by seismic violence, with at least some of its territories collapsed into the writhing sea, Atlas shrugged off some of its population. Migrations of refugees voyaged to Mesopotamia, where they were remembered as the Oannes Men, or Sea People. (See fig. 3.1.) The same name applied to the Fomors in Ireland and the Pelasgians in Greece. At the Nile Delta they were the Mesentiu, or Harpooners. In Mexico and Peru they were "foreigners to the land," the Ah-Auab, and the Ayar-manco-topa. Everywhere they resettled, a syntheses of the venerable homeland's high culture with indigenous influences fostered new societies, sophisticated both materially and spiritually and rooted in common origins, yet increasingly distinct from each other in their development.

Nearly a thousand years of celestial peace allowed the Atlantean seed of civilization to flourish in the Nile Valley, the Indus Valley, the Valley of Mexico, the Fertile Crescent, and a dozen other less ravaged

Fig. 3.1. In this original illustration, survivors in a reed boat flee the late-fourth-millennium B.C.E. cataclysm, the first of four natural disasters that afflicted Atlantis. (Illustration by Kenneth Caroli)

areas of the world. Still reeling from its brush with annihilation, the enervated realm of Atlas suffered the humiliation of alien occupation. With the foreigners' eventual expulsion, the indomitable residents rebuilt their kingdom through their skills as sailors and copper miners.

But the heavens threatened again during 2193 B.C.E., as documented in the *Oera Linda Bok,* or "How the Bad Days Came," one family's heirloom from medieval Frisia. As before, cosmic serpents blazed across the sky, spitting flaming debris across the world. Dynasties fell, whole societies collapsed, and seismically prone Atlantis tottered on the verge of oblivion. More of its people left for less geologically vulnerable climes, founding new domains or reinforcing those pioneered by their forebears. Atlanteans at home knew what it was like to dig out from the rubble and begin anew. But their society emerged more splendid than before because resilience was the hallmark of its people.

Over the next six centuries, they led the civilized world into a new phase of the Bronze Age, with its fresh flowering of art and commerce. But in 1628 B.C.E. this period too was brought to a rude close when the heavens darkened and temperatures plummeted during an immense ashfall. Volcanos in the Aegean and the Pacific, ignited by a recurring barrage of cometary impacts, disgorged destruction and death, prompting yet another Atlantean migration throughout the world.

Although the capital was less damaged than during previous cataclysms, its leaders emerged with a new imperialist mind-set. Atlantis soon after asserted itself as the headquarters of an aggressively expansionist empire, founding colonial dominions on both sides of the ocean it had named after itself and engaging in the power politics of international diplomacy. To back up its claims it built strong armed forces of warships and marines. Concurrent with this military buildup, its chief city expanded in population, size, and material splendor to become the most opulent metropolis in the world. Ambition led to foreign entanglements, however, and the Atlanteans eventually found themselves at war with the other great kingdoms of the world.

Although they were successful at first, their victories eventually soured into defeat. Military disaster on Earth was accompanied by cometary catastrophe in the heavens: A fateful combination of celestial phenomena produced the most lethal assault from the sky ever endured by suffering humankind. Atlantis was not spared. Earthquakes shattered its buildings, colossal waves smashed its harbors, and seismic upheaval tortured Mount Atlas into a major eruption that blasted the island in two. Its fiery, gaping wound gulped millions of tons of seawater in a matter of moments, sucking to the bottom of the ocean Atlantis and its terrified inhabitants. Some fled the ultimate destruction of their homeland, only to find that the world into which they escaped was a dark age of almost universal destruction.

The four global cataclysms were remembered by premodern cultures around the world, sometimes in calendrical systems that used the world-class catastrophe to delineate major epochs. Two systems that used the four natural disasters in this way corroborate each other remarkably well, despite their separation by two oceans. The Aztec calendar, although employed from the fourteenth to sixteenth centuries C.E., was the last development of numerous progenitors going back to the origins of Mesoamerican civilization thousands of years earlier. Its suns, or epochs, were defined by four major disturbances in the earth's history: The first, 4-Ocelotl, or Jaguar, represented a time when humanity was almost devoured by huge packs of animal predators. Human beings survived, built a society—and became rich, idle, and decadent in a cycle that invariably preceded the next epoch, 4-Ehecatl, Windstorm. The penultimate destruction was 4-Quihuitl, Fire from Heaven. The Maya knew the last and most recent planetwide cataclysm as 4-Atl, or Water, the Great Flood, after which their Feathered Serpent cultural hero arrived from his engulfed kingdom on the other side of the Atlantic Ocean. These Aztec 4s coincide with the quartet of cosmic catastrophes now known to have struck the earth around 3100, 2200, 1600, and 1200 B.C.E.

Inhabitants of the Indian subcontinent likewise used the four cataclysms in their calendrical system. According to Caroli's research on the Hindu cycles of time, they were defined by certain constellations, the equivalent of astrological signs in the Western zodiac. Caroli explains that "3112 to 3066 B.C. plausibly represents a dividing line between their first two 'houses.' . . . In Kashmir, the Saptarshi calendar's zero date was fixed when the seven *rishis,* or sages, ascended to heaven to become the stars in Ursa Major, during 3076 B.C." (Caroli 2003). While Madame Helena Blavatsky and her theosophical followers in the late nineteenth century are accused of having gone off the mystical deep end, it nonetheless appears that they based some of their contentions, at least in part, on genuine traditions heard firsthand in India. Caroli claims:

> The Theosophical figures can be rationalized as a sort of lunar deity called a tithi—1/360th of a 354 synodic lunar year, or 371 per solar year. When that reduction is made the interval between the first and the last cataclysms was 2,130 to 2,156 years. Blavatsky's figure for a Zodiacal age was 2,155 years. Now, if we accept these 2,130 years as an entire Maha yuga, or epoch, which began from 3112 to 3066 B.C., we are presented with some interesting results.
>
> There are four *yugas* in this epoch, each progressively shorter than the last. The *Maha yuga*, circa 3100 B.C., ended with another, a *Krita yuga*, which closed sometime between 2260 and 2214 B.C. It was followed by a *Treta yuga* until 1621 or 1575 B.C. Rama Prusha, an avatar of Vishnu in Hindu myth, lived at this time. Appropriately, a great capital remembered as Lankhapura was said to have gone down into the sea during the *Treta yuga*. Before its submergence, a beautiful woman, Sita, was rescued by Rama, hero of several Asian epics, especially the *Ramayana*. Succeeding the *Treta yuga* was the *Davpara yuga*, named after Krishna's capital, which sank at his death to the bottom of the ocean following a mighty war. The *Davpara yuga* ended circa 1231 or 1213 B.C. (Caroli 2003).

Resemblances between the Aztec and Hindu cycles of time suggest they were separately influenced by survivors of the same four catastrophes. No less remarkably, both cycles parallel the recently discovered cosmic events of the late fourth and third millennia B.C.E. and the early seventeenth and twelfth centuries B.C.E. The Aztec suns and quartet of Hindu yugas clearly define the same set of natural catastrophes now recognized by science as having afflicted our planet during the ancient past. Most significantly for our investigation, the Atlantean character of these events clearly appears in the global flood of 4-Atl and Krishna's sunken city in the Davpara Yuga.

The world-changing violence they and numerous other traditions portray signifies an immense story spanning the globe and nearly two thousand years. The scope of its retelling seems almost too broad to comprehend. We are, after all, only just beginning to glimpse a vast panorama that explains the early saga of human civilization. It may be brought into clearer focus, however, by directly comparing myth with science in the context of the four Bronze Age cataclysms astronomers now recognize. The following cataclysm timelines connect some of the leading folk traditions with the archaeological and geologic records. As these connections are made, the world drama begins to describe itself, its players, its plot, and its denouement. Used as interchangeable templates over the epic of Atlantis, these timelines reveal its rise to greatness, its cosmic annihilation, and the fate of its survivors.

FIRST CATACLYSM: 3113 B.C.E.

Celestial Event

- Comet Proto-Encke makes its closest pass to Earth's orbit.
- A comet collides with asteroids in the asteroid belt between Mars and Jupiter, resulting in the Stohl meteor streams; these later form the Taurid meteors associated with Bronze Age cataclysms. The most active recent phase of the Taurid takes place at the turn of the fourth millennium B.C.E.
- As Duncan Steel concludes, "Thus the night sky around 3000 B.C., and for a period of at least one or two millennia after it, was disturbed, contained one or a few major comets recurring annually, coupled with epochs (set by orbital precession) when the annual meteor storm reached prodigious levels" (Wright 2000). According to Steel, a series of four comets spaced one month apart made "terrestrial orbit intersections" with Earth in 3100 B.C.E. (Wright 2000).
- The 500-foot-wide Henbury crater in north-central Australia is created by a meteor impact around 3100 B.C.E.

Geologic Evidence

- An acidity spike occurs in Greenland's Camp Century ice core, which indicates a sudden large increase of ashfall worldwide.
- In *Uriel's Machine* authors Christopher Knight and Robert Lomas note that within the last ten thousand years the direction of the

earth's magnetic field has abruptly changed only twice, most recently in 3150 B.C.E., when a comet struck the Mediterranean Sea.

- Atlantic Ocean vulcanism reaches a peak around the turn of the fourth millennium B.C.E., particularly in Iceland, at Mount Heimay; and in the Azores, the general vicinity of Atlantis.

- Worldwide, erosion values of 20 to 30 tons/kilometer^2 before 2950 B.C.E. jump to 140 tons/km^2. Massive flooding is recorded for the Tigris, Euphrates, and Nile Rivers. In Brazil, the Amazon Basin overflows, creating a now vanished lake, Lago Amazonicas.

Climate Change

- According to Boston University geologist Dr. Robert M. Schoch, Egypt's Great Sphinx shows damage suffered by rainfall predating its official construction in the twenty-sixth century B.C.E. by another 2,500 years. Kenneth Caroli points out, however,

> There was a climate deterioration circa 3090 B.C. The peak of this more moist period was brief, reaching its highest levels of rainfall around 2200 to 2100 B.C. The exact sequence of the climate decline remains somewhat disputed, though it appears to have intensified in stages, punctuated by either extreme, sudden droughts or brief bursts of driving rain (Caroli 2003).

In other words, water damage found on the Great Sphinx need not have occurred seven thousand years ago, about twenty centuries before dynastic Egypt was born, but several centuries after it came into being.

- Tree rings in California's White Mountains show that cooler, wetter conditions prevail in the American Southwest.

- A so-called dust veil event, the abrupt appearance of massive amounts of ash in the atmosphere, occurs, documented by tree rings in Ireland and England. There is increased cosmic dust input coincident with the widespread burning of various northern European bogs.

- The Dead Sea rises three hundred feet. "A bombardment episode may have occurred," according to Caroli (Caroli 2003).

- In Antarctica, a distinct peak in sedimentation occurs at Midge Lake, Beyers Peninsula, Livingstone Island, culminating around 2900 B.C.E.

- A spurt in the growth rate of peat moss at Elephant Island in the South Shetlands peaks around 3100 B.C.E.

Events in Specific Regions

- **Atlantis.** Severe earthquakes and vulcanism triggered by meteoric material striking the geologically unstable Mid-Atlantic Ridge overwhelm large areas of the island. Some territories are broken off and collapse into the sea. Coastal regions are further devastated by 300-foot-high waves traveling at 500 miles per hour. Loss of life and personal injuries run into the tens of thousands. Half or more of the cultural infrastructure is ruined. Although most survivors stay on to rebuild society, large-scale migration to other parts of the world, particularly to the Nile Valley and Mesopotamia, gets under way.
- **Ireland.** New Grange and other megalithic sites at Knowth and Dowth are constructed. In Irish folk tradition, the Fomors, associated with the megalith builders, arrive on the south coast.
- **Britain.** Construction begins on major megalithic sites, including Stonehenge on the Salisbury Plain; the Stones of Stenness outside the village of Barnhouse; and Maes Howe, located at the center of an island, Mainland. The Ring of Brodgar and Skara Brae in the Orkney Islands are erected.
- **The European continent.** Bronze production begins. Corded ware culture arises in Germany, the Netherlands, and Scandinavia.
- **The Aegean.** Stone tombs appear on Crete. Troy I, whose remains are the earliest archaeological evidence for the Trojan city of Ilios, begins. In Greek myth Phorcys survives the first Great Flood. Pelasgus arrives with his Sea People, the Pelasgians, as the first inhabitants of Greece. Writing of the Dardanian flood in the *Statesman,* Plato says that the sun appeared to turn back on its course at midday, during which there was an immense mortality of humans and animals.
- **Egypt.** The Followers of Horus and the Harpooners arrive at the Nile Delta. A fully developed civilization suddenly begins to flourish throughout the Nile Valley. The First Dynasty begins with either King Hor-aha or King Narmer. The construction of the Great Pyramid begins as early as the thirtieth century B.C.E., according to carbon 14 dating conducted during the late 1980s and again in the

early 1990s. The Chalcolithic, or Copper Age, bridges to the Early Bronze Age.

- **Mesopotamia.** The Sumerian Jemdet Nasr culture supersedes the Uruk. Bronze production begins. The Early Dynastic Sumer period commences. A pictographic script, Elamite, the earliest form of writing in the Fertile Crescent, is introduced.

- **Israel.** The Kabbalah, literally "the received tradition" in Hebrew, is a mystical interpretation of the Hebrew Scriptures that relies on their most ancient and original meanings. The kabbalistic term *Atziluth* is its name for the first of four "worlds" or spiritual powers that dominate the globe. Atziluth signifies the World of Emanations, or the Will of God, the beginning of human spiritual consciousness. Philological and mythological comparisons to Atlantis, where modern humans and their first formalized religion were born, appear to be preserved in the Atziluth tradition of the Kabbalah.

- **Iran.** In accounts from the Persian tradition, the Great Flood takes place in 3103 B.C.E. Previous to that global cataclysm the world is said to have been dominated by seventy-two solar dynasties. The same number occurs in Egyptian accounts of the Deluge. An Old Kingdom story, "The Tale of the Shipwrecked Sailor" (see *The Destruction of Atlantis,* 147–49), tells of a distant island ruled by seventy-two serpent kings before it is destroyed by "a fire from heaven" and sinks beneath the ocean. In the better-known Egyptian myth of Osiris, he is murdered by seventy-two conspirators. In arcane Hebrew tradition (the Kabbalah), the total number of angels is seventy-two. The figure appears to be the number of dynasties that governed Atlantis before the late-fourth-millennium B.C.E. catastrophe, as remembered independently by the descendants of survivors in both the Middle East and the Nile Valley.

- **India.** The subcontinent's first written language appears in the Indus-Sarasvati Valley. In the Indian epic the *Mahabharata,* a world age known as the Kali Yuga begins in 3137 B.C.E.

- **China.** Massive flooding forces ancestral Austronesians, who belong to an archaeological culture known as the Dawenkou in southern Shandong and Jiangsu, to migrate from Taiwan to the Philippines. Most of the proto-Malayo-Polynesian peoples who migrate from the East Asian mainland derive their languages from the Dawenkou.

After two thousand years, the Neolithic Yangshao and Hongshan societies are replaced by the Liangzhu culture, a state form that institutes city planning and organized agriculture. Liangzhu cultivation of the peanut, which can be obtained only from the Americas, suggests that transoceanic contacts between the Old and New Worlds are already being made. In mythic tradition, a Great Flood precedes the arrival of Emperor Fu Hsi around 2950 B.C.E.

- **North America.** Massive copper mining operations begin in the Upper Great Lakes region of Lake Superior.
- **Middle America.** Mesoamerican civilization begins with the Olmecs.

    The Mayan calendar starts on August 12, 3113 B.C.E. The Maya's Greater Arrival of culture bearers reach the shores of the Yucatán from the Hun yecil (Drowning of the Trees), a world-class deluge. In the Aztec calendar the first sun, or world age, is brought to a cataclysmic end by 4-Ocelotl, or Jaguar.

- **South America.** Llamas and alpacas are domesticated in the Andes. Ceremonial complexes of the Aspero tradition appear in the western areas of the continent. During the Salavarry period the first Peruvian pyramids with extended forecourts are built along the Pacific coast. In Inca tradition a fleet of civilizers, the Ayar-manco-topa, arrive from the east. Archaeologists regard circa 3000 B.C.E. as the early formative period of the New World high cultures.

SECOND CATACLYSM: 2193 B.C.E.

Celestial Event

- Comets Proto-Encke, Oljato, and Hale-Bopp converge near earth orbit. According to Caroli:

    If Encke is currently about five kilometers across at the core, and the former comet, Oljato, only one-and-a-half kilometers, Halley's may be around twenty kilometers. Hale-Bopp is at least four to five times larger than Halley's, and could be ten times bigger. Prior to its 1997 appearance, computer calculations put Hale-Bopp 15 million kilometers from Earth in 2213 B.C. About a year before it approached our planet, Hale-Bopp neared Jupiter, and could have split into two or more pieces. It does not come as close to any other planets, as it does Earth and Jupiter, yet the former is so massive by comparison, that its gravitational field would have torn Hale-Bopp in twain. The comet could not have adversely affected our planet, unless it had been broken in half from 100,000 to 10,000 years ago (Caroli 2003).

- W. Bruce Masse, an environmental archaeologist with the U.S. Air Force, concludes that "the period 2350 to 2000 B.C. witnessed at least four cosmic impacts (ca. B.C. 2345, 2240, 2188, 2000) and perhaps a fifth (ca. B.C. 2297 to 2265)" (Masse 1998, 201).

  An asteroid explodes over Argentina with the force of 359 megatons, leaving a series of impact craters across the Rio Cuarto area.

Geologic Evidence

- According to Maltese researcher Anton Mifsud, a large land bridge between Malta and the nearby island of Filfla cataclysmically collapsed, generating giant waves that flooded the whole archipelago and brought about the end of Neolithic life on Malta. Traces of major faulting in the submarine Pantelleria Rift, upon which both islands sit, have been dated to 2200 B.C.E.
- Swedish geologists Lars Franzen and Thomas B. Larsson found in their geologic material "indications of strongly increased atmospheric circulation in rhythmically appearing periods" (Palmer and Bailey 1998, 311) throughout the Bronze Age, with a high peak in the late third millennium B.C.E. Ashfall from the Icelandic volcano Hekla-4 dates a major eruption to about 2290 B.C.E.

Climate Change

- In March 1998, a specialist in paleoclimatology, Harvey Weiss, professor of Near Eastern archaeology at Yale, showed that the Habur Plains of northern Syria represented a highly productive agricultural and metropolitan region until all its farmlands and cities were rapidly abandoned. A prolonged, extreme drought forced mass evacuations. Ancient ocean sediments from the Gulf of Oman date the sudden deterioration of what had been a stable climate to circa 2200 B.C.E. Weiss's conclusion was substantiated by Peter DeMenocal at Columbia University's Lamont-Doherty Earth Observatory in New York. He found that chemical signals from the Greenland Ice Sheet Project 2 coincided with the Syrian drought.

- Four years before DeMenocal's confirmation, a researcher at the Swiss Technical University in Zurich analyzed sediment cores from the bottom of Turkey's Lake Van because it lies at the headwaters of the Tigris and Euphrates Rivers. Gerry Lemcke determined that the lake's volume of water declined radically at the same time, with catastrophic effects for the rural and urban populations of Mesopotamia.

- Glaciers renew their advance in Lapland, northernmost Sweden, and the Himalayas.

  Caroli describes:

> . . . a narrow growth event from the American tree rings and the climate instability reported on the Anatolian sequence. Does the burning of the northern European bogs reflect extreme drought, or something else, such as aerial detonations? Lars Franzen found 'spherules' similar to those reported in Syria. He made a comparison of certain rare minerals found in the burned layers of the bogs, possibly cosmic dust, with the site of the Tunguska blast of 1908 (Caroli 2003).

- Irish oak chronologies display evidence of an extraordinary "narrowest ring" event in 2345 B.C.E., which, Baillie believes, "could have a cometary relationship" (Palmer and Bailey 1998, 147).

- Major flooding occurs at Lough Neagh, the largest lake in Northern Ireland.

- Radiocarbon dating of flood-plain deposits in central England's Ripple Brook catchment evidence drastic increases of sediment deposition.

Events in Specific Regions

- **Atlantis.** Widespread seismic violence shatters ceremonial centers and demolishes many residential areas. Vulcanism incinerates croplands and sinks several nearby islands. Tsunamis ravage populations settled along regional shorelines. Many inhabitants are killed, and a second great wave of migration spreads to the

Americas, North Africa, and western Europe across the Mediterranean Sea to the Near East. However, a larger majority of Atlanteans begin reconstruction.

- **Ireland.** The Family of Partholon, immigrants from a disaster at sea, arrive on the south coast. The "World Chronicle" section of the *Annals of Clonmacnois* describes "lakes breaking out" all over the country, accompanied by nationwide panic. The archbishop of Armagh, James Ussher, author of the King James Bible, deduces through evidence in the Old Testament that Noah's Flood occurred in 2349 B.C.E.

- **Britain.** One of the seventeenth century's greatest scientists, William Whiston, successor to Isaac Newton at Cambridge, concluded that the Great Flood of 2349 B.C.E. was brought about by the near miss of a large comet.

- **The European continent.** The Frisian *Oera Linda Bok* reports that the destruction of Atland occurred in 2193 B.C.E.

- **The Aegean.** In *The Laws,* Plato states that "the famous Deluge" of Ogyges took place less than two thousand years before his time—that is, circa 2300 B.C.E. Varo, the Roman scholar, writes that it occurred around 2136 B.C.E. In classical Greek tradition, the Ogygean Flood is accompanied by nine months of darkness (ashfall).

- **Egypt.** The height of Egyptian civilization in the Old Kingdom collapses with the fall of the Sixth Dynasty. A Coptic account in the Abou Hormeis Papyrus tells of a fiery danger that appeared from "the heart of the Lion," the constellation Leo, near the star Regulus. Accompanied by loud thundering in the sky, a rain of burning stones shattered Egypt in "the first minute of Cancer." The Great Flood followed immediately. Caroli states that the report "could refer to a period when the summer solstice left Leo for Cancer, circa 2200 B.C.E. The papyrus sets the catastrophe for 399 years after a prophetic dream which resulted in building the Great Pyramid. If so, the event occurred sometime after 2254 B.C.E."

  A mysterious mass death, occurring simultaneously with widespread fires, strikes the port city of Mendes, which is abandoned until the advent of the New Kingdom.

- **Israel.** According to Masse, evidence for widespread destruction after the start of the twenty-second century B.C.E. "suggests that a cosmic impact may have been a factor, a date which fits well with the estimate of 2188 B.C.E. for the Sodom and Gomorrah impact" (Palmer and Bailey, 1998, 244).

- **Mesopotamia.** The Akkadian empire collapses. In archaeological terms, Ur-III comes to a sudden close circa 2160 B.C.E. Shu Durul, the last king of the Agade empire, dies in 2139 B.C.E. A contemporary epic, *The Curse of Akkad,* tells of "heavy clouds that did not rain," "large fields which produce no grain," and "flaming potsherds that fall from the sky."

- **Syria.** In 1999 archaeologist Marie-Agnes Courty finds collections of petroglyphs that suggest humans witnessed a celestial impact circa 2350 B.C.E.

- **India.** The Banas culture of Rajasthan emerges.

- **China.** The Liangzhu culture is replaced by the first Chinese dynasty, the Xia. Ten "suns" fall from the sky after having been shot by a divine archer, an allegory of the celestial chaos during this period. Nine years of cataclysmic floods follow during the reigns of the emperors Kuan and Yu. Caroli believes "both were connected to sky dragons, probably comets" (Caroli 2003). Using royal chronologies, he dates the "ten suns" incident to circa 2141 B.C.E.

  Emperor Shun writes of a large meteor he saw fall from the sky and strike the earth around 2240 B.C.E., followed by the Great Flood: "The whole world was submerged and all the world was an endless ocean. People floated on the treacherous waters, searching out caves and trees on high mountains. The crops were ruined and survivors vied with fierce birds for places to live. Thousands died each day."

- **Mesoamerica.** In the Aztec calendar, the second sun, or world age, was terminated by a global disaster, 4-Ehecatl, or Windstorm, possibly a characterization of air blasts caused by meteors exploding before they could hit the earth. Ehecatl is the most overtly Atlantean version of the Feathered Serpent, being portrayed in sacred art as a man who, like Atlas, supports the sky on his shoulders. Temples dedicated to Ehecatl, such as his structure at the very center of Tenochtitlán, the Aztec capital, were invariably composed of circular walls, often comprising red, white, and black stones—the same configuration and colors Plato said typified Atlantean building styles.

Votan, the Quiché Maya's founding father, arrives from his Atlantic Ocean kingdom of Valum.

- **South America.** According to Andean folk tradition, the Auarchaki, or Wanderers, seek refuge in Peru from a great flood on the other side of the world. The Kotush tradition begins in the Andes.

THIRD CATACLYSM: 1628 B.C.E.

Celestial Event

- The quartet of killer comets returns to earth, but Hale-Bopp and Halley are too far out to cause mischief this time. Most of the damage is wrought by Oljato or Proto-Encke. All the comets have been substantially diminished in mass from their recurring orbits around the sun, resulting in relatively less destructive consequences for our planet. Even so, another global disaster occurs through meteor impacts, which result in a dust veil event of ash and particularly severe volcanic eruptions in the Aegean and the South Pacific.

Geologic Evidence

- Exceptionally heavy ashfall is recorded in Greenland ice cores. The Nile Delta suffers massive deposition, killing off most plant life across Lower Egypt.
- Iron spherules from Tunisian peat bogs are the result of a comet collision with Earth dated to the late seventeenth century B.C.E. "Their heterogeneous composition," according to Larsson and Franzen, "points to another formation mechanism (other than vulcanism), maybe comet or asteroid impacts in ocean shelf sediments" (Palmer and Bailey, 1998, 212).

Climate Change

- German, British, Irish, and North American tree rings evidence prodigious ashfall.
- Caroli points out that "a Turkish sequence compiled in the 1980s and '90s by a team of dendrochronologists from Cornell University, led by Peter Kuniholm, revealed a sudden growth spurt. A log from a Swedish bog showed a climate regression from 1636 to 1632 B.C. A similar climate horizon turned up in a Chinese bog" (Caroli 2003).

Events in Specific Regions

- **Atlantis.** Although less devastated than in the two previous cataclysms, the island suffers significant damage primarily through earthquakes and tsunamis. Rebuilding begins at once, and the capital enters its most opulent phase as the epitome of a Bronze Age center. Renewed, if relatively small-scale, migration to other parts of the empire and the outside world takes place.
- **Ireland.** The Nemidians arrive on the south coast from Atlantis.
- **The European continent.** The Red Ochre culture ends. The Bell Beaker culture ends. The Old Bronze Age ends. Bronze manufacturing arrives in Scandinavia. Mount Vesuvius erupts in Italy.
- **The Aegean.** The volcanic island of Thera explodes with the force of a major nuclear event. On Crete, the Old Palace phase is decimated, and Mycenaean Greeks invade.

    In Greek tradition, Deucalion survives the deluge.
- **Egypt.** The Fourteenth Dynasty collapses, while a people remembered as the Hyksos overrun the Nile Delta after having been forced from their homelands around the Levant by drastically deteriorating climate conditions. The Egyptian priest-historian Manetho recorded that "a blast of God" prostrated Egypt, allowing the Hyksos to invade without striking a blow.

    The Tempest Stele, found reused in the third pylon at Karnak, tells of an extraordinarily ferocious storm that took place during the reign of Ahmose I. Similarly, the late dynastic El-Arish Text, originally from Persoped in the eastern Nile Delta, describes a deep, prolonged darkness and the death of a pharaoh, whose heir was injured by heavenly fire after his entourage was totally destroyed.

    Caroli notes that "there was a mysterious mass death at Avaris during the XIII Dynasty" (Caroli 2003). Large metropolitan centers destroyed or abandoned around this time include Ithtaw (Residence City) and Hetepsenusret. A Cushite kingdom emerges as Egypt loses control of the area. Baillie suggests that the biblical plagues of Egypt and Exodus were brought about by a severe climate regression due to volcanic ash filling the atmosphere and the effects of a comet's pass near the earth.
- **Middle East.** "There were quite a few destructions in central and southern Canaan," writes Caroli, "after 1630 [B.C.E.], such as at

Jericho. Although burned savagely, the city seems to have been hit by a large earthquake. This evidently released gases into nearby tombs which preserved many perishable items" (Caroli 2003). A dark age descends over Babylon for more than a hundred years as the Amorite capital is sacked. Weakened Mittanni and Hurri overlords lose their hold on Assyria.

- **Asia Minor.** The Hittite Old Kingdom collapses.

- **Mesopotamia.** In an obscured period lasting little more than nine months during Amaziduga's ninth year (i.e., 1629 B.C.E.), the king describes seeing Ninsianna, commonly misinterpreted by modern historians as the planet Venus, but more likely a comet, according to his description.

- **India.** Thousands of congealed "black stones" have been recovered from the ancient Indian city of Mohenjo-daro, which collapsed abruptly and inexplicably around 1600 B.C.E. Travel writer David Hatcher Childress, who visited the site, states that the amorphous lumps "are, apparently, fragments of clay vessels that melted together in extreme heat and fused" (Childress, 1985, 191).

- **Central Asia.** The Afanasevo culture, which introduced pastoral farming fifteen hundred years before, collapses.

- **China.** The Xia dynasty collapses. "The overthrow of the Xia dynasty," writes Caroli, "has been linked to the eruption of Thera" (Caroli 2003). The Shang dynasty emerges on the plain of the Yellow River.

- **North America.** The pace and volume of Upper Michigan copper mining increases abruptly. The city at Poverty Point, Louisiana, is founded. There is a major volcanic eruption at Anniachak, Alaska. The Red Paint culture ends.

- **The Pacific Ocean.** The Lapita Pottery culture, ancestral to the Polynesians, spreads out into the Pacific Ocean. A volcanic eruption in New Zealand compares in strength to the contemporary Thera event.

- **Mesoamerica.** 4-Quihuitl, literally "the Fire from Heaven," is the third of the global catastrophes depicted in its own square on the Aztec Calendar Stone as a sheet of descending flame. It closes a former sun, or world age, from which a few survivors rebuild society. Olmec civilization enters a major cultural phase. According to conventional scholars, the Olmec begins at this time. The Feathered Serpent and his followers arrive from "watery Aztlan."

- **South America.** In South American archaeology, the Middle Formative period begins. Thonapa's people arrive after the Unu-Pachacuti (World Overturned by Water).

FOURTH CATACLYSM: 1198 B.C.E.

Celestial Event

- Comet Oljato or Proto-Encke is nudged closer to earth orbit by the appearance of Halley. Franzen and Larsson offer that

  > . . . relatively large extraterrestrial bodies hit somewhere in the eastern North Atlantic [i.e., the location of Atlantis], probably on the shelf of the Atlantic coast of North Africa or southern Europe around 1000 to 950 B.C., mainly affecting the Mediterranean parts of Africa and Europe, but also globally (Palmer and Bailey, 1998, 212).

- According to Caroli, "the Pleiadian Age, in terms of the vernal equinox, ended between B.C. 1500 and 1100" (Caroli 2003). This period brackets the zenith of Atlantis and concludes with its final destruction. In Greek myth, the Pleiades, as daughters of Atlas, were Atlantises.

Geologic Evidence

- There is a drastic rise in Swedish and Swiss lake levels, especially obvious at Saalachsee, Ammersee, Federsee, and Bodensee, with widespread abandonment of lake-pile villages. Flooding is so great, perhaps unequaled before or since in known history or prehistory, that new lakes form in Germany near Memmingen, Munich, Ravensburg, and Toelz. Lake levels rise dramatically throughout Northern Ireland, such as at Loughbashade. The largest soda lake on earth, Turkey's Lake Van, rises 250 feet in about two years. Climatologists have calculated that such an increase would have required approximately 150 inches of rainfall. Lake levels across central Africa also rise significantly, although not as dramatically. In North America, Utah's Great Salt Lake and Canada's Waldsea Basin reach abnormally high levels, as does South America's Lake Titicaca in the Bolivian Andes and Lago Cardiel in western Argentina. Annual growth rings in Irish bog oaks decline. There is a dramatic climate regression all across central Europe. Frost conditions occur in Tunisia. Sedimentary evidence in North Africa and Scandinavia shows abrupt, general cooling, excessively low tree growth, extremely heavy rainfall, and widespread flooding on a global scale.

- In the late first century B.C.E., while researching at the library of Caesarea, the capital of Mauretania, Diodorus Siculus, the Greek geographer, learned of a catastrophic earthquake that devastated the entire Atlantic coast of North America 1,200 years before his day. Modern geologists have confirmed his report.

- Masse cites "a locally catastrophic terrestrial impact around 1000 B.C." (Palmer and Bailey 1998, 191) that occurred in the badlands of northern Montana.

- West of Broken Bow, Nebraska, lies a mile-wide impact crater created approximately three thousand years ago by a meteor that exploded with the equivalent force of a 120-megaton nuclear blast.

- Greenland's Camp Century ice cores reveal that a global catastrophe threw several thousand cubic kilometers of ash into the atmosphere around 1170 B.C.E.

- Volcanism around the world peaks at the close of the thirteenth century B.C.E. Outstanding eruptions occur in Arabia, from Russia's Avachinsky and Sheveluch volcanoes near the Pacific Ocean on the Kamchatka Peninsula, the Japanese Atami-san, North America's Mount Saint Helens, California's Mount Shasta, Oregon's Newberry and Belknap volcanoes, and Central America's San Salvador volcano. Atlantic Ocean volcanism is widespread, with events in Iceland (Hekla) and on Ascension Island, Candlemas, the Azores (Mount Furnas), and the Canaries (Gran Canaria, Fuerteventura, and Lanzarote).

- Geologist Robert Hewitt describes the end of the Bronze Age (see fig. 3.2) as "a catastrophe which was one of the worst in world history" (Hewitt 1958, 122).

- Franzen and Larsson feel compelled by the geologic evidence to "propose that cosmic activity could offer an explanation for the observed changes. We even suggest that relatively large asteroids or comets (c. 0.5 km diameter) hit somewhere in the eastern Atlantic" (Palmer and Bailey 1998, 301).

Climate Change

- Baillie concludes, "There were two major temperature troughs around 1600 B.C. and 1100 B.C." The latter, "the most marked one, can be traced in many other parts of the world, including Europe, the Americas, the Near East and the Antarctic" (Palmer and Bailey 1998, 175).

- Alaska and the western and central United States grow suddenly cooler and moister.

- Across South America climate deterioration closely corresponds to a neoglacial interval that takes place at the same time.

- In the German Rhineland a vast majority of oak trunks show clear signs of massive flooding around 1000 B.C.E.

Fig. 3.2. This photograph of the Icelandic volcano Hekla depicts a scene reminiscent of the fiery cataclysm that ended the Bronze Age. Nuee's ardentes is fast-traveling incandescent gas ejected by some volcanoes before, during, or shortly after eruption. Similar glowing "clouds" occur when gaseous comets collide with the earth's lower, denser atmosphere or with the planet's surface itself. (Photo courtesy of the Nordic Volcanological Institute, University of Iceland)

- Tree-ring sequences compiled by David Kuniholm show that climate deterioration reached its peak in Turkey from about 1185 to 1141 B.C.E.

Events in Specific Regions

- **Atlantis.** "In a day and a night," according to Plato, the island is obliterated, possibly when Mount Atlas explodes laterally, allowing many millions of tons of seawater to rush into its exposed magma chambers, resulting in a subduction process. (See fig. 3.3.) While most of the population perishes, there are many thousands of survivors who escape to various parts of the world.
- **Ireland.** Waves of survivors arrive: the Fir Bolg, Fir Gailion, Tuatha de Danann, and Milesians.
- **Britain.** Most of the island is depopulated. Development is terminated at Stonehenge; the site is abandoned.
- **The European continent.** The Bronze Age ends. Bavaria's Black Forest is incinerated. Across Scandinavia long-established burial customs are abandoned, *tumuli* (ceremonial mounds) are no longer constructed, and the display of rich funeral objects is drastically reduced. Bronze work comes to a halt, and coastal regions are evacuated. A vast area of low-lying land where several large rivers converged totally submerges the Hungarian Plain in catastrophic flooding. At the height of a rich and active phase, an entire Bronze Age population is wiped out. Italy's Mount Vesuvius erupts on three separate occasions in the century after 1200 B.C.E.
- **The Aegean.** The Bronze Age ends. Caroli writes that

> . . . the massive hydraulic works at Lake Copais, in Greece, used to be attributed to Hellenistic or Roman periods, and no earlier than Mycenaean times. But they now seem to date to later Troy-I and early Troy-II, in the early Third Millennium B.C. The works were abandoned circa 1200 B.C., resulting in massive flooding of the Copais basin (Caroli 2003).

Major earthquake damage and fire occurs in Athens, Mycenae, Tiryns, Knossos, Troy, Urgarit, and Cyprus. In response to unprecedentedly heavy rainfalls, eastern Mediterranean house construction changes from flat to pitched gable roofs.

Fig. 3.3. The eruptions that began to create Surtsey in 1963 likely resembled those that led to the final destruction of Atlantis. (Photo courtesy of the Nordic Volcanological Institute, University of Iceland)

- **Egypt.** The New Kingdom ends, signaling the onset of a decline from which dynastic civilization will never recover. The Harris Papyrus reports prodigious clouds of ash overwhelming the Nile Valley from the west at the time of Ramses III's coronation in 1198 B.C.E. Soon after, he combatted an invasion of the Sea People, who told his scribes that "a shooting star" burned their homeland before it sank into the sea. At the close of the Nineteenth Dynasty (circa 1197 B.C.E.), Pharaoh Seti II describes Sekhmet as "a circling star" that spat flames throughout the known world. The Ipuwer Papyrus records fiery destruction across Egypt.
- **The Middle East.** The Bronze Age ends. At its peak, Assyrian power declines from about 1208 to 1179 B.C.E. A baked clay text from the port city of Ugarit tells of Anat, a star that fell on "the Syrian land, setting it afire, and confusing the two twilights." Many important

and most secondary Bronze Age sites in Asia Minor are burned. The imperial capital of the Hittite empire, Hattusas, is consumed by a conflagration.

- **India.** A celestial war described in the *Mahabharata,* using a thirty-five-year generation, dates to 1200 B.C.E.
- **China.** The final, or Yin-Shang, period of the Shang dynasty begins. The Shang dynasty goes into a sharp decline for less than two centuries before it vanishes. Excavated oracle bones from the period seem obsessed with natural catastrophes. A typical example tries to reassure its client, "In the next ten days there will be no more disasters."

  The last Shang emperor, Chou Hsin, loses a decisive battle to Wu Wang, founder of the succeeding Chou dynasty, in 1122 B.C.E. Chinese myth recounts that simultaneous with this military confrontation a cosmic battle took place between comets in the sky.

  A hurried mass burial at the Shang site of Sanxingdui, in Sichuan Province, includes an abundance of precious goods. The carved jade pieces, elephant ivories, cowrie shells, gold objects, and numerous bronzes are contemporary with Emperor Wu Ding and the Empress Lady Hao, who died in 1189 B.C.E. The extraordinary circumstances of this find appear to have been brought about by the chaotic climate conditions attendant with global cataclysm. Caroli reports, "Legend tells that thousands of Shang partisans fled east by ship, their fate unknown" (Caroli 2003).

- **Mesoamerica.** According to the distinguished sinologist Dr. Mike Xu, Shang visitors arrive from unsettling climate conditions in China on the shores of western Mexico to reform Olmec Civilization.

  In the Aztec calendar 4-Atl signifies the global deluge that destroyed a former sun, or age. It is depicted on the Aztec Calendar Stone as a celestial bucket of water inundating a sinking stone pyramid, a self-evident reference to the final destruction of Atlantis.

  The Aztec Haiyococab, the Water-over-Earth, told how "the Earth-upholding gods escaped when the world was destroyed by the Deluge."

  The Maya's Lesser Arrival of culture bearers takes place on the shores of the Yucatán.

- **North America.** Louisiana's Poverty Point experiences a sudden major increase in population and undergoes its final development. During the height of its productivity, copper mining at Michigan's Upper Peninsula is suddenly terminated. The Chumash culture appears along the California coast. Massive coastal flooding in the southeastern United States, probably caused by meteor and asteroid falls in the Atlantic Ocean, is indicated by a long pattern of impact craters, or "bays," in South Carolina.
- **South America.** Andean tradition recounts that the warlike Ayar-aucca, fleeing defeat and a terrible natural disaster, arrive in Peru. The Andes' Kotush tradition comes to an end. The Sechin-Chavin culture begins in Peru. The Late Formative period begins, signaling a critical sudden development in megalithic construction: "It was as though a spiritual threshold had been reached."

4

ATLANTEANS INTO EGYPT

*But when you depart from here, you shall nevermore see
this island. It will be changed into waves.*

"TALE OF THE SHIPWRECKED SAILOR"

Before the fifth millennium B.C.E. the Nile Valley was sparsely
inhabited by Paleolithic aboriginals, but about six thousand years
ago newcomers were gradually settling in Lower Egypt. Remains of
dwellings from this extended period of influx at Merimda Bani Salamah
show they were oval shaped, lightly constructed huts of wickerwork
posts covered with animal skins, identical to those found in Neolithic
sites across western Asia. Although this people's culture was materially
superior to that of the earlier resident society of Nile dwellers, these
Badarians, as archaeologists call them, did not really foreshadow the
pharaonic Egypt yet to come.

Sometime in the mid-to-late fourth millennium B.C.E., however, the
whole land was dramatically transformed by the sudden arrival of large
numbers of settlers who carried with them all the features of a fully
developed, sophisticated civilization. As Professor Walter B. Emery,
excavator of the pyramid complex at Saqqara and among the most
important Egyptologists of the early twentieth century, concludes:

The rapid advance of civilization in the Nile Valley immediately
prior to the [political] unification [of Egypt] was due to the advent
of the "dynastic race." The theory of the existence of this master

74

race is supported by the discovery that the graves of the late predynastic period in the northern part of Upper Egypt were found to contain the anatomical remains of a people whose skulls are of greater size and whose bodies were larger than those of the natives, the difference being so marked that any suggestion that these people derived from the earlier stock is impossible (Emery 1961, 39).

Already advanced irrigation techniques were applied to the regular flooding of the Nile, and the bounty it now brought forth sparked population growth. The Neolithic villages became *nome*s, or districts, in an evolving political system requiring governmental leaders and centralized authorities to coordinate irrigation, harvest procedures, and food storage and distribution. The Badarians' flimsy wicker huts were swept aside in the construction of massive temples, palaces, and monumental public buildings of huge, finely crafted stone blocks. Emery observes,

It is astonishing that early in the First Dynasty, objects of the carpenter's and joiner's crafts gave ample evidence of an advanced knowledge of working in wood. All the principles of joining, such as both stump and through tenon-tongued, rebate, half-lap and dovetail were known and used; moreover, elaborate carving and inlay of mixed woods with ivory and faience were commonplace. Although their tools were few in number, they nevertheless fulfilled all the essential functions of modern carpentry, with the exception of the plane, which remained an unknown supplement in Egypt until Roman times (Emery 1961, 216).

If these skills did not evolve over a long period of time in Egypt, where were they developed?

Archaic temples and tombs for royalty featured panels decorated with strips of embossed sheet gold from floor to ceiling only about one centimeter apart, recalling Plato's account in *Critias* of Poseidon's shrine "surrounded by an enclosure of gold" and other walls in Atlantis similarly decorated with precious metals. Although weaving had been unknown to the Badarian indigenes, with the advent of the dynastic race the loom, a complex device, abruptly appeared "at a comparatively late stage in the evolution of its design" (Emery 1961, 177).

From the First Dynasty, papyrus was being cultivated for the involved manufacture of writing paper. Emery observes:

> Already evidence has been obtained which shows that the written language was by no means in its infancy, even at the beginning of the First Dynasty. Even the earliest texts show that the written language had gone beyond purely the use of word signs, which were pictures of objects or actions. There were also signs used to represent sounds only, and a system of numerical signs had already been evolved. Apart from the fact that the hieroglyphs are already stylistic and conventionalized, a cursive script was already in common use. All this shows that the written language must have had a considerable period of development behind it, of which no trace has yet been found in Egypt. Some authorities point out that, given sufficient impetus, a written language can develop very rapidly; nevertheless, one would expect to find some evidence of it in the south during predynastic times. Therefore, until evidence to the contrary is forthcoming, we must accept the fact that current with the appearance of a highly developed monumental architecture, there is a fully developed system of writing (Emery 1961, 192).

Before the arrival of the dynastic race the Badarian natives rafted along short stretches of the Lower Nile. But ships of the Archaic period were already bringing back cedar from Lebanon; trading at the Sinai and in Asine, Crete; and engaging in naval skirmishes with similarly seaworthy vessels from Sumer. The 124-foot-long vessel found in its own burial pit on the south side of the Great Pyramid demonstrates an extraordinarily sophisticated level of ship-building skill. Its wooden planks were so precisely fitted that when sewn together by hawsers, the ropes swelled in contact with the Nile, thereby binding the boards into a watertight hull, rendering unnecessary the otherwise standard use of pitch as a sealant. There was even air-conditioning on board: Light winds passing through a contained space over the roof filled with wet branches funneled cooled breezes into the spacious deck cabin. The pyramid boat's remarkably graceful lines bespeak a long tradition of maritime technology, while its high stemposts evidence oceangoing capabilities, not merely royal river outings. These qualities are all the more remarkable when we realize that the vessel was built prior to 3000 B.C.E., three centuries before the first Egyptian dynasty. In the words of Dr. Thor Heyerdahl, "the Egyptians were seafarers long before they arrived at the Nile" (Heyerdahl 1971, 97).

In short, virtually all the features of Egyptian civilization were present from the beginning of its history. "How does a complex civilization spring full-blown into being?" asks the well-known investigator of Egyptian antiquities, John Anthony West.

> Look at a 1905 automobile and compare it to a modern one. There is no mistaking the process of "development." But in Egypt, there are no parallels. Everything is right there from the start. The answer to the mystery is of course obvious, but because it is repellent to the prevailing cast of modern thinking, it is seldom seriously considered. Egyptian Civilization was not a development. It was a legacy (West 1979, 13).

That this legacy did not arrive from the East is certain. The waterless desert tracts that acted as a buffer against the incursion of Asian tribes for so many centuries—until the infiltration of barbarian Hyksos charioteers in the mid-seventeenth century B.C.E.—were an even more effective barrier against cultural influences. Moreover, nothing remotely resembling or approaching the development of the high civilization of Egypt existed anywhere in western Asia. The various and seemingly contradictory Egyptian cosmogonies agreed at least that the earliest primeval deities came from the Distant West.

Modern researchers are supported in their conclusions about a dynastic race that delivered civilization to the Nile Valley from the Distant West. The "father of history," Herodotus, while traveling though sixth-century B.C.E. Egypt, quotes the priests of Memphis as having said that their ancestors came from a land in the far west. Two hundred years later, Manetho, an Egyptian priest writing in Greek, reports that the first civilized people came to Egypt with all the makings of a highly sophisticated society after a catastrophic deluge. The Greek geographer Diodorus Siculus, Mantheo's contemporary, reports, "The Egyptians themselves were strangers who in very remote times settled on the banks of the Nile, bringing with themselves the civilization of their mother country, the art of writing, and a polished language. They had come from the direction of the setting sun, and were the most ancient of men" (Leonard 1904, 92). He claims that the ancestors of the Egyptians came from Ethiopia. As described in chapter 2, the Ethiopian prince Memnon, who died defending Troy, was an Atlantean leader. During the Early Classical period, Ethiopia was synonymous with Atlantic North Africa, the Atlantic Ocean just outside the Pillars of Heracles (Gibraltar), or Atlantis itself.

Meh-Urt, the Celestial Cow, symbol of birth from nothingness, was among the deities they brought to the Nile Valley. Her name means, literally, "Great Flood." Chapter 175 in the Book of the Dead features a description of the event she personified: "The Earth was covered by the Flood. All life was destroyed." Some virtuous humans did survive, however. Their leader was Osiris, who was memorialized in the Osireion, located twenty-six feet behind the Temple of Seti-I (flourished 1360 B.C.E.) at Abydos (Abdu). It is an underground vaulted hall surrounded by a channel representing the Great Water Circle, or ocean, and thus created an allegory in stone of Atum's "primeval hill." According to Egyptologist Rundell Clarke, a scale model of the structure was centrally installed in it with a statue of Osiris at its summit. This strange subterranean building was a ritual simulacrum of civilized humankind's origins from Atum's island kingdom in the middle of the ocean, a transparent reference to the sunken Atlantean land, the homeland of the Egyptians' ancestors. The Old Kingdom "Destruction of Mankind" was discovered, appropriately enough, in the Osireion itself. The account tells of Aalu, the Isle of Flame, likewise known to North America's Apache Indians by the same name. It obviously describes a volcanic island suggestive of Atlantis.

According to "The Destruction of Mankind," Aalu was located far onto the Great Water Circle, west of Tuat, the Otherworld residence of the gods, at the ends of the world where the sun goes down, surrounded by lofty mountains separating heaven from the earth. It was a great island kingdom with luxuriant crops of wheat, and its palatial city was surrounded by an iron wall "of many gates, to which converged far-spreading roads." Each morning, the sun god appeared at Aalu through a "door" situated at the center of the island. But one day, Atum, father of the gods, summoned Tefnut, portrayed as "a bloodthirsty lioness.

Her mane smoked with fire, as her faced glowed like the sun" (Mercatante 1978, 184). Tefnut was a mythic image of the comet (also known to the Egyptians as Sekhmet) that menaced the Bronze Age and destroyed Atlantis, along with dozens of cities that were its contemporaries, in the late thirteenth and early twelfth centuries B.C.E.

Atum ordered Tefnut to destroy Aalu with a celestial conflagration, for its inhabitants had grown to despise the gods. Aalu is also mentioned in the sixteenth century B.C.E. Book of the Dead (chapter 61), a collection of mortuary texts placed in tombs with the deceased. The island kingdom is here depicted with navigable streams similar to the regulated canals of Plato's Atlantis. Less obvious is the "door" through which the sun god appeared at dawn, the implication being that Aalu lay in the east. But the island was specifically identified in the far west, beyond Tuat, itself of western and Atlantean significance: Tuat's mountains were said to separate heaven from earth, as Mount Atlas did, and personified Shu (see fig. 4.1), the Egyptian Atlas, who separated Geb (earth) from Nut (the sky).

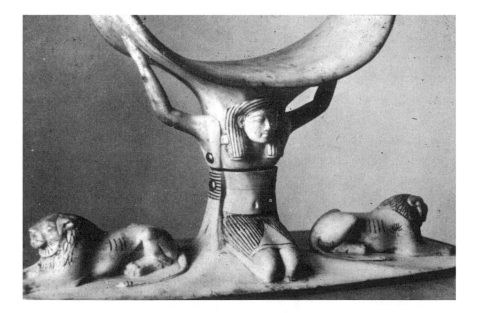

Fig. 4.1. Depicted in this acacia wood head rest, Shu bore the sky on his shoulders at the center of the world as defined by twin lions representing east and west. Dynastic Egyptians claimed their descent from survivors who escaped the inundation of their island realm in the Western Sea. (National Archaeological Museum, Cairo)

The sun god's "door" at Aalu can only have been the astronomical feature of a megalithic temple not unlike Britain's Stonehenge, that masterwork of calendric genius. In fact, the notches at Stonehenge used to sight the alignments of celestial targets are still known as "windows," suggesting the same concept behind the Egyptian "door": a stone frame deliberately oriented to catch the sun's first rays. For example, the so-called heel stone at Stonehenge, rather than signifying a heel, is instead derived from the Old Welsh *haul* (pronounced "hayil"), meaning sun. Because astronomically oriented temples flourished "beyond the Pillars of Heracles," the far western location and identity of Aalu seem credible. Atum's association with the Primal Mound and his involvement with the flood are closely related to Atlas and his mountain, which collapsed into the sea. Atum was, in short, an Egyptian version of Atlas, an identity underscored by the philological resemblance between the Egyptian god and the Greek Titan.

According to the oldest Egyptian traditions, several waves of Emery's "dynastic race" swept over Lower Egypt, the foremost being the Semsu-Hor, or Followers of Horus. They were immediately followed or accompanied by the Mesentiu, or Harpooners. The harpoon was also carried as an emblem by the Semsu-Hor in their Lower Nile *nome* on the western Delta, where the falcon sky god himself was sometimes known as Hor-tchema, Horus the Piercer, as he stood poised to harpoon his nemesis, Seth, in the guise of a hippopotamus. Because the Semsu-Hor were the first kings of Egypt, every pharaoh of the thirty-one dynasties, with the lone exception of the heretical Amenhotep IV, the self-styled Akhenaton, personally identified with Horus. As Mercer explains, "Horus himself, according to tradition, was the last of the divine rulers of Egypt. They, as well as the dynastic rulers, were considered the incarnation of Horus, that is, Horus kings, and as such were treated as gods" (Mercer 1960, 78). The Book of the Dead makes it clear that the Semsu-Hor were Atlanteans: "Horus will be exalted on the throne which is set up on the Isle of Flame," a name descriptive of volcanic Atlantis.

But Horus as a religious figure may have been the result of some compromise between the newly arrived Harpooners and the natives. Mercer suggests that the dynastic race of immigrants, "on establishing themselves in Egypt, perhaps in the Delta, may have located themselves at first in a town or district whose inhabitants already had as their ensign and god a falcon, which the newcomers adopted and made their own, and which developed into a falcon- or Horus-worship" (Mercer 1960, 93). He points out that the root of *horus,* "falcon," is *hor,* "face," which stood for heaven, *hort,* and that therefore the foreign dynasts combined their own sky deity or heaven deity with the resident falcon god. This peaceful syncretism is reflected in the legend of Horus as the son of Osiris, the god of rebirth and the fructifying principle of nature, who came from afar to impregnate his wife, Isis, the personification of the new motherland, Egypt. Horus (the power of pharaohood) would then be considered the offspring or natural result of a union between the incoming civilizers from the Distant West and the indigenes of the Nile Valley. Accordingly, Osiris's title Prince of the Westerners is particularly appropriate.

As their harpoon emblem implied, the Semsu-Hor and the Mesentiu were seafarers. The founders of pharaonic Egypt from the Distant West arrived suddenly at the delta, carrying with them the art and science of a full-blown civilization after a great flood. But looking to the west, we can find no evidence of that civilization's homeland in Libya. Still farther west are only the shores of North Africa, and beyond, a vacant ocean. Yet Plato said that the Egyptians preserved the history of a mighty empire whose capital was on a large island out in the near Atlantic.

The civilizing Followers of Horus were graphically defined in Upper Egypt's Dendara zodiac, which represents identical pairs of falcon-headed human figures on bent knee holding up the heavens. Atlas was the legendary founder of astrology, envisaged in Greek myth as supporting the vault of the sky. He was born among sets of twin brothers like those shown in the Dendara zodiac. Chapter 20 in the Book of the Dead relates that the "homestead" of the Semsu-Hor was in Sekhet-Aaru. Researcher Martin Bernal demonstrates in his book *Black Athena* that the Greek name Atlas was derived from the Egyptian *aru,* making the identification of Sekhet-Aaru with Atlantis all the more clear.

The Greek version of Egypt's civilized origins told of Aegyptus, the first pharaoh, from whom the land took its name. His grandfather was Poseidon, the sea god creator of Atlantis, whose emblem, like that of the Followers of Horus and the Harpooners, was the trident. The mother of Aegyptus was a mortal woman, Libya. His legend reflects the same migration depicted in the Egyptians' own foundation narratives: Aegyptus was a second-generation Atlantean whose parents trekked across Libya during their long flight from their "homestead" at Poseidon's island, Sekhet-Aaru. Underscoring this tradition, Orpheus, the first-century B.C.E. Greek historian, regarded Egypt as a "daughter of Poseidon."

Aegyptus was one of the Semsu-Hor, whose historical reality was confirmed in Egypt's first king, Hor-aha. The lineage he instituted in 3100 B.C.E. set the precedent for kingship that would endure for the length of dynastic times. Emery writes,

> According to tradition, the god Horus reigned in prehistoric times in Egypt, but he was always represented by an earthly king, who was a 'Horus', or a Horus king. Such kings were called in historic times, 'Followers of Horus', Semsu-Hor. Horus himself, according to tradition, was the last of a line of divine rulers of Egypt. They, as well as the dynastic rulers, were considered the incarnation of Horus, that is, 'Horus kings', and, as such, were treated as gods (Emery 1961, 95).

In other words, the very concept of pharaohood that dominated the whole history of dynastic Egypt was instituted by the Atlantean Semsu-Hor.

The historical reality of King Hor-aha and his Atlantean identity was strongly supported in the early twentieth century by the renowned Egyptologist Sir Flinders Petrie. While excavating at Abydos, where the Osireion is located, Flinders found a small ivory tablet inscribed with the likeness and name of a King Aha. Behind the figure appears a bull running over wavy ground into a net stretched between two poles, almost exactly the same scene embossed on the Vapheio cups. These are two perfectly preserved gold artifacts found at a Mycenaean site in Laconia, Greece, just south of Sparta. The cups had been imported from Minoan Crete about 3,500 years ago. One of them depicts a scene Plato describes in his account of Atlantis, where sacred bulls were ritually captured with nooses.

Petrie discovered the King Aha tablet in a shrine dedicated to the goddess Neith, an even more direct connection to Atlantis, because it was in her temple at Sais, on the Nile Delta, that the original account of the oceanic civilization was preserved, according to Plato. Neith was worshipped as the First Birthgiver, said to have woven the world on her loom, which she invented and bequeathed to humanity. In this role she was the mythic personification of the Atlantean Followers of Horus, Emery's "dynastic race" that introduced weaving into the Nile Valley, along with all the other benefits of high civilization. But Neith had a terrible aspect as well. When offended, the goddess was known as She Who Would Have the Heavens Fall upon Earth and threatened celestial catastrophe. Under such dire circumstances she was appealed to as "the protectress against the encroachment of water."

Besides being the most primeval goddess, historically her city witnessed the joining of the Lower Nile *nomes* (districts) prior even to national unification in dynastic times. Significantly, one of her symbols was the Red Crown of Lower Egypt. So ancient and ancestral an account as that of Atlantis could not have been enshrined in a more apt place; keeping it at her temple in the presence of the First Birthgiver was symbolic of the Atlantean Semsu-Hor arrival on the shores of the Nile Delta, and of their story. No more appropriate location for preserving the story of Atlantis existed, because it was near Sais that the Atlanteans had been turned back by Ramses III in their final attempted conquest of Egypt.

An abundance of physical and traditional evidence from ancient Egypt clearly reveals that the rural inhabitants of the Nile Valley were hosts to technologically advanced refugees from the far west, where some natural disaster had driven them from their oceanic homeland more than five thousand years ago. Together both peoples built a new civilization, whose most splendid achievement still stands on the Giza Plateau. Beside it, buried in its own crypt, is a 124-foot-long ship. It is not alone. Four more are entombed nearby. Nor were these merely ceremonial craft for leisurely outings down the placid Nile; they were seaworthy vessels that had actually sailed long and hard enough to bear enduring traces of wear.

Dating as they do to before the official founding of pharaonic civilization, the sophisticated maritime technology they demonstrate belonged to a highly advanced predynastic race, the Followers of

Horus—the same people who built the Great Pyramid. These are the vessels in which they arrived from their Atlantean homeland, an interpretation that alone adequately explains why such magnificent ships were allowed to share the same sacred precinct with the foremost monument the world.

The cataclysmic event from which they carried refugees to far-off safety at the Nile Delta was preserved in a document known as *The Book of What Is in the Duat,* or Otherworld. "When the Creator wished to punish humanity," its anonymous author reports, "he dispatched his right eye, Sekhmet, the sun, who fell into the waters of the abyss."

5

NOAH WAS ATLANTEAN

*Though you be sought for, yet shall you never
be found again.*

EZEKIEL 17:19

Prolonged seismic violence during the late fourth millennium B.C.E. fomented large-scale evacuation from the slowly subsiding Atlantic land mass. Its human migrations spread mostly eastward by caravan through the still-verdant Sahara and along the coast, and by flotilla across the Mediterranean Sea, skirting North African shores. These Atlantean masses who settled in the Nile Valley triggered the abrupt rise of dynastic civilization, while those who erected the first cities in the Fertile Crescent between the Tigris and Euphrates sparked the equally rapid development of Mesopotamian civilization.

Publicly, at any rate, no archaeologist would so much as consider such an interpretation. Yet it competently explains the common features (some of them identifiably Atlantean) of Early Dynastic Egypt and Sumer. While they undoubtedly shared some cultural contacts, both peoples remained essentially insular to outside influences of any kind. More to the point, their resemblances did not come about gradually, as would be expected through evolving communication, but appeared simultaneously from the outset of both societies, suggesting they were rooted in a common source. According to Egyptologist Dr. Walter Emery, "Indeed, the existence of a third party whose cultural achievements were passed on independently to Egypt and Mesopotamia would best explain common features and the fundamental differences of the two civilizations" (Emery 1961, 107).

Some of those common features include the use in their respective cults of symbolically composite animals, such as winged griffins, serpent-necked felines, and pairs of entwined beasts, or a hero dominating two lions. In portraits of their kings, both Sumerian and Egyptian artists represented them as larger than life-sized and surrounded by smaller figures. For Sumerian monarchs and Egyptian pharaohs, wearing a beard was indicative of strength. Moreover, both rulers were known by the same title: Bull of the Heavens. The Egyptian bull, Hap, was a fertility cult figure associated with kingship, whose rituals were virtually indistinguishable from the Son of Enlil bull ceremonies at Ur. The bull, as described in Plato's account, was the center of a special royal ceremony in Atlantis. And while the bull is a symbol common to a great many cultures, its veneration in identical or near-identical rituals among different societies is not common and suggests a prehistoric relationship among Egyptians, Sumerians, and their ancestral Atlanteans.

There are similarities beyond those of ritual. Archaic Egyptian and Sumerian architects simultaneously used a specialized recessed-brick technique, with the methods differing only in the size of the bricks used. The contemporary Jemdet Nasr period in Sumer and the Egyptian Archaic featured *totons,* or window facades, that were practically identical, while palace design in both cultures "undoubtedly had a common origin" (Emery 1961, 191). First Dynasty pharaohs sacrificed retainers at their funerals and entombed them in the precincts of the royal sepulcher, as did the early monarchs at Ur. Predynastic religion originated in a monotheistic solar cult associated with the supreme god, Ra, while in Mesopotamia in the late fourth century B.C.E. the Sumerian "first god," Dingir (Shining), represented the same kind of beginnings. Interestingly, the original inhabitants of the Canary Islands, off the Atlantic coast of Morocco, initially worshipped only a sun god associated with the high mountains of Tenerife and Gran Canaria. So too the Egyptian pyramids were venerated as Mountains of Ra, and the ziggurats of Sumer were looked upon as monumental staircases to Dingir. A cultural continuity begins to appear that stretches from its source in the Atlantic Ocean eastward to Egypt and then into Mesopotamia.

That continuity becomes especially clear in parallels between the Sumerian Asari and the Egyptian Ausar (better remembered in his

Greek guise as Osiris). The similarity only begins with their names. In both civilizations Asari-Ausar was regarded as a man who achieves divinity after spreading the values and technology of civilization throughout the world. Later he is treacherously murdered and his corpse dismembered, its pieces scattered far and wide. His wife—Innini in Sumer and Eset or, more famously, Isis in Egypt—is also his sister in both versions. She collects his body parts, then restores him to eternal life through the power of her mystery religion. Both Innini and Eset were fertility goddess, and both were represented as weeping figures in their respective cultures.

Asari's title was Faithful Lord of the Tree, and Ausar's symbol was the *Tet* amulet, the trunk or "pillar" of a tree that was part of his resurrection story. Coincident with his appearance in both cultures were the simultaneous beginnings of civilization in the Nile Valley and in the alluvial plain created by the Tigris and Euphrates Rivers around 3100 B.C.E. By that time the Followers of Horus, who had delivered civilization to Egypt, were busy trying to fuse the various nomes into a unified state. A similar political process was undertaken by the newly arrived Atlantean ancestors of the Sumerians. "The impression we get," Emery concludes, "is of an indirect connection and perhaps the existence of a third party whose influence spread to both the Euphrates and the Nile" (Emery 1961, 119). Researchers continue to postulate, even stress, the existence of a "third party" as the common source for Egyptian and Sumerian civilizations, and not only because both were so culturally insular. Connections between the two were severely restricted by the extensive, waterless desert that sealed off Egypt from the east. Moreover, the general impression of an Atlantean third party is underscored by the nature of both the similarities and the far more numerous and fundamental differences between the two civilizations.

For example, a scene depicted on an ivory knife handle from Gebel-el-Arak, and repeated in greater detail among the wall paintings from a late predynastic tomb at Hieraconopolis, shows the Followers of Horus engaged in a pitched sea battle with foreigners. While the Egyptians are portrayed commanding typically native vessels, their enemies man the high-prowed, high-stemmed boats of Sumer. The implication seems to be that contact between the two civilizations was infrequent and less than cordial.

Racially, the Sumerians continue to puzzle archaeologists. They were neither Semitic nor Indo-European, and their language was agglutinative, a kind of Finno-Urgic tongue suggesting some Caucasian connection. Referring to themselves as the "black-headed people," their eyes were light, their complexion fair to tan, and their build short and slender. They were apparently related to the same stock as the Followers of Horus, the Guanche aboriginals of the Canary Islands, the pre-Celtic inhabitants of the British Isles, and the ancient Iberians, of which today's Basque population may be the lone surviving remnant. In other words, they were part of the Atlantean race.

The most obvious point of comparison between Sumer and Egypt is pyramid temple design, which appeared shortly after, if not simultaneously with, the separate beginnings of both civilizations. Like most of the other similarities that link the two cultures, Egyptian and Sumerian pyramids are similar in fundamentals but differ greatly in details. This would explain their origins from a common outside source, while accounting for their individual treatment at the hands of two cultures growing away from each other, like different branches of the same tree. The sacred mountain with its "lofty stage-tower" was memorialized in the Sumerian ziggurat. The name itself is descriptive, meaning "mountain peak" and reminiscent of the Egyptians' reference to their pyramids as "mountains of Ra."

Campbell writes of the ziggurat "towering in five stages, in imitation of the holy mountain" (Campbell 1961, 137). Plato reports that the sacred numerals of Atlantis were five and six, representing male and female energies respectively. To create a proper balance of spiritual energies, the Atlanteans incorporated these numbers in their monumental architecture, the same numerical symbolism at work in Sumer. But the decisive point here is that the pyramids and ziggurats were built entirely independently of each other. They were not the results of cross-cultural contacts. The step pyramid, a style most resembling the ziggurat, developed from the mastaba, or free-standing tomb of a single story, whereas the ziggurat grew out of temples raised on platforms. In other words, both concepts sprang from a common inspiration that predated their own civilizations, but their methods of evolution were completely unrelated.

Clearly, the most important feature linking pyramid to ziggurat was their common function as monuments to the ancestry of their people—

to those who journeyed eastward from the sacred mountain island in the distant western sea. In the Babylonian version, after Utnashpitim survived the flood, he erected a temple on a mountain peak, where he offered thanks to the gods. His sons then went down into the world to found its races and nations. As before, there are similar fundamentals and differing details. Zoser's man-made Mountain of Ra at Saqqara and the ziggurat at Ur are both five-step pyramids (again, the Atlantean sacred numeral, 5) constructed of mud brick. But unlike the Egyptian pyramids, the ziggurats contained no internal chambers or passageways. The name of the volcanic mountain that signaled the Deluge was the Sumerian Adad. Likewise, a mountain "in the place of the setting sun" was the Arallu, which compares with the Egyptian Aaru, also described as located in the Distant West. Here, then, in the preeminent structures of Egypt and Sumer, are the surviving monuments to that third party from which both claimed descent: the Atlanteans.

The Sumerian myth of Enki seems to reflect this divided development from a common root: After a golden age during which all humans spoke the same language and embraced each other as brothers and sisters, Enki "changed the speech in their mouths, put contention in it, into the speech of men, that until then had been one." Enki was a water deity who traveled in his great ship, the *Ibex of the Abzu,* on a worldwide mission to civilize humankind. The ibex was a wild goat with large, curved horns. Here is the motif of the goat as sea symbol that is repeated from earliest historic times throughout virtually every Western and some Near Eastern cultures.

Enki provides an Atlantean point of comparison between Sumer and Egypt, where temple art sometimes represented the goat-headed Khnemu, a creation god, as the captain of the "solar boat" that ferried the first gods and humans to the Nile Delta. Similar to Oannes, the Babylonian civilization god, Enki was associated with traveling over vast tracts of open sea. The Abzu was the primeval waste of waters out of which arose his "mountain of life." The cosmogonic myth of the Sumerian Abzu is virtually identical to that of the Egyptian Atum, god of the primal sea, who raised a mound from its depths.

In *The Feats and Exploits of Ninurta,* the Abzu is repeatedly distinguished as salty, hence oceanic. Once more, we are confronted with examples of cross-cultural influences. Or were both peoples of the

Nile Valley and southern Mesopotamia inheritors of a common tradition from a third party? Evidence does indeed point to that outside source from far across the sea. For example, in *The Affairs of the Water-God,* we read that "after the water of creation had been decreed, Enki built his sea house of silver and lapis lazuli. He ornamented it greatly with gold. He made it float over the water like a lofty mountain." The caretaker of this sea house was Nashe, the "mountain of heaven and Earth."

Near it was a green, fruit-bearing garden with many birds and fish. The "lofty mountain" had been raised in primeval times upon the peak of a dragon's back to become Ninhursag, Nin-of-the-Mountain. This sacred island was blessed with all kinds of herbs, wine, honey, trees, gold, silver, and bronze, together with "all four-legged creatures." It was Ninhursag, also known as Queen of the Cosmic Mountain, who, in the words of the eminent Sumerian language expert Noah Kramer, "set the stage for the organization of the universe, the creation of man, and the establishment of civilization" (Kramer 1969, 321).

In *The Begetting of Nanna* Ninhursag's great city is described: "Behold, the Bond-of-Heaven-and-Earth, the kindly wall, its pure river, its quay where the boats stand, its well of good water, its pure canal!" Here, at the birthplace of the gods, they "built the lofty stage-tower on the nether-sea, and chapels for themselves," devised the first laws, and founded the science of astronomy-astrology. The Babylonian version of the Sumerian Ea was Marduk, who "made supreme the glorious city, the seat dear to their [the gods'] hearts, constructed an enclosure around the waters." In a liturgical text Ea is described as "the lord who dwells in a fane in the midst of the ocean" (Gaster 1969, 135).

These mythic accounts of Enki's "sea-house," Ninhursag's "cosmic mountain," and Ea's "glorious city in the midst of the ocean" are self-evident portrayals of the same homeland of civilization that Plato depicts in his Atlantis dialogue. Ninhursag's Bond-of-Heaven-and-Earth is Atlas (fig. 5.1), the Upholder of the Heavens, inventor of astrology-astronomy, and so forth. Reaffirming the Atlantean identity of the Sumerian accounts, the cosmic mountain (that is, Mount Atlas) lay in the Distant West, beyond a vast stretch of sea; it is depicted on the cylinder-seal impression of a ziggurat positioned over a twisting

Fig. 5.1. This Roman statue circa 100 A.D. depicts Atlas, the first king of Atlantis, supporting the zodiac. (Naples Archaeological Museum, Italy)

rope, the symbol of water. *Tarkullu* (Rope) was the Babylonian sea god. Included on the same seal is the image of a fox (for the Fox Star), indicating West.

The Sumerians' supreme god was Enlil (fig. 5.2), who, like Atlas, separated heaven and earth, and was known as the Father of the Gods, King of All Lands, and Secret of the Great Mountain—epithets evocative of Atlantis as the dominant spiritual and political power of the early Bronze Age.

In *The Epic of Gilgamesh*, when the hero goes in search of the Great Flood survivor, he finds him in the Distant West, dwelling at a mountaintop upon which rests the vault of heaven, and whose base is at the bottom of the sea. In short, the gods were born on an island dominated by a great mountain and located across the ocean in the far west. There they built the first city and civilization, which reached its height in a splendid palace, Enki's "sea-house." That this Atlantis-like myth served as the cosmogony of a whole people 2,600 years before Plato wrote his dialogue points to the credibility of both accounts.

Fig. 5.2. The Sumerian god Enlil, who was said to have ruled the world during the Lam Abubia—an "age before the Flood"—holds up the bowl of the heavens in this gypsum votive statuette from Iraq, circa 2700 B.C.E. (Museum of the Oriental Institute, University of Chicago)

The bull played a revealing role in Sumerian religion: At cities such as Ur and Nannar, it was revered as the Son of Enlil, that supreme god, Secret of the Great Mountain, who "separated heaven and earth," practically the same words used two-and-a-half millennia later to describe him in his Greek guise as Atlas. Campbell points out that the ziggurat at Nippur was dedicated to the Atlantean Enlil, "the Lord of the Air [the same title for the Egyptian Atlas, Shu], who reigned from the summit of the world mountain" (Campbell 1961, 78). The bull was synonymous with kingship in both Sumer and Atlantis.

Certainly, the Sumerians' most indelible impact on the Near Eastern civilizations that followed was the story of the Deluge. Although, not surprisingly, details were altered and new mythic elements introduced as it passed through subsequent cultures, the account remained essentially unchanged. Its Atlantean implications are highlighted by the great mountain of Ninhursag memorialized in the ziggurat. During each New Year's festival, the *Enuma Elish*, a poem recalling the flood, was recited around the ziggurat at Easgila, affirming that structure's Atlantean association. It described how the chief of the gods (the Lugallugga, or Big Chief of the Chiefs) "dragged off all of them into the midst of the sea, who occupies the middle thereof."

The ziggurat at Sippar marked the location where Xiusthros, the Babylonian flood hero, buried a history of the world until his time. His Deluge account generally coincides with the sudden beginnings of both the Mesopotamian and Nile civilizations following the arrival in the eastern Mediterranean of culture bearers from seismically wracked Atlantis—the Sumerian Akkadi and the Egyptian Followers of Horus. As Filby explains, "The Genesis account envisages the end of an ancient civilization and the rise of a completely new race, the descendants of Noah, who spread across the world from the Middle East." The Old Testament describes these "descendants of Noah" as the builders of the Temple of Babel (the ziggurat at Etemenanki), raised to memorialize their ancestry.

Babylonian and Assyrian scribes write of an "age before the Flood," the Lam Abubia, known to the Egyptians as the First Time, and they describe an antediluvian king, Enmemduranna, as the founder of divination, just as Atlas was later revered by the Greeks as the father of astrology. Similarly, Adapa was the Sumerians' first astrologer. Magic rituals of expiation were handed down as secret instructions from the "ancient sages of the Lam Abubia." The Assyrian monarch Assurnasirpal (reigned 883–859 B.C.E.) loved to read the "monumental inscriptions from before the Flood," recalling Plato's description of the laws and major decisions arrived at and inscripted on posted tablets by the kings' council at the Temple of Poseidon in Atlantis. The Tablets of Fate were composed by the gods when they met every year in the Ubsukinna, the assembly hall of Enlil, that Wind of the Underworld Mountain, whose "head rivals the heavens, whose foundation is laid in the pure abyss [the Abzu, or 'primal sea']."

Plato described ten kings of Atlantis before it was destroyed, and ten kings reigned prior to the Great Flood in both Sumerian and Babylonian versions, while Genesis mentions ten "antediluvian patriarchs." Plato's *Critias* ends with "Zeus, god of gods, perceiving that an honorable race was in a most wretched state, and wanting to inflict punishment on them, collected all the gods into his most holy habitation." When the

Sumerian god Enki warns Ziusudra of the coming Deluge, he tells him, "This is the decision, the command of the assembly of the gods" convened by Enlil, the supreme deity, to punish sinful humankind. The two accounts, although widely separated in time, obviously refer to the same catastrophic event.

The destruction that followed was truly Atlantean in scope: "Against the standing-place [temple] of the gods it [the cataclysm] has directed its terror. In the sitting-place of the Annunaki [lesser deities] it has led forth fearfulness. Its dreadful fear it has hurled upon the land; the mountain, the dreadful rays of fire, it has directed against all the lands. All the windstorms, exceedingly powerful, attacked as one."

The oldest Syrian account, preserved in Lucian's *De Syria Dea,* tells how the gods sent "waters boiling from the Earth," a theme repeated in the Koran, which records that the flood "boiled over" from the oven of an old woman. Her name, Zula-Cupha, refers to a spring of hot water. Clearly, these three sources describe a flood caused by volcanic activity. The theme is taken up again in the Sumerian *Saga of Ninurta:* "From the mountain there went forth a pernicious tooth [volcanic outburst] scurrying, and at his side the gods of his city cowered on the Earth. Oh, mountain-stone, who in the hostile land has raised a roar of wrath [an eruption], who utters a roar as in battle, wrathfully, terribly."

The Babylonian version of *The Slaying of the Labu* is no less dramatic: "The mighty Irra seized away the beams [of the dams], and Ninurta coming caused the locks to burst. The Annunaki bore torches, making the land to glow with their gleaming. The noise of Adad [the volcanic mountain] came unto heaven, and a great water-spout reached to the sky. Everything light turned to darkness. For one day, the hurricane swiftly blew like the shock of battle over the people." Ishtar wailed, "Like a brood of fish, they [the people] now fill the sea!" After six days, "the sea became calm, the cyclone died away, the Deluge ceased. I [Xiusthros] looked upon the sea, and the sound of voices had ended."

It is difficult to understand how conventional historians can insist that the world-class deluge portrayed so vividly in Mesopotamian tradition was nothing more than a local inundation caused when the Tigris and Euphrates overflowed their banks. Descriptions of a mountain with "dreadful rays of fire" and repeated mention of the sea hardly qualify it as the result of rising river conditions, however severe. More to the point of our discussion, the cataclysm depicted by Sumerian and Babylonian sources is identifiably Atlantean, even to the similar language in Plato's account.

These Mesopotamian flood stories are particularly distinguished by the destruction of a former kingdom, from which survivors land in the Near East to respark civilization. For example, the Babylonian version tells how "over mountain and sea went the throne-bearers" to establish new empires after the flood. The same antediluvian culture bearers appear in Genesis, where Noah's sons father the post-Deluge human races, dividing up the world and establishing new nations. One of these was Shumer, after whom the civilization he founded, Sumer, took its name. Indeed, the Old Testament portrays this eldest son of Noah as the architect of the oldest kingdom in Mesopotamia.

The name Noah likewise demonstrates how the flood story not only predated the composition of the Old Testament (circa 800 B.C.E.), but was known far beyond Israel. The name is apparently derived from the Hurrian name Nuach. The Hurrians were Bronze Age inhabitants of Asia Minor but were originally from Caucasia. Planetwide climate changes produced by the cometary disasters of 3100 B.C.E. decimated their ancestral croplands, forcing them to migrate in search of better conditions elsewhere. The Phrygians, a related tribe who migrated into Asia Minor from Thrace, but with roots in Armenia, knew a Deluge myth whose hero was Nannakos.

Surviving Phrygian coins carry the Greek letters NOE above the representation of a floating square chest with passengers aboard, while a dove bearing an olive branch flutters overhead and a man and woman step ashore. These various Noah tales have him landing his ark in Armenia on Mount Ararat or Mount Nisir. Such mountainous locations may have meant that Caucasian versions and perhaps a flood-hero cult left Sumer with some native Hurrians, who returned to their native Armenia after Sargon, the conquering Akkadian king, occupied Sumer with his Semitic forces around 2260 B.C.E. In all Sumerian accounts of the Great Flood the ark does not come to rest on an Armenian mountaintop, but lands instead at the seashore.

Parallels are also suggested between the earliest Sumerian Noah (Ziusudra) and Zarathushtra, founder of the Zoroastrian religion. The

Persian Deluge story is closer to the Sumerian original than either the Babylonian or Semitic versions. In the language of the oldest sacred literature of the Iranian people, Zend, the story related how Yima, the first patriarch of Persia, was saved in the Arg of the Magus (the Ark of the Magician). Significantly, the *Zend-Avesta* was the holy book written by Zarathushtra, and his first Iranian legend portrays him as a royal descendant of invaders from another land across the sea. While Ziusudra was certainly a symbol of Atlantean migration to Mesopotamia in the mid-to-late fourth millennium B.C.E., he too may actually have existed.

The Babylonian priest Berosus recounted that Xiusthros (Ziusudra), among his divine instructions prior to the Deluge, was commanded to compose a history of the world to his day and to bury it at Sipparah. Giving life to this myth is a terra-cotta tablet discovered during a dig at Sipparah and preserved at Istanbul's Ottoman Museum. Its translation tells of a "safety ship" riding out a cataclysmic flood after the destruction of a great city and its kingdom. The scribe, Ellit-Aya, dates himself in the text to fourteen years before the close of the Shutural, the last of the Akkadian dynasties, circa 2140 B.C.E. He writes that he copied the account from a source so ancient he was unable to identify it, and that parts of the original were *hibis,* or "illegible," with age. The surviving fragment, titled "While the Men Rested," is the tenth section of a yet unrecovered twelve-part epic. Ellit-Aya's tablet is the oldest example of the Mesopotamian Deluge story, even though, as he reported, the source he copied it from was already in his time a very ancient document. Its discovery at the same city mentioned in the myth itself is remarkable.

A telling indication that the Flood story was not only prebiblical but essentially alien to the Jews is the foreign word chosen in Genesis to describe the ark, because there was no Hebrew equivalent: *Tebah* is derived from the Egyptian *tebet.* The Deluge was not unknown to the earliest pharaonic scribes, and while the Old Testament version mostly relied on Babylonian sources, its authors also seem to have been familiar with a much older tradition from the Nile Valley. The ark itself lends credibility to the story. As Filby discusses in some detail in *The Flood Reconsidered,* it was, in fact, a seaworthy vessel, or else the author of the Babylonian account was a shipbuilder with expert knowledge of seaworthy vessels. Filby points out that in 1604 a Dutch merchant, Peter Jansen, built a faithful reconstruction of Noah's ark at Hoorn, using the same ratios given in Genesis: 300 by 50 by 300 cubits. The result was a 120-by-20-by-120-foot craft that proved remarkably stable with its cargo full and able to weather heavy sea swells. Genesis, in fact, describes Noah as a shipwright, implying that he belonged to a "sea people" with an oceangoing maritime tradition.

Was Noah an Atlantean? In his Sumerian guise as Ziusudra, he belonged to that first series of geologic convulsions that struck the Atlantic land mass and prompted many of its inhabitants to seek shelter on foreign shores. The seismic upheavals shook civilization free from its isolated homeland to take seed in the Near East. There, sometime after 3100 B.C.E., the Atlantean culture bearers introduced the virtues of a more complexly organized society to the Neolithic natives. The evidence of Mesopotamian myth and history not only adequately preserves the story, but also helps to confirm Plato's account. If his *Critias* had never been written or had been lost to posterity, we should still know of the oceanic homeland of civilization, thanks to Sumerian records, the oldest traditions of lost Atlantis.

6

THE GREEKS KNEW IT ALL

There is a connection between this place [the Garden of the Hesperides] and the land of Atlantis, as recounted by Plato.

JEAN MARKALE, *THE TEMPLAR TREASURE AT GISORS*

The ancient Greeks recalled not one but four major cataclysms. Interestingly, each one paralleled planetwide natural disasters scientists now know to have actually ravaged the earth in the early millennia of civilization. No less remarkably, these Greek catastrophes coincide with time parameters arrived at by modern academics in geology, astrophysics, and climatology. A general consensus of specialist opinion has assigned these cataclysmic episodes to 3100, 2200, 1629, and 1198 B.C.E. In Greek terms they correspond respectively to the floods of Phorcys-Dardanus, Ogyges, Deucalion, and Atlantis.

As the first of the Deluge heroes in Greek myth, Phorcys is associated with the calamity of the late fourth millennium B.C.E. because he was regarded as the founder of Aegean civilization. His title, He Who Was Borne Away, refers to the natural catastrophe that annihilated a former age. Phorcys was the leader of a people known as the Pelasgians, or Sea People, the same characterization (Pulasta) used by Pharaoh Ramses III, documented on the walls of his victory temple at Medinet Habu in West Thebes, to describe the Atlantean invaders of the Nile Delta. In other words, terms for the Egyptian Pulasta and Greek Pelasgians—both Sea People—were used to describe the same outsiders from Atlantis.

The Pelasgians derived their name from Pelasgus, the "First Man" to set foot on the Greek mainland, a son of Gaea, the Mother Earth goddess, and a prince who arrived in the Aegean with the rest of his fellow refugees. He was depicted in vase art as a bearded man being disgorged headfirst from the mouth of a monstrous sea snake before the goddess Athena. In this obvious symbolism Pelasgus signifies the arrival of the Pelasgians and civilization in Greece. The same image appears on the other side of the world in Mesoamerican representations of the culture-bearing Feathered Serpent, who is portrayed as a fair-skinned bearded man emerging from the jaws of an enormous snake. Remembered by the Toltecs as Tollan, he was believed to have come from the east, over the Atlantic Ocean, fleeing the natural destruction of his homeland. Pelasgus likewise arrived in the Peloponnese after a terrible deluge from the west. It seems logical to conclude from a comparison of these two foundation myths, widely separated geographically, that an Atlantean catastrophe was responsible for both.

Said to have reunited scattered humanity in Greece following the Great Flood, Phorcys was the son of Inachus (Rapid Current) and Melia (Ash, from which tree his ark was made). Inachus, too, possessed an Atlantean heritage from his father, Oceanus, and his mother, Tethys, the Lovely Queen of the Sea. Their son led survivors from mountaintops, which had become islands, across the waters to Argos, where he become the first king. Oenotros, his great-grandson, was the founder of Etruria in the tradition of Atlantean culture bearers arriving in foreign lands to establish new civilizations. Etruria, according to Plato, was an early Atlantean conquest.

At the north end of the temple to Olympia Zeus in Athens stood a pair of 360-foot obelisks memorializing the Great Flood of Phorcys. Twice a year each was ceremoniously scaled to commemorate humankind's escape from the catastrophe by climbing mountains. Cakes were then tossed into the clefts near the temple to honor those who perished in the cataclysm. Both obelisks were still standing as late as 180 C.E.

Even in early classical times, when the Pelasgians were a dying race, the Greeks could still distinguish them from the other peoples of the Troad (the Trojan sphere of influence in northwestern Asia Minor) as the Pelargoi, or Storks, the implication being that, like storks, they come and they depart. In a broader sense the term Pelasgian or Pelagic came to describe things maritime or oceanic. The bay at the top of the Aegean Sea formed between Thessaloníki and the Greco-Turkish border was known as Pelagos. The term *Pelagic* has also come to refer to the so-called cyclopean masonry typical of Bronze Age Troy, Minos, Mycenae, Etruria, and Atlantis. The name combines the folkish origins of Aegean civilization, its architectural style, its naval prowess, and its Atlantean scope. When Atlantis is described as a Pelasgian city, we may envision its physical features, even its residents. An important historian of preclassical Europe explains, "The Pelasgian tribes in Italy, Greece and Asia were united in times reaching high above the commencement of history by a community of religious ideas and rites, as well as letters, arts, and language" (Graves 1961). In other words, Atlantis, like Ilios, Knossos, or Mycenae, was a cultural variation on the Pelasgian theme threading through the Bronze Age.

For example, Aeneas, the Trojan leader who brought his followers to Italy, tells an Arcadian (Greek) king:

> Dardanus, who sailed away to the Teucrian people [of Minoan Crete], and who was first father to our city, Ilios, and made her strong, was, as the Greeks relate, sprung from Electra, the daughter of Atlas. For Atlas the mighty, who sustains the spheres of the heavens on his shoulder, begot Electra. The father of your family is Mercury. He was conceived and born by fair Maia on Cyllene's cold mountain peak. Now, if we put faith in what we are told, Maia was begotten by Atlas, the same Atlas who supports the constellations of the sky. Thus our two families are both branches sprung from the same original stock.

Here, *The Aeneid* clearly defines the common heritage of Trojans and Greeks in the Atlantean origins of both peoples. This organic connection between the Pelasgian Sea Peoples in the Aegean and their Atlantean kinsmen appears in some of the Trojan and Achaean (Mycenaean) Greek names of characters in the epics of Homer and Virgil. For example, Nestor, son of Priam, the last Trojan king, shares the same name with the eighth king in Plato's story of Atlantis. Another

Trojan was named after the Atlantean flood hero Deucalion.

The Trojan Otrynteides' "birthplace was by the Ogyges Lake [the Atlantic Ocean, after the oceanic deluge figure, Ogyges], near your father's demesne." Otrynteides' father lived at the foot of a snowcapped mountain known as Hyde. These few details about Otrynteides clearly describe Mount Teide, known to its natives as Heyde, the volcanic mountain of Tenerife in the Canary Islands, part of the island empire of Atlantis. Otryn*teide*s contains the name of the Atlantic volcano, the highest mountain in Europe.

Just as Kleito gave birth to the first kings of Atlantis in Plato's account, the *Posthomerica* by Quintus Smyrnaeus portrays Kleite as a Trojan mother who lived "near the Gygaean Lake," a reference to the Ogygian flood, the second cataclysm to shake Atlantis, around 2200 B.C.E. Several other Trojans he mentions have decidedly Atlantean names. These include Evenor, Eumaeus, and Agamestor. In Plato's account Evenor was an early inhabitant of Atlantis; Euaemon and Mestor belonged to its original ten kings. Quintus also described an Achaean soldier, Elasippos, who shared his name with the seventh Atlantean king in Plato's *Critias*.

One of the Pleiades—and, consequently, an Atlantis—was Merope, after whom a Trojan ally, Merop, was named. A Trojan Merops appears in *The Aeneid*. The Achaean officer in charge of war horses was Eumelos, the Greek name, appropriately, of the second Atlantean king, according to Plato. An officer under the Atlantean general Memnon, was known as Alkyoneus, named after the leader of the Pleiades, Alkyone. These names demonstrate that the Trojans were blood relatives of their cousins in Atlantis.

What Phorcys was to Greece, Dardanus was to Troy. As Aeneas explained, he was the son of Electra, another daughter of Atlas, an Atlantis. She sent him away in time to escape the geologic upheavals that afflicted her oceanic homeland. He sailed the length of the Mediterranean Sea, landing on the northwestern shores of Asia Minor. There he lent his name to the Black Sea straits, which still bear his name, the Dardanelles, then moved to a coastal area where he founded a new state, Dardania. His grandson, Tros, expanded it into a power-ful kingdom still remembered as Troy. Its chief city was Ilios, after Ilus, and was modified by successive generations of descendants from

Dardanus. Remarkably, the improvements of these royal builders parallel the various phases and levels archaeologists uncovered in their excavations at Hissarlik, site of the Trojan capital in Turkey.

Electra was familiar as "the vanishing Pleiade," after losing her place in the constellation. The Greeks believed she turned her face away from the earth in mourning for the destruction of Troy, but perhaps she disappeared when she sank into the sea with her island home, as implied in the myth. The Romans, in fact, referred to her as Atlantis.

A variation of the Trojan foundation story recounts that Dardanus wanted to erect a new kingdom at the foot of a mountain known as Ate, but Apollo told him that to do so would doom the capital to destruction. Heeding the sun god's warning, he laid the foundations at Mount Ida instead. There, Dardania grew up to become a great city. Later, however, his great-grandson, Ilus, struck another foundation at Ate, with eventually dire consequences for all Troy.

Apollo's admonition was a clear reference to Atlantis. Ate was a mountain whose name echoed the drowned homeland from which Dardanus had escaped to Asia Minor. The Atlantean theme survived in the descendants of Dardanus, who "reigned for a while over the Arcadian kingdom founded by Atlas, but were parted by the calamities of Deucalion's flood," according to Homer. As Robert Graves observes, these Atlantean Dardanians were more than legendary. They were depicted as the Drdny, allies of the Sea People, in the wall texts at Medinet Habu. Similarly, the Dardanians were allies of Troy, according to Homer, who stated that the Trojans themselves were descended from Pelasgians and Dardanians—in other words, two lines of Atlantean descent.

Poseidon built the walls of Atlantis and Ilios, and both were laid out on the same plan: high, decorative walls interspersed with watchtowers and enclosing a citadel of shrines, temples, barracks, public buildings, and gardens. In *The Flood from Heaven*, Bernard Zangerer concludes that resemblances between the two cities were so numerous and close that the Trojan capital must have been Atlantis itself. At the very least, the many convincing comparisons he cites demonstrate that Atlantis (in its final phase) was a Late Bronze Age metropolis.

Troy's archaeological record coincides with the floods described in Greek tradition. Dardanus left the sinking motherland of Electra to rebuild civilization in Asia Minor. His escape parallels the first migrations from the Atlantean lands in 3100 B.C.E., the same date for the earliest human settlement at Troy. As some indication of its rise to commercial importance, Sumerian merchants operated a trading post there three hundred years later.

Around 2200 B.C.E. the Troad experienced an abrupt population increase so great that many Trojans migrated to Egypt. They established a permanent community opposite Memphis on the right bank of the Nile, at the foot of a nearby hill that shared its name with the new settlement: Tarau, the modern city of Turra. Newcomers who arrived suddenly at Troy during the early third millennium B.C.E. were forced to flee their Atlantean homeland by the second world catastrophe, known as the Deluge of Ogyges.

Ogyges' father, Poseidon, was the same sea god who created Atlantis. His followers were "giants" like himself, just as the Atlanteans were known, after Atlas, as Titans. Riding out the inundation of the late third millennium, Ogyges and company washed ashore in Greece, where his followers immediately took over and installed him as king. Little else is known about him save what Homer wrote concerning his abandoned homeland, Ogygia, an island in the Atlantic Ocean, where Calypso (herself an Atlantis, the daughter of Atlas) was high priestess of a magic cult. Using a genealogical chronology long since lost, the Greek travel writer Pausanias believed the Ogygian Flood took place in 1764 B.C.E., although no major natural catastrophes are known to have occurred at that time, at least in the ancient Old World. Since Ogyges came after Phorcys but before Deucalion, he is associated with the cataclysm of 2200 B.C.E.

A more precise date may be fixed for a third deluge familiar to the Greeks. During 1629 B.C.E., the Aegean island of Thera exploded in a major volcanic eruption accompanied by simultaneous geologic upheavals in other parts of the world. Yet again, the Atlantean lands were badly shaken, and many of its residents fled to Europe. Their flight was epitomized by Deucalion, "the One who has been through the Water." He and his wife, Pyrrha, were the only survivors of a great deluge that exterminated the rest of humankind.

The human race was believed descended from this pair, a way of expressing in myth the Atlantean heritage of every Greek born thereafter, because Deucalion's uncle was none other than Atlas himself. Deucalion's father, who warned him of the coming flood, was Prometheus, the brother of Atlas. Clymene (Wave-tossing Sea) was his mother. Deucalion's descendants, like Noah's, were the founders of civilizations after the Deluge. His son, Hellen, was the founder of Hellenistic culture; Hellen's sons in turn were Dorus, progenitor of the Dorians, and Xulthus, first of the Achaean Greeks whom archaeologists call the Mycenaeans. Apollonius Rhodius, the third-century B.C.E. chief custodian at the Great Library of Alexandria, refers to Greece in his *Argonautica* as "the Pelasgian land, ruled by the sons of Deucalion."

Deucalion's ark was said to have come to rest on Mount Parnassus, at the Gulf of Corinth, where the most important religious center of the classical world, Delphi, was instituted. In other words, the Delphic Mysteries were imported from Atlantis. Indeed, it was here that the sacred Omphalos stone was regarded as the Navel of the World. Like the Sumerian Ziusudra, Deucalion was a vintner and "builder of shrines," implying both civilizations received a common tradition— namely, from survivors of the penultimate Atlantean cataclysm arriving separately in Greece and Sumer.

The last deluge was the final destruction of Atlantis described by Plato and corresponded to a natural disaster that devastated much of the world around 1200 B.C.E. These Great Floods not only parallel the four Bronze Age catastrophes and their respective time parameters known to science, but also are dominated by Atlantean themes, suggesting that each cataclysm provoked its own mass migration from the afflicted island. Refugees fled to various parts of the world, including the eastern Mediterranean, where their arrival and impact on Greece were enshrined in myth.

7

ATLANTEANS ACROSS
THE SAHARA

They subjected parts of Libya as far as Egypt.

PLATO, *TIMAEUS*

In 1926 a German author announced the discovery of Atlantis. Paul Borchardt was a serious investigator dedicated to scientific methodology and the accumulation of hard data. No armchair archaeologist, he sought tangible proof himself across the sands of North Africa. In Libya's Ahaggar Mountains he met Berbers who had preserved oral traditions of a lost City of Brass. Not only was the legend similar to many details found in Plato's account, but the Berbers' tribal name, Uneur, resembled the name of the first man of Atlantis mentioned in *Critias,* Euenor. Another tribe at Shott el Hameina, in Tunisia, bore the even more striking name of Attala, which they translated as "Sons of the Source."

The Attala also knew tales of a drowned City of Brass, suggesting the metallic decorations for which the great walls of Atlantis were widely famed. All this persuaded Borchardt that he was on the trail of the lost civilization. His suspicions were reinforced by a modern Berber scholar, Ouzzin, who found names and situations in *The Slaying of the Labu,* a Sumerian Deluge epic virtually identical to those he knew in Moroccan culture. It described the foundation of the city of Tangier by Tangis, a princess who died at sea. Her husband became involved in the war against Atlantis, which, in the midst of battle, was destroyed by an earthquake and disappeared under the waves in a terrific cataclysm (Hope 1970, 237).

The Berbers belong to the Tuareg, nomads of North Africa. They are a mixed people of largely Moorish and Negro stock, whose ancestors predate the establishment of Islam, well into the earliest centuries of the ancient world. A racial anomaly, or recessive trait, persistent among the Rifians of Morocco and the Braeber and Shiloeh of the Great Atlas is occasional blondness. Berber legend recounts that their first monarchs had "hair of bright gold," suggesting Plato's description of the "fair" Atlantean kings. The Berbers' language, like their racial character, is a mixture of influences.

A basis for all Berber dialects, however, is Hamitic, the language of the ancient Egyptians. A particularly important word shared by both peoples is *ba,* "soul." Their script, Tifinagh, is a mix directly descended from the lost Libyan and Mauretanian languages, themselves inheritors of an even earlier Atlantean tongue. Today's Berber chieftains maintain a custom of special significance: The elders of a village, when meeting together in council, sit in a circle wearing ceremonial robes dyed dark blue. In *Critias* Plato tells how the Atlantean kings, bedecked with azure cloaks, convened in a circle.

The ancestors of the Berbers were described by several writers in classical times as the Atlantes, Atlantioi, Autochthones, or Atarantes— a "remnant race" dwelling on the coast of northwest Africa. The Greek geographer Diodorus Siculus writes that a people who called themselves Atlantioi, on account of their linear descent from Atlas, the eponymous king of Atlantis, still maintained a kingdom of sorts on the shores of the Outer Sea—that is, the Atlantic Ocean—during his lifetime in the late first century B.C.E. In his *On the Nature of Animals,* the Roman historian Aelian writes that the "dwellers by the ocean that tell the story of the ancient kings of Atlantis, who traced their descent from Poseidon, wore headbands of the skin of male sea-rams as a sign of authority. The queens likewise wore fillets of female sea-rams." What animal Aelian meant by "sea-ram" has never been determined.

Borchardt was familiar with these Atlanto-Berber parallels, and he studied the *History* of Diodorus Siculus. It described a catastrophic earthquake that ripped much of the North African shoreline, tumbling cities into the Mediterranean Sea during the midthirteenth century

B.C.E. The German scholar's research in Libya established that the coasts had indeed been wrenched by a particularly disastrous seismic event in prehistory. Geologists confirmed that the upheaval took place between 1250 and 1175 B.C.E. and was undoubtedly part of the natural catastrophe that obliterated Atlantis in 1198 B.C.E.

Then Borchardt dug from a southern Tunisian swamp the ruins of a sizable town laid out in concentric walls enclosing what appeared to be a central palace. The site, which seemed to support his suspicions, was Shott el Jerid, locally known as Bahr Atala, the "Sea of Atlas." Nearby hills were still called the Mountains of Talac, or the "Great Atlantean Water." As the excavation progressed, it began to resemble the city described in Plato's *Critias*. The local Atlantean names, together with Berber myth, tended to confirm Shott el Jerid as the location of the lost civilization.

But it was only a town, after all, never the major capital Plato detailed. And it sank not into the ocean, but beneath the Tunisian sand. Structures such as Borchardt found appear throughout the Atlantean sphere of cultural influence on the shores of the Atlantic and into coastal North Africa. *Timaeus* states that the Atlanteans "subjected the parts of Libya as far as Egypt." If he had not exactly uncovered Atlantis itself, Borchardt did trace, in folk tradition and physical remains, the most eastward evidence of Atlantean expansion—an influence extending in practically a straight line across North Africa out into the Atlantic. In fact, a pattern of Neolithic centers spread from Iberia south and east over North Africa toward Egypt, as indicated by a series of sites stretching through the Sahara from Mascara, Tiaret, and Setif to Haidra, in Libya.

Even in classical times, the Greeks spoke of the fabled Hecatompylon, the City of a Hundred Doors, which Heracles is said to have erected somewhere in northwest Africa on his way to visit Atlas in the Fortunate Isles. Such a place does indeed exist at Zora in Morocco. It is a large site of the early third millennium B.C.E. and was originally composed of one hundred upright stone slabs closely resembling doors arranged in a circle. This forgotten monument was doubtless the Greeks' Hecatompylon. Its existence confirms the validity of Hellenic (actually, *pre*-Hellenic Bronze Age) myth and tends to identify Heracles as the personification of seafaring megalith builders, who sailed the Atlantic Ocean and the Mediterranean Sea, raising monumental stone

structures from Britain and Morocco to Majorca and the Balaeric Isles.
These Neolithic Sea People were Atlantean, and it was from their concentric architecture, most famously represented at Britain's Stonehenge,
that the Bronze Age city described in the Platonic dialogues as Atlantis
was to evolve.

But the story of Atlantis was preserved in more than North African
ruins. The Latin historian Avienus wrote at greater length than Plato
about the drowned capital in his *Ora Martima,* which survives only in
fragments. Avienus worked with original documents at the Great
Library of Carthage until it was gutted by fire during the Second Punic
War. The obscure and isolated Maxyes people of coastal Morocco
claimed descent from Trojan veterans fleeing the destruction at Ilios.
Well into Roman imperial times they continued to domesticate ele-
phants, the only such creatures in northwest Africa, from a time
unimagined millennia before, when their ancestors crossed long-sunken
land bridges from Morocco to the island of Atlantis.

No pyramids have yet been discovered in the Sahara, nor are any
likely to be found there. The eastward-wandering Atlanteans probably
observed that the rapidly encroaching desert would soon make permanent habitation impossible. During the mid-to-late fourth millennium
B.C.E., the sands were inexorably winning their struggle over the retreating fertile plains. Herds of bison and cattle, which once roamed its
grasses in great numbers, had begun to dwindle. But the passing
Atlanteans left their mark here too.

Drawings at Jabbaren and Aouanrhet, painted with the same red
ochre the Egyptians used in their temple murals, show women wearing
wreaths and headdresses identical to those of their Nile counterparts.
The girls pictured with European facial features and blond hair at
Tassili-n-Ajjer, in the Oran Province of Libya, wear Egyptian robes,
including Wadjet tiaras. Wadjet was a cobra goddess, protectress of the
Lower Nile. The figures are poised in worshipful positions—with raised
palms in the Egyptian manner—before animal-headed gods commonly
represented throughout the Nile Valley. Those portrayed most often are
the lion, the falcon, and especially the cow, who sports a solar disc
between its horns.

In Egyptian religion these beasts were, in their best-known mani-
festations, Sekhmet, the goddess of celestial destruction associated by

Twentieth Dynasty Egyptians with the Atlantean cataclysm; Horus, whose followers arrived at the Nile Delta to spark civilization there; and Meh-Urt, who personified the Great Flood from which they came. These three deities, among the most ancient in the Egyptian pantheon (all of them predynastic) were said to have journeyed from the west. Their mythic imagery perfectly depicts a people migrating across North Africa toward the Nile Valley, where they came to be worshipped, in the wake of a natural catastrophe.

The Pastoralists, as archaeologists have come to call these Atlanteans in transit across the Sahara, practiced deformation of cattle horns, a curious practice they shared with only the dynastic Egyptians, and employed animal-breeding procedures used in the Upper Nile. While the Atlantean migrants left no monumental architecture to mark their passage through Libya, the same cannot be said of their presence in northwestern Africa. Strabo, a Greek geographer who became a Roman historian, wrote of an age long before his when "more than three hundred cities" lined the coasts on either side of the Pillars of Heracles (today's Straits of Gibraltar). Perhaps he had in mind one city in particular, Lixus.

Lying about seventy-five miles south of Gibraltar along Morocco's Atlantic coast, the earlier foundations of Lixus (see fig. 7.1) were built upon by the Romans after they seized the city from the Phoenicians, who themselves took it over from someone else. They called it Maquom Semes, "City of the Sun." But a stele at the Phoenician capital of Carthage commemorating Admiral Hanno's first voyage to Maquom Semes, already ancient at the time of his arrival, records that the place was populated exclusively by "foreigners." He reported that the city was located "on an island within an island," whose walls were intersected by canals and encircled a temple-palace complex at the very center of the innermost island. His description is generally identical, although on a smaller scale, to Plato's portrayal of Atlantis in *Critias*.

One of the few surviving fragments of legend about the city from pre-Phoenician times relates that its last queen was named Shimisa (Little Sun). To this day the resident Arabs refer to its ruins as Shimish (Sun). The Romans renamed it Lixus, the City of Light. They created a large, beautiful mosaic of Neptune (Poseidon) on a spot sacred to the god of the sea. Hercules was supposed to have been buried under its massive stone plaza, and the Hesperides were at one time said to have

Fig. 7.1. The bizarre ruins of Lixus, site of the Atlantean colonial capital of Autochthones on the Atlantic shores of present-day Morocco

guarded the golden apples of immortality near its walls. The original city, whatever its name may have been, was built on a hill by the Lucas River, which, in earlier times, may have surrounded the site on all sides, rendering it an island in the stream. Lixus was constructed of huge encircling walls on the cyclopean scale of Plato's Atlantis. Virtually nothing is known of its builders or original inhabitants save that they worshipped a solar deity, as suggested by the name both the Phoenicians and Arabs applied to it and the name of its last queen.

Lixus and the Berbers who live among its ruins are all that remain of the North African connection between Atlantis in the west and Egypt in the east. The people of both Lixus and the Nile Valley worshipped a sun god above all others. Architecture in both lands was massive and was raised during the early history of civilization. The city's encircling, monumental walls are reminiscent of the battlements that encompassed Atlantis. The capacious harbor at Lixus, built and abandoned long before either the Phoenicians or the Romans arrived to claim it, accommodated vessels from Plato's oceanic island, perhaps during the evacuation. Recurring blondness among the Berbers is a genetic remnant of that final period of large-scale migration 3,200 years ago. But the Hamitic connection between Berbers and Egyptians implies contacts earlier by some twenty centuries, when the geologic convulsions of the ancestral island forced the Atlantean migrations in the late fourth millennium B.C.E.

Lixus is not the only mystery city of Atlantic Morocco. Farther down the coast lies Mogador, as the Phoenicians called it, known today by its Berber name, Essaouira (Safe Anchorage). The port's stone breakwater, among the largest of its kind in the ancient world and still standing after more than three thousand years of erosional wave action, was part of a colossal harbor, an enigma in itself: The need for even a small docking facility, let alone one of such extensive dimensions many hundreds of miles from the nearest commercial centers, seems lacking. The closest city of importance, Lixus, lies 350 miles to the north. Mogador is an apparent anomaly left in a littoral no-man's-land fronting what is now an empty sea. Yet its position begins to make sense when we realize that this ancient harbor is near one of the sunken land bridges that long ago connected Morocco with the Atlantic islands. Safe Anchorage is the closest point on the North African coast to the Madeiras, a location that suggests the city must have once, very long ago, served as an important port for oceangoing ships sailing between the Atlantic isles and Morocco.

Another clue to Mogador's Atlantean identity was its other, even earlier name, Karikon Teichas, or the "Carian Fort." *Carian* is derived from the Persian *karka*, or "cocks," referring to the high-plumed horsehair helmets, the so-called rayed crown—armored headgear worn by the Sea People of Atlantis and portrayed on the walls of Ramses III's victory temple. In fact, *carian* was the term regularly used by classical writers to describe all things Atlantean, such as the *caryatid*, a supporting pillar in human form, still referred to as an atlantean column. The most famous examples of such columns support the porch of the Erechtheum in the Athenian Acropolis.

Mogador, or Karikon Teichas, appears to have been deliberately founded by the Atlanteans as the nearest land connection between their oceanic islands and North Africa. It probably prospered by trade with the Madeiras, once rich in timber for ship building, when they were part of the Atlantis empire. What other causes could justify the construction of so large a harbor far from any known trading center, and at so remote a period in antiquity? Unfortunately, this question is left to speculation; pitifully inadequate archaeological work has been carried out at

Mogador. The same holds true for Lixus, which, by its position almost directly opposite the suspected location of Atlantis, was perhaps specifically founded to serve as the capital of the North African colony.

Autochthon (literally, "Sprung from the Land") is listed in Plato's *Critias* as the sixth Atlantean king, who probably ruled the area currently comprising modern Morocco. Diodorus Siculus writes of a native people dwelling in coastal Mauretania (modern Morocco), facing the direction of Atlantis, who called themselves the Autochthones. They were descendants of the Atlantean colonizers who established an allied kingdom on the Atlantic shores of North Africa. Autochthon was a name by which the Greeks knew the Pelasgians, or Sea People, another name associated with the Atlanteans.

While the ruins of Lixus and Mogador still exist, far less may be seen of another originally Atlantean site in North Africa that developed into one of the most powerful cities of the ancient world. Today all that remains is an almost indistinguishable archaeological zone in a residential suburb of Tunis, but once, long ago, the citadel of Carthage, known as the Byrsa, stood on a low hill surrounded by a wall sheeted with precious metals. Alternating rings of land and water were arranged around the Byrsa in a concentric pattern interconnected by roofed canals. Each land ring was encircled by its own wall, abutted at regular intervals by high watchtowers. A vast harbor fronted the broad plaza serving as a marketplace in an enclosed basin or fortified docking facility known as the Cothon (drinking cup). From here a channel ran 1,396 feet into another harbor used to accommodate mercantile vessels from all over the known world (and doubtless parts of the officially unknown world, as well).

The foremost Atlantologist of the early twentieth century, Lewis Spence, muses,

> I think that a comparison of these resemblances, which include most unusual features, will leave no doubt in any unbiased mind that the plan of Carthage was substantially the same as that of Atlantis. The inevitable question of course arises, how is this to be accounted for? We can only answer by either the assumption that Carthage was herself Atlantis, or that her plan was an architectural memory of the city (Spence, 1968, 18).

Obviously, Carthage was not Atlantis, because during Plato's day the Phoenician city prospered. It would not be destroyed for another 250 years, and then by military action, not a natural catastrophe.

Kart-hadshat, or the "New City" of Carthage, is believed to have been founded at least four centuries after the events of the Trojan War, which destroyed the thalassocratic tradition in the Aegean world and opened up the Mediterranean to the mercantile prowess of the Canaanites, or Phoenicians. They followed in the wake, culturally as well as commercially, of those Atlantean-descended Sea People—the Minoans of Crete, Greek Mycenaeans, and Trojans from Asia Minor—who squabbled for dominance in the eastern Mediterranean during the Late Bronze Age.

The Roman writer Strabo reports that the Phoenicians began their Atlantic colonial expeditions after the Trojan War: "They occupied before the Age of Homer [circa 800 B.C.E.] the best of Iberia and Libya." The Phoenicians were not given to originality, synthesizing instead the sometimes diverse forms of different cultures, hence their mosaic blend of Egyptian, Assyrian, Greek, and other styles in art and manufacturing. The resemblance between Carthage and Atlantis can therefore be explained by the venerable Atlantean architectural heritage the Phoenicians found in North Africa.

In other words, the Phoenicians built Carthage on a site originally occupied by an Atlantean colonial city, or they may have been in league with descendants of Atlantean survivors. Virgil has Aeneas arrive at Carthage, his implication being that the city stood even before the out-break of the Trojan War. Perhaps it did, contrary to what historians imagine, if not as a Phoenician metropolis at that time, then as an Atlantean port upon which the Phoenicians later built.

The Atlanteans left faint but imperishable traces of their long sojourn among the ruins, ancient history, myth, and surviving cultural and even racial heritage of North Africa. That so little survives of what was once the greatest human drama ever experienced on the continent is as much a testimony to the effects of time as to the fragility of civi-lization, however powerful.

8

AMAZONS VERSUS ATLANTIS

Great precipices form a wall of rock, believed by the Tuaregs to be the fortress of the Amazons, ruled by a white goddess: the old fable of Atlantis.

COUNT BYRON DE PROROK, *IN QUEST OF LOST WORLDS*

Although Plato's account of Atlantis is the best-known version from classical times, it is not the only one. Another far less famous version was written about three hundred years later by a fellow Greek born in Agryrium, Sicily. Diodorus Siculus was a peripatetic scholar who traveled widely throughout the Mediterranean world, gathering information firsthand for a huge world history he was compiling. Around 5 B.C.E., he visited Caesarea, newly renamed by Caesar Augustus himself. Previously known by its Carthaginian name of Iol (Sun City), it was the recently revived capital of Mauretania, a semi-independent kingdom spread over what is now Morocco and western Algeria.

The Mauretanian king was Juba II, more scholar than statesman, the former prince of Numidia (modern Libya) and now a thoroughly Romanized monarch. Juba had helped create the first modern library system in Rome, later assembling his own vast collection at Caesarea. It was one of the greatest athenaeums of the classical world, containing manuscript copies found nowhere else, for Juba had managed to save part of the immense library at Carthage before that city's obliteration almost 150 years before. The documents were among the oldest in existence, going back to early Phoenician times, and recorded ancient information otherwise lost during the four-hundred-year-long dark ages that almost totally obscured all knowledge of the preceding Bronze Age. This was the special library where Diodorus Siculus learned a tale that those few investigators familiar with it still dismiss as myth.

To Diodorus, however, it was historical fact, not fanciful legend, and was worthy of inclusion in his encyclopedic life's work. The result of extensive travels throughout the Mediterranean, this massive world history consisted of forty books divided into three main parts. While most were lost with the collapse of classical civilization, the first five installments escaped destruction. In volume 1 Diodorus writes that long before the birth of Greece, when Egypt was the great kingdom of the world, another power swept out of the Caucasus Mountains of Central Asia. This was a tribe of warrior women, the renowned Amazons, led by Queen Merine and comprising thirty thousand infantry and twenty thousand cavalry. The queen came to the aid of an Egyptian king, Pharaoh Horus, and helped him deter an invasion from Libya. Victorious, the Amazons extended their conquest across North Africa to the shores of the Atlantic Ocean. There they took over Hesperia, a nation near the Tritonides, a fen created by the River Triton, where Merine built a new metropolis, Chersonesus. From this "City of the Triton" she staged an overseas assault on Atlantis itself, just a day's sail from the North African coast.

According to Diodorus, despite stiff resistance the invasion gained a foothold, and Cerne, the Atlantean capital, fell after its high walls (see fig. 8.1) were breached. The old city was renamed after the triumphant Merine, but she was generous in success, repairing the damage caused by the fighting, and concluding an alliance with the defeated Atlanteans. Peace prevailed until Atlantis was attacked again, this time by a people known as the Gorgons, who were seeking to expel the occupiers. The Atlantean-Amazonian union stood firm, however, and the threat was repulsed. Undeterred, the Gorgons soon returned in force, landed at several places along the coast, and inflicted stinging reverses on the queen's army.

Merine was driven from Atlantis and pursued across the sea to Hesperia, where a desperate battle bloodied both sides. After sacking and burning Chersonesus, the Gorgons went back to Atlantis, restoring

Fig. 8.1. A model reconstruction of a typical defensive wall around a city of the late Bronze Age matches Plato's description of the fortified perimeter that surrounded Atlantis. (National Museum of Athens, Greece)

the capital's original name, while Merine collected and buried her dead warriors under three Mounds of the Amazons. Retreating with her battered veterans across the Libyan desert, she finally arrived in Egypt, where she was consoled by Pharaoh Horus.

What are we to make of this account? It is utterly unlike Plato's version and seems to lack any basis in comparative myth or history. Although Diodorus writes that he learned it in Mauretania (probably at King Juba II's great library in the Mauretanian capital, Caesarea), it seems entirely legendary: Atlantis, supposedly the greatest power of the ancient world, humiliated by a band of rootless women? Yet Diodorus thought enough of Queen Merine's life to include it in his history of the world. Does it at least contain fragments of real events, however garbled, as he apparently believed? If so, they might reveal something of a lost episode in the long history of that sunken civilization.

A closer look at the details suggests it was not, after all, entirely a piece of fiction. For example, Hesperia's location, supposedly in what is now Morocco, recalls the Hesperides, daughters of Atlas who protected his garden of golden apple trees, where *Atlantis* meant "daughter of Atlas." No less suggestive are references to the River Triton at the Tritonides and Chersonesus, the new capital built by the Amazons. The triton was the scepter of Poseidon, the sea-god creator of Atlantis, according to Plato.

Curiously, Diodorus tells us that the capital of Atlantis was Cerne. The name occurs nowhere else but in the Dorset countryside outside Dorchester, in the south of England. At the outskirts of the town of Cerne-Abbas (Abbot of Cerne) lies the 180-foot image of a naked man wielding a club in his right hand (fig. 8.2). Archaeologists believe it is well over two thousand years old, although dating techniques are unable to assign a precise time frame for its creation. During the 1970s subsurface investigations under the giant's extended left arm revealed the outline of what appeared to be a hanging cloth. Researchers

Fig. 8.2. Aerial photograph of the Cerne-Abbas Giant, a three-thousand-plus year-old memorial to Britain's flood hero (photo courtesy of the National Trust of Britain)

assumed the hill figure depicted Hercules, who was commonly portrayed with club and cape. However, subsequent testing showed the underarm outline had been added centuries after the effigy itself was cut into the chalk layer just beneath the surface of the ground. Roman legionnaires probably altered the original figure to resemble Hercules, the divine patron of soldiers.

The Cerne-Abbas Giant was actually meant to represent Gogmagog, who was said to have wielded an immense war club. With its proper identification, the figure's Atlantean connection begins to appear in its gigantic proportions: Gogmagog was a leader of Britain's first inhabitants, descendants of the Titan Albion, brother of Atlas. This tradition seems related to the giant Fomors, the earliest residents of Ireland. Culture bearers from Atlantis arriving in several other parts of the world, as far away as the shores of Peru, were often described in local folk memory as "gigantic."

Four centuries before Diodorus Siculus, the Greek historian Herodotus reported that a people dwelled on the Atlantic shores of North Africa near the River Triton, which flowed into a great lagoon known as Tritonis. The natives called themselves "Atlantes, named after the mountain. Those who live around Lake Triton sacrifice chiefly to Athene, and after her to Triton and Poseidon" (*Histories*, Book IV). He goes on to write that the Atlantes of his time (circa 490 B.C.E.) held an annual festival "at which girls divide themselves into two groups, and fight each other with stones and sticks. They say the rite has come down to them from time immemorial, and by its performance they pay honor to their native deity, which is the same as our Greek Athene." It seems all the more significant, then, that at the Panathenaea, the Athenian festival dedicated annually to Athena, dancers wore the peplum, a kind of broad, flouncing skirt decorated with scenes from the Greek war with Atlantis. No less cogent was preservation of the identical story at the Nile Delta temple of Neith, an Egyptian incarnation of the same Amazonian goddess.

Herodotus believed the Amazons were not entirely mythical but were an actual band of warrior women who represented a force to be reckoned with in preclassical times. He describes them as tall of stature and dressed in leather skirts, their tribal emblem.

During the mid-1960s a circular burial mound 80 feet across and 3 feet high was excavated from the sands of Abalessa, some thirty-four miles west of Tamanrasset in Algeria. Inside its chamber French archaeologists discovered the well-preserved corpse of a 5-foot, 8-inch Caucasian female still wearing a leather skirt. Tuareg natives at once identified her as Tin-Hinan, the legendary foundress of their tribal nation. Her remains were carbon dated to the late fourth or early third millennium B.C.E., the period in which Diodorus set his account of Amazons in North Africa. Both he and Herodotus appear to have been validated by the Abalessa find.

Queen Merine supposedly came from beyond the Black Sea, but her name, "Sea Goddess," does not suggest origins in the Caucasus Mountains. More likely, she received it as a title from the conquered Atlanteans with whom she struck an alliance. The three Mounds of the Amazons in which Diodorus reports she interred her dead warriors actually exist and tour guides still point them out to visitors. Today Moroccan Berbers tell stories of Al Azoun, the People of Azoun, great women warriors who conquered North Africa thousands of years before the coming of Islam. *Amazigh* is Berber for "noble language," referring to the forgotten tongue of the Amazons. Count Byron de Prorok, the famous Hungarian archaeologist, explored the French Ahagghar Mountains during the mid-1930s. One peak in particular, he learned, was singled out for special reverence by the Tuaregs. "Legends connected with the mountain are many," the count wrote, "mostly including the mysterious white Queen who lived there with an army of Amazons. Benoit used the story in his *Atlantide.*"

Despite Merine's apparently Atlantean name or title, the Amazons' traditional Black Sea origins are sometimes suggested by linguistic evidence. For example, the name Amazon is not Greek but derives from the Georgian word for "moon," *maza,* with earlier related meanings in the Hittite *amargi,* "return to the mother," and *hamaxzun,* "fellow countrymen." More to its proper definition, the name Amazon is Armenian for "moon woman," which accurately describes the Amazons' cult of the lunar Mother Goddess. Their shields were *paltae,* crescent shaped, like the moon. Merine's priestesses did in fact bear arms in the Libyan Gulf of Sirte (Sidra), while the Amazon founder was an armed priestess from the Minoan colony of Ephesus. Her name was Cresus, from which the modern Crete derives. Amazonian imagery brings to mind famous representations of bare-breasted Minoan priest-esses holding snakes in their outstretched hands, which in turn recalls Herodotus's description of the shirtless Amazons with their serpent symbols.

Plato's own account of Atlantis contains internal evidence of an Amazonian connection. He states that the first lady of the Atlantean island was Leukippe (White Mare), an apparent reference to the foam-ing waves of the sea. Variations among other Amazon names are Melanippe (Black Mare), Lysippe (Who Lets Loose the Horses), and Hippolyte, described by Claudian as "leading her snow-white, beauti-ful troops into battle." Plato stresses the Atlantean devotion to horses, which were provided with their own separate baths. The whole second land ring of Atlantis was a racetrack.

Leukippe's name is part of a Bronze Age tradition associating the white horse, particularly the mare, with royalty and divinity. Troy's sacred horses, outfitted with gold and silver trappings, were pure white; early worshippers at Pontus harnessed a team of four white horses to a chariot and drove them into the sea as a sacrifice to Poseidon. The sea god who invented the animal was also credited with the creation of Atlantis, where his colossal statue stood among four winged horses at the city's sacred center. Images of the horse were the leading emblems of the Amazons as well. The Amazonian lunar goddess, Artemis, rode a white steed, and Arabs still refer to a white horse as "moon colored." Cooper, recalling the Atlantean Leukippe, identifies the white horse as a "lunar sea symbol."

The hillsides of Britain still preserve images of the sacred white horse, which, like the Cerne-Abbas Giant, have been cut into chalk just beneath the surface of the ground. The most famous of these is the White Horse of Uffington in Dorset. At 374 feet long and 120 feet high, it may be seen from as far away as twelve miles, even after countless centuries, because local residents regularly clear off the outline. The same activity long ago involved surrounding communities in an old cer-emony known as Scouring the Horse. Every seven years people rede-fined its outline by walking along it in a commemorative procession, preserving the image as they honored it.

Until the mid-1990s the White Horse of Uffington was generally considered a remnant of Celtic ritual practices going back no earlier than the third century B.C.E. However, its elongated design suggested comparable Bronze Age renditions, a suspicion confirmed when improved dating procedures revealed that the hill figure was actually 3,500 years old, making it contemporary with the florescence of Atlantis. The geoglyph represents a British version of the Atlantean Leukippe: Ceridwen, a sea goddess who likewise ruled over a distant realm and was referred to by Druidical bards as the White Mare. The renowned author and mythologist Robert Graves tells how "the goddess will suddenly transform herself into a mare. She often figures as the 'White Lady', and in ancient religions from the British Isles to the Caucasus as the 'White Goddess'" (Graves 1948, 209). Her incarnation at the Greek Argos was as Io, daughter of the flood hero Inachus. A moon goddess, she bore Epaphus, the founder of Memphis and Libya, whose name signifies "the beginning." She was also worshipped as Leukippe and gave her title, White Goddess, to pre-Celtic Britain: Albion, the "White Land." These complementary Greek and British mythic figures feature distinct traces of Atlantean origins, with their themes of the flood and far-off realms.

Scouring the Horse was not the only British folk ceremony involving the representation of a sacred white mare suggestive of lost Atlantis. A pre-Christian May Day festival at Padstow, in Cornwall, included a mock horse ridden into the ocean as an offering to the sea god. Known as Dipping Day, the occasion commemorated a beautiful white horse that escaped the Great Deluge. The same ceremony was performed at Minehead, Somersetshire, where it was called the Sailor's Horse. The Cornish legend of Lethowstow recounts how a lone flood survivor escaped on a white horse over the engulfing waves. The Trevellyan family coat of arms depicts their ancestor's white mare swimming through the turbulent ocean.

Ireland had its white-horse rituals too. Every would-be king of Ulster endured an inauguration wherein he achieved symbolic union with the Great Mother Goddess in the form of a white mare. The horse was sacrificed and the potential monarch tasted its meat and drank a cup of its broth, then bathed in the elixir. This done, he was confirmed at last as rightful sovereign and "husband of the White Goddess." In midsummer an effigy greeted as the White Horse was carried in procession through a bonfire, but it was not allowed to burn. Immediately following the "survival" of the White Horse, peasants dashed through the bonfire themselves, and their children were flung harmlessly across its flames into the arms of relatives and friends. In Dublin on May Day boys cut white-thorn May bushes, symbolic of the White Horse's mane. Together with the bleached skull of a horse, they were cast into the midst of the bonfire.

Interestingly, all these May Day goings-on commemorate the arrival of the Tuatha de Danaan in Ireland in 1202 B.C.E. Regarded as early civilizers of Ireland, the Followers of the Goddess Danu were described in the Old Irish *Book of Invasions* as culture bearers from a natural catastrophe that had destroyed their kingdom, which was lost beneath the sea. Such peculiar ceremonies seem to memorialize the fiery destruction of a sunken homeland and the arrival of survivors who revered the memory of their ancestress—Plato's Leukippe, the "white mare" of Atlantis.

Across the ocean that took its name from the drowned realm, Ixchel was the White Lady, the divine founder of Maya civilization, who arrived on the shores of the Yucatán following a terrible deluge that destroyed a former age. In temple art she is sometimes portrayed scooting on a gigantic wave, which scatters her possessions across the surface of the sea. This same Atlantis-like theme is taken up again along the eastern shores of Mexico in the coastal regions of a later people, the Huaxtecs. Their army featured auxiliary troops, women warriors led by Tlazolteotl. Her name meant "Woman Who Sinned before the Deluge." Their weapons, like those of their Amazonian sisters, were the bow and snakeskin shield. The Guayaqui Indians of far-off Paraguay also told of female warriors dressed in snakeskins.

According to the mestizo chronicler Enrique Camargo, Tlazolteotl came from "a very pleasant land, a delectable place, where are many delightful fountains, brooks and flower gardens. This land was called *Tamoanchan,* the Place of the Fresh, Cool Winds" (Davies 1982, 42). It was here that she committed some offense against the gods, who destroyed the "Place of the Fresh, Cool Winds" with a terrific flood. Sailing with a remnant of her warrior women, Tlazolteotl eventually arrived on the shores near Veracruz.

Greek myth recounts that Heracles dealt the Amazons their worst defeat and drove them far from their homeland, beyond the known world, after he stole the girdle of their leader, Hippolyte. The fate of the

Huaxtec women warriors seems logically to complete the Greek story of their European counterparts. Here too, Heracles makes his appearance. Could the Amazons he pursued have crossed the ocean from Tamoanchan-Atlantis before its destruction, arriving on the Mexican coast? Were Tlazolteotl and Hippolyte the same person? In any case, it seems remarkable that two myths from such diverse cultures at opposite ends of the world should so wonderfully complement each other, even to the inclusion of Tamoanchan-Atlantis. Indeed, Camargo's description of Tamoanchan closely resembles Plato's portrayal of the balmy midocean climate Atlantis enjoyed. Parallels between the Huaxtec and Greek versions defy coincidence to suggest a real transfer of information or mutual experience from one continent to the other.

And what about Queen Merine's meeting with Pharaoh Horus, as depicted by Diodorus? Did such a king ever rule Egypt? We may recall the words of the British excavator of Sakkara, Walter Emery, quoted in chapter 4: The god Horus was always represented by an earthly Horus king of the smsu-Hr. The Egyptians treated these dynastic rulers as gods. In other words, all the kings who ruled after Horus himself ruled in prehistoric times passed under his divine name, receiving it as a royal title. Therefore, any pharaoh may have been the King Horus who met Queen Merine.

Yet there *was* an Early Dynastic monarch with a similar name, Hor-aha. He may have been a very important man, if Emery's identification of him with Menes, the first ruler over a united Egypt, is correct. Should Hor-aha have been the same king described by Diodorus Siculus as Pharaoh Horus, then his story of Atlantis took place around 3100 B.C.E. This is a particularly important period in our discussion of Atlantis: At this time the island kingdom, wracked by natural disasters, was being partially evacuated. Masses of refugees settled in safer parts of the world, leaving their oceanic homeland underdefended. Caught in the aftermath of a devastating cataclysm, with hardly enough natives left to rebuild their shattered civilization, let alone fend off foreign aggression, the Atlanteans were easy prey to invasion.

The Gorgons Diodorus mentions appear to have been fellow Atlanteans from the Canary Islands who were determined to liberate Atlantis from its foreign conqueror. In 40 C.E., the Roman scholar Pomponius Mela refers to the Canary Islands as the Gorgons in his

Geography. Other Latin scholars refer to the Canary Islands as the Gorgonian Isles. Not far from where Pomponius Mela lived at Tingentera, near the Pillars of Heracles (the Straits of Gibraltar), was the Atlantis-like city of Tartessos, founded by Gargoris, a mythic character associated with the Atlantic Ocean. The Canary Islands' identification with the Gorgons finds additional foundation in the names its original inhabitants, the Guanches, gave to different districts of Tenerife, the largest of the islands: Gorgo and Gorgano.

When the Spaniards landed at Tenerife, among the Guanche natives was a class of women warriors, the Vacaguare. Their leader, Guayanfanta (Royal Lady), was so powerful that she picked up a Spanish officer in her arms and ran off with him!

During 1530, on the other side of the Atlantic Ocean, another conquistador, Francisco Pizarro, discovered an island off the northwest coast of Colombia that the natives called Gorgone. It was inhabited by women warriors similar to those of the Huaxtec, armed with small, moon-shaped shields. Like many tribal peoples in the New World, they did not survive the Spanish conquest.

The Gorgons' legendary power to turn humans and objects into stone suggests the numerous islets in the vicinity of the Atlantic islands, such as the Canaries, many of them fashioned into fantastic simulacra by the action of wind and waves over time. *Gorgon* means "grimfaced" and implies "the works and agencies of Earth," referring to geologic upheaval. The early-twentieth-century mythologist Lewis Spence explains:

> Thus we find the Gorgon women connected with those seismic powers which wrought the downfall of Atlantis. . . . It was indeed the severed head of Medusa, the 'witch,' which, in the hands of Perseus, transformed Atlas into a mountain of stone. The proof, therefore, is complete that the myth of the Gorgon sisters is assuredly a tale allegorical of the destruction of Atlantis and of those evil forces, seismic and demonic, which precipitated the catastrophe (Spence 1942, 117).

The Amazons were almost certainly not women warriors; the image is too mythic for reality, although they may have been led by an actual queen. Egypt, after all, had its real-life female rulers, most notably

Hatshepsut around 1500 B.C.E. While Diodorus Siculus was in Mauretania learning about the Amazon invasion of Atlantis, the North African kingdom was effectively ruled by Cleopatra Selene. Most likely, the Amazons represented a military force composed in the usual manner of men who worshipped a bellicose goddess like the Greek Athena or the Egypto-Libyan Neith. Even today among the Moroccan Tuaregs already cited for their Amazonian traditions, male followers of the Atlas Mountain goddess sometimes wear skirts and veils in reverent imitation of women.

Resemblances between classical descriptions of the Amazons and archaeological evidence of the Minoans undoubtedly demonstrate a relationship of some kind. As the Amazons were powerful, shirtless women who worshipped the moon, so the Minoans were led by bare-breasted lunar priestesses. Emery points out that an early Nile Delta nome featured a Minoan emblem, suggesting a Cretan connection with Pharaoh Horus or, at any rate, some First Dynasty king. Even so, a military confrontation between ancient Crete and Atlantis in the late fourth or early third millennium B.C.E. is unlikely, given the low material level of Aegean civilization at this time. More likely, the Amazons who invaded Atlantis belonged to the same culture that sparked Minoan civilization.

The four centuries of dark ages from which classical Greece arose debased the Atlantean Gorgons into monsters through the agency of myth. All that survived was their parentage in Phorcys, remembered as "the old man of the sea," and Ceto, a daughter of Ocean. The Gorgons are connected to Atlantis through Phorcys, leader of survivors into Greece from the first destruction of the Atlantean lands. His most infamous mythic daughter, Medusa, was associated with Atlantic North Africa, where Merine fought it out with the real Gorgons. They liberated their fellow Atlanteans, chasing the occupiers back over the seas to Mauretania, where the queen's defeat forever disabused her Amazons of further military ambitions in the west. This interpretation of the strange story recounted by Diodorus is suggested by the details of its internal evidence relative to events during the late fourth millennium B.C.E. If it is correct, he has preserved what would have been an otherwise forgotten episode in Atlantis's critical transition from a geologically crippled Neolithic society to a new Bronze Age empire.

9

GONE TO HADES

Atlantis, which was extremely large, for a long time held sway over all the islands of the Atlantic Ocean.

MARCELLUS

At first sight the Canary Islands appear to be the ideal setting for Plato's description of Atlantis. Lying, as he wrote, "beyond the Pillars of Heracles," not far from the Atlantic coast of northwest Africa, they were rich in the fruits he described and in natural springs of hot and cold water that gushed from volcanic fissures. Until little more than five centuries ago, the islands were thickly forested. There was a broad lake at Tenerife, the largest of the seven islands, while rivers flowed across extensive, fertile plains. Tenerife's great volcanic peak, Teide, might easily pass for the mountain that stood near the northern outskirts of Atlantis. Indeed, the islands' geological background complements Plato's story. As recently as 1867 a volcanic mountain rose thundering to the surface near the island of Terceira, but it sank back into the ocean a few days after its dramatic appearance. The red, white, and black stone the Atlanteans were supposed to have used for their walled structures is still found in great abundance throughout the Canaries as tufa, pumice, and lava.

But the Canary Islands' superficial resemblance to Plato's lost civilization is not unique. The Azores and Madeiras may just as suitably fit his description of Atlantis. They too were once heavily forested, are still temperate and mountainous, and possess the hallmark red, white, and black construction stone, with natural springs of hot and cold water. The Madeiras' Corral de Feiras is no less appropriate a setting for the legendary capital than Tenerife or Gran Canaria. Of course, all three island groups are disqualified as the original Atlantis because they still exist. Nevertheless, the geologic features of the Canaries, Azores, and Madeiras are characteristic of most mid-Atlantic islands. Consequently, the oceanic setting for Plato's account is borne out by their physical correspondences to events he portrays in *Timaeus* and *Critias*. Etruscans and Phoenicians dominated the western Mediterranean in his day, so what lay beyond Sicily was virtually unknown to Greeks in classical times. Plato's accurate description of a geologically average mid-Atlantic island implies that his information about Atlantis must have come from some outside source familiar with the real world on the other side of the Straits of Gibraltar. His location for the oceanic kingdom is appropriate of all volcanic islands that typify the eastern half of the Atlantic.

Unlike the Madeiras or Azores, however, which were uninhabited when rediscovered during the fifteenth century, the Canary Islands reveal part of the Atlantis riddle because of their unique human history. In 1331 the first Portuguese to land at Tenerife encountered a strange native people who, when asked by the foreign explorers to identify themselves, replied that they were Guanche—literally, "men." Actually, these aboriginals were the Mahoh, but modern European historians still remember them as the Guanche. Although their islands lay just fifty-six miles from the North African mainland, the Guanche were a fair-skinned Caucasian people of tall, erect stature, with light eyes and often blond hair. Their material culture resembled in every respect a former Bronze Age civilization that had degenerated to its Old Stone Age origins, together with a curious mix of continental western European and Egyptian-like influences. Millennia of isolation from the outside world resulted in genetic decay from too much inbreeding: Their well-preserved human remains at Tenerife's Mummy Museum, in the capital city of Las Palmas, show numerous curved spines, bone deformations, cranial irregularities, and many varieties of inheritable disease. The visiting Portuguese were puzzled by the contrast between these primitive islanders, who lived in caves and went about in animal skins, and the great stone pyramids, massive walls, and lofty pillars of their environment.

The Phoenicians had arrived in the Canary Islands two thousand years earlier and had set up the so-called Anago Stone, a stele covered with Punic inscriptions, at the extreme northern tip of Tenerife. On the big island of Tenerife the stone image of a fish was found inscribed with an ancient Berber word, Zanata, the name of a Phoenician goddess (Reid 1999, 145). But the Phoenicians built no permanent settlements on the island; they came only for fresh water, then pushed on along the African coast in their efforts at colonization. In 1968 a Roman amphora was found at Graciosa, an islet north of the Canary Island of Lanzarote. Since then, the capital city museum at Arricefe has expanded its collection to include a dozen Phoenician and Roman jars. Sometime after the decline of Carthage, Roman freighters occasionally put in at Tenerife for fresh oranges.

The first-century geographer Pliny the Elder describes an expedition to "Canaria" sometime during the reign of Juba II (29 B.C.E.–20 C.E.), the enlightened monarch of Mauretania. While their Guanche hosts were apparently in hiding, the Mauretanians came upon evidence of a civilization already ancient and mostly abandoned by the natives. Juba's expedition reported that the island was uninhabited, although among some ruins they found the remains of a structure dedicated to Juno (rather, the Canary Islands' equivalent thereof): "In ea aeicullum esse tantum ex tructam"—"This whole stone (statue) had collapsed into the building."

During Atlantean times (and for many centuries thereafter, until they were renamed by Pliny the Elder), the Canaries were collectively known as Gorgonia for the original name of their inhabitants, the Gorgons (Guanches). Later, Greek myth corrupted them into monsters who possessed the power to turn men and objects into stone. In *The Odyssey* Homer describes how a ship is turned into stone just outside the harbor of an Atlantis-like city as a warning from Poseidon. This theme is in keeping with the marine environment of the Atlantic islands. In fact, the Gorgons were identified with the Canary Islands by the Iberian geographer Pomponius Mela, who lived at Tingentera, near the Pillars of Heracles, in 40 C.E.

After Portugal ceded the Canary Islands to Spain, the Guanche were destroyed for staunchly resisting all efforts to Christianize them. Before their extermination their language showed influences from other apparently unrelated cultures from long ago and far away. For examplc, the Guanche word for "virgin," *magada,* is *Magath* in Old High German, just as Guanche *hari* ("sacred") is related to the German *heilig,* or "holy." The Guanche *ec* for first person singular is similar to the German *ich.* When inhabitants at the northern end of Fuerteventura were asked by French explorers in 1339 for the island's native name, they replied, Ma Hoh—"My High Place," or "My Highland"—referring to the nearby mountains of Sombrero and Ecantaga. Ma Hoh is unquestionably Indo-European, similar to the German *Mein Höh,* or "My High (land)."

The Guanche word for a goat fold was *cabuca; capra* is Latin for the same term. Guanche *vincter* (he is conquered) is identical in Hittite, and both Etruscan and Guanche share the same word for "god": *ais.* The Guanche *cel,* or "moon," resembles the Greek *selene,* just as the Guanche *corja* (bird) is echoed in the Latin *corvus,* or "crow."

By far the most intriguing linguistic parallel occurs in a Guanche word for the great volcano of Tenerife. At 12,198 feet, Mount Teide is the tallest mountain in Europe. The native Canary Islanders believed its fiery vent opened into the subterranean kingdom of death presided over by Echeyde, "I Heyde," or, more usually, Heyde. Aides was the earlier name of Hades, in Greek myth the king of the dead whose underground realm lay in the Distant West. His father was Kronos, synonymous with the Atlantic Ocean and known even to the later Romans as Chronus Maris (Sea of Kronos). Resemblance between the Guanche Heyde and the Greek Hades or Aides, together with Hades' Atlantic location, cross-references the Canary Islands' Mount Teide (a Spanish corruption of the Guanche *Heyde*) as the original Kingdom of Death that the Atlanteans must have described to their descendants in Greece.

Guanche speech additionally demonstrated affinities with North African Berber. An important term in Berber and Mandingo (a black African language strongly influenced by Berber) is *mensa,* or "king." *Mency* in Guanche was "prince," while *taoro mency* meant "king." The Guanches knew the Canary Island of La Palma as Benehoare, suggesting the Beni-Howare tribe of the Middle Atlas Mountains. So too the Canary Island of Gomera appears related to the Ghomera tribe of Morocco's Rif people.

Gomera features several Neolithic dolmens, or standing stones, aligned with megaliths stretching across Europe as far as Italy and the

Baltic. In keeping with these New Stone Age structures, Plato's description of Atlantis, particularly the concentric plan of its city, implies that the site was originally a megalithic center upon which a Bronze Age citadel was later imposed.

The Canary Islands were so named by Pliny the Elder. He reported that an expedition setting out from Mauretania in 40 B.C.E. visited Tenerife, where large numbers of dogs *(canarii)* were tended by the natives. Their dog cult, like that of the Egyptian Anubis (Anpu), surrounded the rites of mummification and passage to the afterlife. Anubis was often portrayed as a stylized dog, still sometimes misinterpreted as a jackal. But Anubis was no scavenger: He assumed the title First of the Westerners, meaning he was among the first deities to arrive in Egypt from the Primal Mound described in myth as sinking in the Distant West.

Pliny was writing of subjects that were common knowledge long before his time. Nearly five centuries earlier Herodotus described the Kynesii. Of all men, they dwelt the farthest away, beyond the Pillars of Heracles. *Kynesii* means "dog worshippers," and the Guanches did indeed place the dog near the center of their religious beliefs after Ataman, the Canary Islands' Atlas. Centuries before the islands were officially rediscovered by the Portuguese, medieval European legends spoke of the Cynocephali, a dog-headed people dwelling somewhere in the vicinity of northwest Africa. In Egyptian temple art, Anubis was popularly envisioned as a man with the head of a dog.

Here too an Atlantean theme emerges. In *The Odyssey,* the hero arrives at the palace of Phaeacia, the Homeric Atlantis, and finds the royal residence ornamented with the golden statues of life-sized dogs fashioned by Hephaestus. The Divine Artificer was, appropriately enough, the mythic personification of volcanoes, those geologic emblems of his forge. Hephaestus was also the husband of Maia, eldest of the Pleiades, daughters of Atlas, and therefore an Atlantis. As in so much of our research, historical fact and informative myth are interwoven into complementary, albeit sometimes indistinguishable, forms. But here is no minor motif. Rather, the dog is a distinct cult figure that retraces connections between the Canaries and Atlantean links to the Nile Valley.

In fact, this animal always played a significant role in Egyptian society. Herodotus described how the Egyptians shaved themselves in mourning after the death of a family dog, just as they did for humans.

In Book II of the *Histories* he wrote that no one should consume wine and bread or any other food that happened to be in the house at the time of the dog's death out of respect for the departed animal's spirit. The wealthy had lavish tombs built specifically for their dogs. An entire city, Cynopolis, the capital of a canine cult, was named after the dog. Only in Egypt and the Canary Islands was this animal raised to such a high religious status.

The dog-headed Anubis was companion to the cultural hero Osiris on his civilizing mission throughout the world. When his master was murdered, it was Anubis who found the body and embalmed it so skillfully that it was impervious to decay. From then on burial rites were associated with loyal Anubis. He was envisioned as a spirit guide who led the human soul through the darkness of death, just as Seeing Eye dogs lead the blind. Even the Egyptian New Year began June 15 with the heliacal appearance of Sopdit, the Dog Star, at dawn (hence, our own "dog days" of summer).

Although the Guanches and Egyptians were spiritually focused on the dog, the animal figured into the mythic concepts of other ancient peoples as well, and often in an Atlantean context. A Sumerian epic recounting the beginnings of Mesopotamian society, *The Transfer of the Arts of Civilization from Eridu to Erech,* told how the goddess Inanna took the "divine decrees" of medicine, art, technology, letters, and law from a distant land over the sea in her chariot drawn by seven dogs. Seven was numerically symbolic for the completion of cycles (the seven chakras, the seven musical notes, etc.) and the sun (the seven days of the week, for example). In conjunction with the appearance of the dog in her myth—to say nothing of her voyage of civilization to Mesopotamia from over the sea—Inanna's legend suggests the Atlantean Guanches with their solar and canine cults.

In *The Cults of the Dog* Howey examines the Old Testament story of one of Japheth's sons, who, after the Great Flood,

> . . . abandoned the society of his fellow men and became the progenitor of the *Cynocephalii,* a body of men who by this name denoted that their intelligence was centered on their admiration for dogs. Following this line of thought, we note that when men are represented as dog-headed, one interpretation is that they are to be

regarded as pioneers of human progress through hitherto untrodden ways (Howey 1972, 45).

Appropriately, Japheth's son institutes his Cynocephalii dog cult after
the Great Flood, when he became one of the pioneers of a new civilization. In Genesis the sons of Noah are described as founders of the first
nations after the Deluge, and their names have been identified with the
earliest peoples of antiquity. Ham, for example, was the progenitor of
the Hamites, who included the Egyptians and Guanches, just as Shumer
was the eponymous founder of Sumer.

It seems clear, then, that dog worship was essentially the same for
both the Guanches and Egyptians. Howey's characterization of the dog
as a "pioneer of human progress through hitherto untrodden ways"
suggests the animal's rank in the pantheon of the world's seminal civilization, whose early inhabitants were compelled to migrate over a long
North African trek from the shores of Morocco across the Sahara into
the Nile Valley, carrying with them their faithful canine deity. From
Phaeacia's golden dog statues to the Guanche dog cult and its descent
in the Egyptian worship of Anubis, the line of Atlantean progression
from west to east is discernible.

A clue to the sacred nature of the dog among Guanches and
Egyptians may be found among Greek followers of the Orphic
Mysteries, who regarded the animal as special because the souls of virtuous people were said to return to earth temporarily in the canine form
as a final phase before entering heaven.

But a fundamental connection linking the Canary Islands with the
Nile Valley is not confined to spiritual parallels. Practical and technical
comparisons can also be made. For instance, similarities between
Guanche and Egyptian mummification are remarkable considering the
thousands of desert miles separating the mid-Atlantic islands from the
Nile Valley. Essential techniques involved were nearly identical,
although the Egyptians reached higher levels of sophistication and
refinement. Both Guanches and Egyptians embalmed the bodies after a
ceremonial bath and removal of the heart, lungs, and hair, which were
placed in separate canopic jars. Bandages were similarly applied, and
food, flowers, honey, and grave goods were laid beside the deceased as
offerings to his or her spirit. Offering libations of milk was standard

practice in Guanche ritual, just as the Egyptians poured milk in ceremonies honoring Eset, the inventor of mummification. Interestingly, Guanche morticians, like those in Egypt, were despised by the rest of society.

Howard Reid, whose recent investigations of ancient mummification are probably the most comprehensive, admits:

> [T]he sun-worshipping, mummy-making Guanches had rather a lot in common with the ancient Egyptians, rather more than coincidence could account for. Having now spent several years studying mummy cultures worldwide, I had not encountered any other mummy makers whose techniques so closely resembled Egyptian techniques" (Reid 1999, 149, 162).

Reid tells how during examination of a Guanche mummy an archaeologist was surprised by the resemblance of its hair to counterparts in the distant Nile Valley: "Her immediate reaction was that it had been styled and treated after death in almost exactly the same way that the ancient Egyptians styled their mummies' hair" (Reid 1999, 161).

Other Guanche practices and traditions paralleled those of Egypt. As in Egypt, Guanche trepanning (a kind of primitive brain or skull surgery) achieved high success rates. Even traditional Guanche wrestling holds are displayed identically in numerous examples of Egyptian temple art. When Reid and his archaeologist companion witnessed a display of Guanche martial arts on Gran Canaria, she remarked, "This is exactly like the stick fighting you see on the walls of the temple of Ramses III at Medinet Habu, not far from the Valley of the Kings. It's identical" (Reid, 1999, 156).

The Canary Islands' Egyptian-like influences particularly illuminate an Atlantean connection. The Guanche language itself, for all its numerous Indo-European cognates, is strongly paralleled in the earliest Hamitic dialects of ancient Egypt. These language similarities are complimented by a Smithsonian report that comments on "the peculiarly Egyptian type of face of one of the women" (Gambier 4 June 1903, 111) sketched shortly after the Spanish arrival.

The most compelling material comparison between the Canary Islands and Egypt involves the pyramids found in both parts of the ancient world. Although built on a smaller scale than those of pharaonic civilization, the pyramids of Tenerife resembled early specimens of Egyptian design, as in Zoser's step pyramid at Saqqara. Canary pyramid styles varied from island to island for reasons not understood. While step pyramids appeared in Tenerife, a conical design was unique to Lanzarote, the Canary Island closest to North Africa. Here the Guanches erected tall, pointy structures resembling sundials. Apparently, Lanzarote's seismic instability toppled all but one of the 35-foot cones made of black, white, and red volcanic rock. It stands in a park near the sea, in the city of Arricefe.

Two pyramids in good condition still stand on opposite sides of Tenerife, in Guimar and near the town of Icod de los Vinos. Both structures are aligned with the sunrise at the summer solstice. A 45-foot-high stone pyramid of seven steps leading to a flat top may still be visited on La Palma. All three Canary Islands pyramids were deliberately located between the sea and a volcanic mountain. They are surrounded by the ruins of terraced farming, which show strong resemblances to the agricultural techniques used by the Inca and pre-Inca peoples of South America.

Like their Egyptian counterparts, the Canary Island' pyramids are links to the story of Atlantis. Central to Guanche religious belief was a ritual fear that their chief pyramid would collapse, signaling the collapse of the entire island into the sea. Part of their litany, chanted by half of the assembled congregation, was, "Ee Iguida, ee Igan, Idafe!" ("It will fall, Idafe!"). Idafe, the spirit of the pyramid, replied through the other half of the celebrants, "Gueguerte, ee guantaro!" ("Give to it, and it will not fall!"). It would appear that some previous catastrophe so deeply impressed the Guanches that they incorporated a preventive ritual against its recurrence in their leading religious ceremonies.

The earliest Egyptian creation myth at Heliopolis told how Ra led gods and men from a Primal Mound in the Distant West because he predicted it would sink back into the sea. Guanche religious thought was obsessed with a similar impending disaster. To forestall it, the Harimagada, a Guanche college of "holy virgins," annually leapt into the ocean as voluntary sacrifices. The Harimagada grew out of a Guanche oral memory that recalled an epoch, very long before, when the Canaries were part of a larger homeland lost under the ocean. Some of their ancestors survived the catastrophe by climbing to the summit of Mount Teide. The last line of the Guanche flood epic reads, "Janege quayoch, archimenceu no haya dir hanido sehec chungra petut" ("The powerful Father of the Fatherland died and left the natives orphans").

These apparent references to the Atlantis story were preserved by the Guanches in far greater detail before the arrival of European Christians, who sought to demonize every aspect of native culture. Perhaps the most revealing of all surviving material connecting the Guanches with Atlantis is found in the *Tois Aethiopikes,* by the Roman writer Marcellus in 45 C.E.:

> Historians speak of the islands of Prosperpine and three others of immense extent of which the first was consecrated to Pluto, the second to Ammon, and the third to Neptune. The inhabitants of the latter had preserved a recollection, transmitted to them by their ancestors, of the island of Atlantis, which was extremely large, and for a long time held sway over all the islands of the Atlantic Ocean. Atlantis was also consecrated to Neptune.

Marcellus describes Atlantic island groups known in modern times as the Azores, Madeiras, and Canaries. Appropriately, the gods he mentioned, Pluto and Neptune (the Greek Hades and Poseidon, respectively), play important roles in the Atlantean drama: The former is Tenerife's Mount Teide, while Poseidon, in Plato's account, created Atlantis. In this fragment from the *Tois Aethiopikes* we learn that the Guanche inhabitants, even as late as imperial Roman times, "preserved a recollection, transmitted to them by their ancestors, of the island of Atlantis."

Pliny the Elder supports Marcellus's description of the Guanche by reporting that they were in fact the children who survived the disaster that sank their capital. A Greek philosopher writing in 410 C.E. notes that the story of Atlantis was still retold by the inhabitants of the Blessed Isles, one day's sail off the coast of Mauretania. Eight centuries later—and four centuries before the islands were officially discovered by the Portuguese—Monk Cosmo describes the Canaries in his *Topographia Christiana* as "the land where man dwelt before the Flood." In addition, the Arab geographer Edrisi writes of them about the same time Cosmo penned his *Topographia Christiana,* and Don

Inigo, an early-sixteenth-century chronicler of the conquest in the Canary Islands, states that the Guanche nobility claimed descent from the earliest kings of Atlantis.

The natives of Gran Canaria enthusiastically welcomed the Spanish (much to the inhabitants' inevitable disappointment) as fulfilling the long-preserved prophesy of "a great white ship" sent by a sea king to restore glory to the islands. Was this a folk memory kept alive by tradition from the golden days of the Atlantean empire? Perhaps it was the promise, never fulfilled, of a "sea king" to someday return after the destruction of Atlantis.

Like the Atlanteans in Plato's account, the Guanches met for prayer in a circle around a sacred pillar, a dolmen, with arms raised and palms open in the Egyptian manner. The Christians threw down all the dolmens they could find, but at least one example survives at Tenerife's Barranco de Valeron. Like the king's council area for the creation of new laws in Plato's description of the Temple of Poseidon at the very center of Atlantis, the Tagoror (Place of Assembly) was where Guanche princes met, laws were promulgated, and vital matters of state debated.

Another Guanche parallel right out of the pages of *Critias* was their Efeguen. These unusual temples were mostly demolished by the Christian conquerors, but reliable eyewitness descriptions (such as the personal observations of Galindo, a literate Spanish army commander of the late fifteenth century, cited in Mercer 1973, 104) confirm their Atlantean character. Exhibiting a structure similar to the concentric design Plato defined as the hallmark of Atlantis's sacred architecture, the Efeguen comprised two circular walls, a smaller one within a larger, with a raised altar positioned at the very center, just as the altar of Poseidon stood at the center of the concentric walls of Atlantis. To clinch the comparison, many Efeguen were constructed of red, white, and black stone—the same color scheme that, according to Plato, was favored by the Atlanteans.

The best-preserved such temple is located on Las Palmas. Its unique structure is paralleled only by the architecture of Plato's oceanic capital. The Canary Islands' proximity to the suspected location of Atlantis, together with the lost civilization's recollection by the Guanches, makes a strong case in favor of Plato's *Critias* as history, not allegory.

Three well-crafted copper spear heads from Michigan's Upper Peninsula. Their manufacture between 3100 and 1200 B.C.E. coincides with the ancient Old World's Bronze Age, which depended on such rich mineralogical sources and was dominated by Atlantean copper barons.

"Oxhide" copper ingots from a ship that sank in the eastern Mediterranean Sea during the late Bronze Age (Iraklion Museum, Crete)

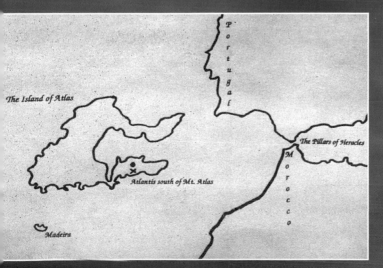

The location and configuration of the island of Atlas, with Atlantis as its chief city, based on sea floor features "beyond the Pillars of Heracles" (Straits of Gibralter) as described by Plato in his fourth-century dialogues *Timaeus* and *Kritias*.

This eruption on one of the Canary Islands, Lanzarote, typifies Atlantic Ocean volcanic activity of the kind that Plato said destroyed Atlantis.

The final moments of Atlantis must have resembled the geologic violence associated with the catastrophe on another Atlantic island, Surtsey, during the 1960s. (Photo courtesy of the Nordic Volcanological Institute, University of Iceland)

The Titan Kronos, whom both Greeks and Romans associate with the Atlantic Ocean, is depicted in this statue in Linz, Austria, as the pitiless destroyer of human life, a mythic reference to the traumatic Atlantean catastrophe.

The portrayal of a pair of terra-cotta winged horses from an Etruscan temple exactly matches Plato's description of those with Poseidon's chariot at the sacred center of Atlantis. According to Plato, the Atlanteans occupied western Italy, where the Etruscans became their descendants.

Part of a state plaque honoring Wisconsin's partially destroyed man mound (Baraboo), which has been revered by various regional tribes as a memorial to the gigantic flood hero who saved their ancestors from a deluge of fire and water.

George Catlin's painting of the Mandan Bu Dance, which he witnessed in the early nineteenth century. It commemorated the arrival of a single survivor from a terrible flood that obliterated a land in the east.

This prehistoric earthwork in Ohio was sketched before it succumbed to the farmer's plow in the middle of the nineteenth century. Its physical resemblance to Plato's vivid description of the drowned Atlantis complements innumerable North American tribal accounts telling of ancestral origins in a sunken realm.

The costume for the Apache Crown Dance, which recounts "the old Red and Black Land" that was inundated during a world flood in the ancient past (Museum of the American Indian, New York)

As seen in this model at the Poverty Point Archaeological Museum, Poverty Point's Atlas-like mound and layout of concentric and alternating land rings and canals mirror the Atlantis that Plato describes. (Poverty Point Archaeological Museum, Louisiana)

In the center of Mexico City's Plaza Mayor lies this scale model of Tenochtitlán, surrounded by a representation of its artificial lake. The Aztec capital was patterned after the Atlantic island home of Quetzalcoatl, the founding father of Mesoamerican civilizations.

In this eighth-century temple relief from Copán, Honduras, Itzamna, the Yucatán Maya's deluge hero, supports a representation of the sky, much as the Greek Atlas, the first king of Atlantis, is depicted holding up the heavens.

Located at the precise center of Tenochtitlán, the Aztec capital, the Temple of Ehecatl embodied the sacred numerals, colors, and concentric arrangement found in Atlantis. (National Museum of Anthropology and Archaeology, Mexico City)

One of numerous pre-Inca (Mochica) terra-cotta artifacts portraying bearded foreigners who, according to widespread folk traditions, were associated with the arrival of flood heroes in Peru.

An original painting of Atlantis commissioned by J. Douglas Kenyon, publisher of *Atlantis Rising*. (Photo © L. Thomas Miller)

There can be no question that the Las Palmas ruins and the first city of the Atlantic empire were conceived in the same architectural style. Guanche monumental construction is tangible proof that an Atlantean mode did in fact exist, and in the area of the ocean Plato said it did. As such, the ancient remains at Las Palmas represent hard physical evidence of Atlantean civilization.

Less dramatic material proof underscores an Atlantean presence in the Canary Islands. Some of the most common prehistoric pottery found on Gran Canaria features stylized handles resembling a bull's horns, suggestive of ancient Crete, although the majority of Tenerife pottery, in the words of a Smithsonian report, show "the influence of early Etruscan art." The *labrys,* or double-headed axe emblematic of both Minoans and Etruscans, is likewise in evidence throughout the Blessed Isles. Also common to Tenerife, Crete, and Etruria are the *tumuli,* or stone burial mounds, where the Guanche Sigones, or Chosen Nobles, were interred.

Still performed at Las Palmas is the prehistoric Canario, a community dance very similar to the Jewish hora, itself the last survivor of its kind popularized throughout Asia Minor and particularly associated with the Trojans during the Late Bronze Age, more than three thousand years ago. Even an obscure Guanche goat cult has been traced to the Dardanians, blood relatives and allies of the Trojans. Guanche officials, such as their *faycag,* or priest-judges, carried an *anepa,* a ceremonial staff of rank, the equivalent of the *lituus* borne by Etruscan, Hittite, and Trojan augurers.

All these ancient Germanic, Berber, Egyptian, Latin, Minoan, Hittite, Trojan, and Etruscan linguistic, architectural, mythic, and cultural themes coursing through the Canaries could not have arrived there together from the east. Such a variety of influences swept from the west into continental Europe, the Nile Valley, the Near East, and Asia Minor. Their far-ranging impact was generated by the mass migration of culture bearers carrying all the powers of a dynamic, even seminal, civilization from the direction of the Atlantic Ocean. And only a major natural catastrophe there could have uprooted an entire population, forcing it to migrate throughout the world.

Indeed, the most ancient traditions of all these peoples tell of their ancestors arriving after a Great Flood that obliterated a former civilization in the far west. The Canary Islands stood closest to the epicenter of cultural diffusion, which explains the diversity of themes evident among the Guanches. They were themselves Atlanteans, residing in one of the nearest outposts to the island capital, only some 200 miles to the north. The Canaries stood at the oceanic crossroads of Atlantis, North Africa, the Mediterranean, and the high civilizations that lay beyond to the east.

Among the Guanches' most identifiably Atlantean material remains were their massive ramparts. One cyclopean wall ran for 12 miles, bisecting the island of Lanzarote. Another still cuts Fuerteventura in half. According to Henry Myhill, in his study of Canary Island archaeology, "All the architectural finds made in recent years in the Canaries go to prove that these islands were the outposts of an earlier, higher culture, however provincial and barbarized. Large, city-like settlements have been discovered, imposing grave layouts and finds of inscriptions keep coming" (1968, 27).

Examples of the Guanches' written script are still being found throughout the Canaries, but none has so far been translated. An outstanding example stands near the shore facing Africa, on the island of Lanzarote. Several lines of inscription appear on a 12-foot-high monolith beneath five concentric circles separating six spaces—a possible representation of Atlantis itself: 5 and 6, according to Plato, were deemed sacred numerals by Atlanteans and were incorporated into their city planning.

The historical Guanches are no less obscure than the Atlanteans from whom their Gorgon ancestors descended. Indeed, enough survives of their legacy to confirm that the homeland of Atlantis did in fact exist. That confirmation was graphically expressed in the Guanches' most important deity: Gran Canaria's Montana de Cuarto Purtas was the sacred residence of their supreme being, Ataman, the Upholder of All, envisioned—just as Atlas, the Upholder, was—as a mountain separating heaven from the earth. Underscoring this common identity, a recurrent petroglyph found mostly in prehistoric caves represents the god bearing the sky on his shoulders. The Guanche Ataman and the Greek Atlas were undoubtedly one and the same figure, the first king of Atlantis.

10

CHILDREN OF ATLANTIS

On this island of Atlantis had arisen a powerful and remarkable dynasty of kings, who ruled Europe as far as western Italy.

PLATO, *TIMAEUS*

At the center of Atlantis, according to Plato, sprawled the monumental Temple of Poseidon. The ornate building of stone and precious metals contained his colossus standing in an immense chariot drawn by six winged horses. A smaller version of this Atlantean work still exits in Rome's Giulia Museum. Yet another contemporary copy is on display in the Tarquinian Museum. Poseidon's figure is missing from these terra-cottas; however, both are known to have originally adorned temples to the sea god. The likeness from Praeneste was made by Etruscan craftsmen sometime during the early sixth century B.C.E. But who were the Etruscans? And what were they doing with copies of the most important statue in Atlantis?

The Etruscans were a pre-Roman people who dominated western Italy from about 800 B.C.E. A previous period, once referred to as Villanovan by archaeologists who assumed it represented a different culture, is now regarded as an earlier Etruscan phase beginning five centuries before. By 750 B.C.E. the early classical historian and mythologist Hesiod refers in *The Agony* to "the far-famed Tyrsenoi," Greek for the Etruscans. He declares them to have been the first civilizers in Italy, prodigious seafarers who established a powerful thalassocracy that dominated the western Mediterranean until the rise of Carthage. Others remembered how they contested Phoenician sailors for the distant Azore Islands in the mid-Atlantic Ocean, nine hundred miles from Europe.

Archaeologists know the Etruscans built magnificent cities that incorporated architectural feats such as the 350-foot-high tower of Lars Prosena, hung with half a dozen enormous bronze bells. They also mass-produced high-quality bronze on an unprecedented scale. When Roman forces captured the Etruscan city of Volsinii in 280 B.C.E., they confiscated no less than two thousand bronze statues. In 205 B.C.E. the Etruscan city of Arretium provided thirty thousand shields, fifty thousand javelins, and forty fully equipped warships in fifteen days to supply the invasion fleet of Scipio Africanus. The Etruscans were also master irrigationists, as exemplified by the Graviscae Drain, a labyrinth of subterranean water courses, pools, and lakes created by the mammoth excavation of ingenious drainage canals.

They were high-minded statesmen who set up the Populi Etruriae, or Omnis Etruria, a league of independent city-states whose rulers wielded broad powers but were subject to a centralized authority. Etruscan cavalry were unmatched for versatility and splendor. One of the New York Museum of Art's most precious possessions is a full-sized, perfectly preserved Etruscan chariot of bronze decorated with sculpted gold and silver appointments. But their accomplishments also reached beyond the realm of design and bronze production: They were great lovers of music, assembling large groups of harpists, lutenists, flutists, drummers, trumpeters, pipers, singers, and other performers in what may have been the first musical orchestras or bands in history. Surviving Etruscan tomb art is similarly sophisticated, vivid, and dynamic.

The ruins of many Etruscan cities are still visited and studied; thousands of related artifacts are scattered around the world in museums and private collections. Yet the Etruscans are European archaeology's greatest enigma. Although numerous specimens of their written language exist, after more than a century of scholarly effort they continue to resist translation, save for yielding an important name now and then.

To add to the confusion, the Etruscans referred to themselves as the Rasna. Investigators are divided over whether the term is in fact a proper name or merely descriptive. In other words, calling the Etruscans Rasna may be like referring to the whole German people of 1900 as the Kaisers, even though only the king was Kaiser. A mountain chain still known as the Rassenna stands near the ancient city of Arretium, whose Etruscan residents contributed heavily to the Roman war effort against Carthage.

Etruscan origins are no less enigmatic. Some researchers speculate they were native Italians, but their sudden appearance at the beginning of the twelfth century B.C.E. suggests otherwise. Herodotus's claim that the Etruscans came from Lydia, in southwestern Asia Minor, is still being debated after 2,500 years. The Egyptians knew them much earlier, when Pharaoh Merenptah included them among his worst enemies, the vaunted Sea People.

They were mentioned again by his successor, Ramses III, when he had to battle the same alliance of invaders, and are listed in the roll call of captured prisoners on the walls of his victory temple as the Trs.w or Twrws.w, the Egyptian-language version of the Greek Tyrsenoi. Trs.w's philological identification with the Etruscans is supported by Ramses himself. He singled them out because they came from the northwest, the direction of Italy, unlike the rest of the Sea People, who attacked from the north and northeast. The Trojans were part of the Atlantean confederation that invaded the Nile Delta, and *rasnes* or *rasne*—the Etruscans' name for themselves—refers to "public affairs" in the Trojan tongue.

Of the ten origins for the foundation of Rome recorded by Plutarch in the "Romulus" chapter of his *Lives,* two are identifiably Atlantean. He reports that the Pelasgian Sea People, "wandering over the greater part of the habitable world, and subduing numerous nations, fixed themselves here, and from their own great strength in war, called the city 'Rome.'" Virgil agrees, recalling how "the ancient Pelasgians long ago were the earliest occupants of the Latin land." He wrote that Roman ancestors were refugees from Troy led by Prince Aeneas, whose own forefather was "the same Atlas who uplifts the starry heavens." These origins parallel both Ramses III's report of the Trs.w invaders he dispersed and older Greek references to the civilizing Pelasgians.

Plutarch continues, "Some say again that Roma, from whom the city was so-called, was daughter of Italus and Leucaria." Italus was the Latin version of Atlas, while Leucaria was a sea goddess, one of the sirens, an inflection of Leukippe, the first woman of Atlantis. Plato, after all, outlines the limits of Atlantean influence in Europe by extending them to western Italy, and thereby includes the Etruscans as part of an oceanic alliance that menaced the Aegean and Egypt. His character-ization of these events as the Atlantean War falls like a perfectly matched template over Homer's Trojan War and Ramses' invasion of Sea People. Indeed, all three sources portray different aspects of the same confrontation. The Trs.w were Sea People allies who sailed from the defeat and final destruction of Atlantis back to Italy, where they rose to power as the Etruscans.

The sea power they commanded from Etruria and their accom-plishments in city planning, public works projects, irrigation, bronze manufacture, and the arts were all drawn on a truly Atlantean scale. Ruins of Etruscan cities at Fiesole, Volterra, Tarquinii, and Sutri still exhibit the same kind of concentric walls with watchtowers and inter-connecting bridges arching over canals that Plato describes for Atlantis.

The Etruscans prospered almost a thousand years after the cata-clysm that overwhelmed their kinsmen beyond the Pillars of Heracles. Succumbing to the same moral decadence that preceded the destruction of Atlantis, they thoroughly intermarried with the Roman conquerors, so much so that their language as well as their cultural identity vanished long before the onset of another catastrophe—the collapse of classical civilization.

The dark ages that followed likewise obscured Atlantean legacies at the other end of the Mediterranean. Part of that legacy still survives in the Spanish city of Cádiz, known even in late Roman times as Gades. Earlier still, the Greeks called it Gadira, after Gadeiros, the second king listed in Plato's account of Atlantis, "presumably the origin of the pres-ent name" (Caroli 2003).

But Gadeiros was not the only Atlantean city in Iberia. Tartessos once stood in what would now be Huelva, on the River Tinto, or per-haps on the site of Asta Regia, north of Cádiz, at the source of the Guadalquivir River. Tartessos may have arisen as a direct consequence of survivors arriving in large numbers from the ocean. Strabo, the important Roman historian, reported that a sea people built the city in 1150 B.C.E., less than fifty years after the final destruction of Atlantis. With its sudden disappearance, a power vacuum developed in Spain, then part of the Atlantean empire. Deprived of its imperial headquar-ters, the political center shifted away from Gadeiros, resulting in the building of a new Iberian capital.

There is an etymological resemblance between the names Tartessos and Tyrsenoi (Greek for Etruscans), and Tartessian bronzes are not unlike Etruscan examples from Caere. An even earlier name the inhabitants of Tartessos used to refer to themselves, Turduli, is similar to Tursha, Egyptian for Trojans. The Tursha were listed by Ramses III among the Sea People who attacked his kingdom after the turn of the thirteenth century B.C.E. Supporting a Turduli-Tursha relationship is the double of a Tartessos tablet, dated to the Late Bronze Age, found on the island of Lemnos, some thirty miles off the coast of Troy. Sometimes the ancient Iberians were referred to collectively as the Turdentani. These comparisons demonstrate the heritage they, the Turduli, the Etruscans, and the Trojans all shared in their Sea People origins as well as their common experience in the Atlantean War.

During the 1920s American archaeologist Dr. Ellen M. Whishaw excavated the presumed ruins of Tartessos at a forbidding place shunned locally as the Cave of the Bats. There she found a dozen human male and female skeletons arranged in an orderly circle around one more, that of a woman, at the very center. Judging from the costly nature of their accompanying grave goods, she determined that the remains belonged to a wealthy family whose members had committed mass suicide by overdosing on opium. Were they royalty from the house of Gadeiros who died of despair over the tragedy of their Atlantic homeland? Or maybe they were participants in ritual sacrifice, as suggested by their number. In Pythagorean numerology the number 12 was associated with cosmic order, as we see in the signs of the zodiac, number of Olympian deities, solar Labors of Hercules, months of the year, half of the hours of one day, and so forth. Thirteen was known as the Numeral of Misfortune because its presence upset the cosmic order, resulting in chaos. Could the discovery in the Cave of the Bats have been a ceremonial attempt to reestablish the harmony of a world shattered by the Atlantean catastrophe?

Perhaps an answer lies in the polychrome statue of an ornately dressed woman unearthed in 1897 not far from the Mediterranean Sea in southeastern Spain, near the town of Elche. A masterpiece of terracotta art, it is unlike anything comparable in Roman, Phoenician, or Greek portraiture. The Lady of Elche was a product of the Turduli, descendants of the Atlantean colonists who occupied Spain during the Late Bronze Age.

Proof of her identity was found in the form of an otherwise unique bronze candelabrum retrieved from the same excavation. Its only other known counterpart came from the suspected location of Tartessos, near the Huelva River. Also convincing was a singular golden necklace from Tartessos that was identical to the ornament depicted on the statue. These costly items and her elaborate headgear portray a person of obvious importance, but her noble expression suggests someone who is more than an aristocrat. She may have belonged to the royal house of Gadeiros during neo-Atlantean times in Tartessos. Or perhaps the Lady of Elche was one of those who died in the city's ring of suicide. Was she the woman at its center? In any case, to see her statue is to behold the face of an Atlantean in Spain.

As director of the Anglo-Spanish-American School of Archaeology, Whishaw displayed particular courage by announcing that, in her opinion, "Tartessos derived more or less directly from . . . the lost continent of Atlantis" (Whishaw 1924). Her colleagues condemned any serious talk of the sunken city as the worst form of academic heresy, and her research was ignored. But the names of these naysayers have since been forgotten, while her research is still consulted by both unconventional and mainstream archaeologists. She was led to her controversial conclusion by comparing the Turduli with Plato's description of the Atlanteans: Like them, the Turduli were extraordinary sailors, plying the Atlantic to Cornwall in Britain and to Lixus or even Mogador along the North African coasts of Morocco.

Their oceangoing ships were usually heavily laden with cargoes of ingots. Atlantis was said to be the affluent metal broker of the Bronze Age; likewise, the miners of Tartessos were responsible for their city's wealth. One of their kings, Arganthnios (literally, Silvery Locks) allegedly sold so much precious metal to Phoenician merchantmen that they had their ship's anchor cast in solid silver. The king's name is derived from the Etruscan word for silver, *arcnti,* another link between Tartessos and Etruria. Tartessos was a major producer of copper and bronze just as the Atlanteans achieved their prosperity through the manufacture of orichalcum, or high-grade copper. Ezekiel said of Tartessos in the Old Testament, "Tarshish was thy merchant by reason of the multitude of all kinds of riches; with silver, iron, tin and gold they traded in thy fairs."

During their campaigns to wrest the Iberian peninsula from its inhabitants, the Romans learned Celtic traditions of overseas origins. The Gauls believed that their ancestral ruling class came from the splendid Isle of Glass Towers, which disappeared in a natural disaster. A first-century Greek writer, Timogenes, describes a widely held belief among the "barbarians" that their Gallic forebears came to western Europe from a lost island in the Atlantic Ocean. Survivors landed at the mouth of the Douro River, where they built their first town, the harbor city of Porto. From there they migrated throughout Iberia and France, where they were the first chiefs of the Gauls.

The tale is not without historical foundation. A Celtic settlement on the Douro that natives called Porto Galli (Port of the Gauls) became the Roman Portus Cale, from which the whole Lusitanian province eventually derived its modern name, Portugal. Its capital, Lisbon, was earliest known as Elasippos, the same name Plato assigns to the seventh king of Atlantis. (See fig. 10.1.) In Greek myth the Titan Iberus, after whom the entire Spanish peninsula was named, is the brother of Atlas. None of this would have surprised the Romans, who referred to all Iberians as "the children of Atlantis."

Fig. 10.1. Near the Castle of St. George atop the highest hill in Lisbon, these broken columns are all that remain of Elasippos, the Atlantean colonial capital of Bronze Age Portugal.

11

ATLANTEAN KINGS FOR IRELAND AND WALES

In Conan's veins flowed the blood of ancient Atlantis.

ROBERT E. HOWARD

How deeply into pre-Celtic Irish folklore the American fantasy writer Robert E. Howard delved to create his famous Conan character may only be guessed. Even so, a Conann does appear in the *Leabhar Gabhata,* or the Irish *Book of Invasions,* the oldest known history of Ireland "from before the Flood." A compilation of Druidic and other pagan folk traditions transcribed by Christian monks around 580 C.E., it relates Conann's command of a stronghold at Tory Island, off the coast of Donegal, the county whose name is a corruption of the Gaelic Dun Nan Gall (Fort of Foreigners). This name referred to Conann's people, the Fomors or Formorach, Ireland's earliest inhabitants, who arrived prior to the first deluge. They were seafaring giants whose name meant "Under Wave," a reference to their original homeland, Falias, before it sank beneath the sea.

Conann and the Fomors are also mentioned in the *Annals of Clonmacnois,* in which they were said to be ruled by Queen Cessair. She was additionally known as Banba, the earliest name for Ireland. Of the three vessels that fled the inundation, hers alone escaped shipwreck to land safely on the shores of Cora Guiny, carrying her father, Bith, and fifty maidens dedicated to her care. They stepped ashore with Ladru, another son of Noah, and Fintan, the chronicler of Ireland's pre-Celtic history.

They were followed three centuries later by the Family of Partholon, the tribe of a thousand men and women named after their leader. Partholon and his people were the only survivors of Gorias, also known as Mag Meld (Pleasant Plain), which had been dragged to the bottom of the ocean by a ferocious storm. They were skilled irrigation-ists and immediately began working to organize the land into alternat-ing divisions of land and water as the basis for a new agricultural society. But they were opposed by the resident Fomors. Defeated in too many battles and plagued by widespread illness, the Family of Partholon sadly pulled up stakes and once more entrusted their future to the sea. They were not heard from again, save for a small commu-nity that remained behind, quietly surviving in Ireland long after the Fomors passed away.

But the monumental public works projects Partholon left behind were found and used by another group of newcomers. The Nemedians came from the sunken land of Finias. While in the process of expand-ing Partholon's irrigation by a dozen new lakes, they too clashed with the Fomors, who demanded as tribute two-thirds of their children each year. In response the Nemedians stormed Conann's castle at Tory Island and slew him along with a large number of his retainers. Victory, however, was short-lived. Weakened by an epidemic and suf-fering a string of unbroken defeats on the battlefield, the Nemedians followed the example of their immediate predecessors and quietly slipped away from Ireland, never to return. They counted only forty survivors.

Then fresh waves of foreign immigration, all from the drowned land of Murias, swept over Ireland in rapid succession. First to land were the Fir Gailion and Fir Bolg. Rather than fighting the inhabitants, Breas, the Fir Bolg king, forged an alliance with them by marrying a Fomor princess. Thus the three peoples were united against a common threat: Storming ashore were the Tuatha de Danann. Outnumbered as they were, these Followers of the Goddess Danu nevertheless inflicted a decisive defeat on the coalition ranged against them at the Plain of Carrowmore. The ghosts of the Fomor dead were believed to have returned to Falias, their primeval homeland at the bottom of the sea. Soon after, they were joined by the last wave of pre-Celtic invaders, the Milesians, led by their eponymous ruler, Miled.

The Fir Gailion pledged their fealty to the Tuatha, but Fir Bolg survivors escaped to the offshore islands of Man, Aran, Islay, and Rathlin. The stone ruins still standing there are commonly associated with the Fir Bolg. Meanwhile, the victorious Tuatha de Danann reigned peacefully over a united Ireland for many generations. The Celts who arrived from continental Europe six centuries later absorbed not only their blood and culture, but the whole invasion legacy of ancient Ireland. For example, the last poet-king of the Fir Bolg was Fathach, from whose name was derived the Irish term for Druid, Fathi. Celtic genes as well as manners and mysticism were heavily influenced by the previous inhabitants. The humbled Fomors continued to serve as the high priests and priestesses of Ireland's megalithic sites, which their forefathers had erected.

The foregoing is a concise outline of Ireland's deep past as related by the Irish *Book of Invasions*. Although most scholars dismiss it as nothing more than a garbled collection of historically unaccountable legends, they nonetheless admit that at least flashes of Bronze Age and even Neolithic elements sometimes illuminate the text. The *Leabhar Gabhata* is far more enlightening, however, than skeptics believe. It is nothing less than a chronicle of major events preceding Celtic Ireland's birth around 600 B.C.E., told in terms of the Atlantean experience. Each "invasion" represented one of the waves of immigration that washed over the country from the first catastrophe in the late fourth millennium to the final destruction of Atlantis around the turn of the thirteenth century B.C.E. The Old Irish account tells of four lost cities—Falias, Finias, Gorias, and Murias—each associated with one of the various peoples who arrived before the Celts.

Remarkably, the *Book of Invasions* not only parallels Greek and Native American traditions of the same four floods, but each deluge coincides with one of the cataclysms only recently discovered by science. The earliest, in 3100 B.C.E., corresponds to Ireland's first immigrants, the Fomors. The cataclysm of 2193 B.C.E. is associated with Partholon, followed by the Nemidians in 1629 B.C.E. The final destruction of Atlantis scattered a wave of various escaping peoples—the Fir Gailion, Fir Bolg, and Tuatha de Danann—in 1198 B.C.E. Late-fourth-millennium upheavals on the island of Atlas compelled the Fomors to seek safety in Ireland, where they were remembered as flood survivors.

Plato characterized the Atlanteans as titans whose mighty fleets conquered most of the world. According to the *Annals of Clonmacnois,* the Fomors "possessed a fleet of sixty ships and a strong army," comprising a *sept,* or part of a tribe descended from Chem, the biblical Shem, a son of Noah. They lived by "piracie and spoile of other nations, and were in those days very troublesome to the whole world." Their name is derived from *fomor,* meaning "giant" and "pirate."

Fomor settlement in Ireland was said to have taken place before the Great Flood, but their legacy continued throughout the subsequent history of Ireland, contributing to the country's most common name: Murphy is derived from O'Morchoe, or Fomoroche—from Fomor. The Murphy crest features the Tree of Life surmounted by a griffin or protective monster and hung with sacred apples—the chief elements in the Garden of the Hesperides (Atlantises). Visitors to the seacoast in the western part of County Wexford may still see Mount Ard Ladran, where, tradition has it, one of Fomor queen Cessair's male companions, Ladru, was buried with the remains of their ship. Her father, Bith, another son of Noah, lies in Slieve Beagh, a mountain on the borders between Counties Fermanagh (from Formorach) and Monaghan. Both his and Ladru's memorialization within these mountain sepulchers recalls the Mount Atlas of their drowned homeland. Queen Cessair herself was buried on a high hill. Located on the banks of the River Boyne, it continues to be known as Cuil Cesra.

As though to confirm her legend, down the Boyne, not far from Cuil Cesra, stands a Neolithic cemetery dominated by the oldest structure of its kind in Ireland and the world. New Grange, seventeen miles northwest of Dublin, is a circular mound about 250 feet in diameter, surrounded by twelve megaliths. Thousands of pieces of white quartz completely cover the exterior of the curb facing due east. The upper section of the mound is arranged into a boxlike configuration of stone slabs cut with channels to carry away rainwater. Four minutes after sunrise every winter solstice, light blazes through this "roof box" down the 62-foot-long corridor into the otherwise dark interior. A shaft of light brightly illuminates the 9-foot-square, 18-foot-high burial chamber carved with many spiral designs. Meanwhile, the monument's eastern face, as though joyous at facing the dawn on this special morning, becomes a blaze of white light reflected from the wall of quartz aligned with the sunrise. The spear of light rises to point at each of the spirals linked together at the far end of the innermost chamber. In a few moments, it retreats down the corridor, returning the mound's interior to its former darkness until the next winter solstice.

This annual light-and-shadow drama has been going on at New Grange for the last 5,100 years. Reliable carbon dating obtained through a pair of large charcoal samples from early construction caulking in between roof slabs indicates that New Grange corresponds to the late-fourth millennium B.C.E. upheaval and the arrival of the first Atlanteans, who are remembered as the Fomors. New Grange has no forerunner in Ireland. The high architectural and astronomical standards it exemplifies, together with lofty concepts of the human soul's rebirth, did not emerge from nothing and most certainly needed more than a few generations of continuous development. As no evidence for such preparation exists, the know-how and spirituality that created New Grange must have been imported from an outside culture already well advanced in monumental construction techniques and metaphysical ideas. Ireland's mythic traditions suggest the Atlantean identity of that culture. The name New Grange is derived from the old Gaelic Am Umah Greine (Cave of the Sun), which means that the solar orientation of its roof box was known centuries before it was discovered by archaeologists in the 1960s. Although the Fomors built the monument, it was used by the conquering Tuatha de Danann, who gave it its name because they knew the sun as *grian*. Additionally, the last of their monarchs was Mac Grene.

New Grange was known still earlier as *Oengus an Broga*, the "Cave of Oengus," after the Tuatha de Danann prince. A sorcerer as well, he saved the goddess of youth and beauty, Bride, from annual abduction at the hands of Bera, lord of the Underworld. Oengus carried her off to the Island of Youth, Tir-nan-Og, another title for Murias, the same kingdom in the middle of the ocean from which the Tuatha de Danann left for Ireland. It is also known as Crannog, or Ruined City of Kenfig. These names testify to the enduring memory of an Atlantis-like homeland in Irish consciousness. A Scottish version of the myth tells how Tir-nan-Og's sacred well was sinfully uncapped, resulting in a worldwide deluge that engulfed the entire island. In these folk memories appear not only apparent references connecting New

Grange to Atlantis, but also the Atlantean flood of Ogyges described in Greek tradition.

The people composing the second wave of Atlantean migration, corresponding to the 2193 B.C.E. cataclysm, were described in Ireland as the Family of Partholon, with Partholon recognized as their chief. Also remembered as Bartholon, his name was a compound of *bar,* "sea," and *tolon,* "waves," not unlike that of another culture bearer on the other side of the Atlantic Ocean—Peru's Kon-tiki-Viracocha, or Sea Foam. He was the son of Baath, the sea god, just as Atlas was the son of Poseidon, who, according to Plato, arranged Atlantis into alternating rings of land and water. The *Leabhar Gabhata* describes Partholon as also quartering Ireland into divisions of land and water. Much of that account was reluctantly narrated in the late sixth century C.E. by one of the last living descendants of Partholon's family, Tuan MacCairill, when it was transcribed by St. Finnen, a monastery priest.

Plato states that the Atlanteans venerated a sacred number, 5, in the creation of their kingdom, which resonates with the Fir Bolg's division of the country into five provinces. The Atlantean identity of the Fir Gailion is less clearly defined, perhaps because they were not from Atlantis. Instead, their name implies that they were Trojan allies in the Sea People's confederacy that ravaged the eastern Mediterranean at the end of the Late Bronze Age. After the fall of Troy and their defeat by Ramses III, they may have sought refuge from the pursuing Achaean Greeks beyond the Pillars of Heracles in the Atlantic. This speculation may explain why they and their Fir Bolg companions, sailing directly from the final debacle in the Near East, arrived in Ireland a few years before the Tuatha de Danann. These slightly later Followers of the Goddess Danu were refugees, not from war but from the natural disaster that drowned their city. Fir Gailion means, literally, the "People of Ilion," and Ilion was the name of the Trojan capital.

On their heels were the Tuatha de Danann. Their leader was Ogma, from Tir-nan-Og, the Irish Atlantis. He introduced a new written language named after himself, which comprised notches for five vowels and lines for fifteen consonants. These were etched into natural stone or the walls of cut tombs to memorialize the dead and/or prominent visitors. Although the earliest surviving examples of Ogham date only to the fourth century C.E., it's connections to runic and Etruscan alphabets bespeak its antiquity; its ultimate roots as an elemental script appear to lie in the Middle-Late Bronze Age. Ogham's identity as an import is evidenced in its signs for *h* and *z*, letters that do not appear in Old Irish. It may be at least one of the original written languages developed and used in Atlantis, but it is more likely a simplified version of Atlantean script modified to accommodate later Celtic speech. Significantly, most Ogham inscriptions are found at Munster, Ireland's southernmost, earliest inhabited province, where the Tuatha de Danann were alleged to have landed and built their first settlement. Og's Atlantean provenance is clear from the name of his sunken homeland, the Island of Youth—Tirnon-Og.

According to a classic authority on early Ireland, Henry O'Brien, the Tuatha de Danann arrived at the south coast of Ireland in 1202 B.C.E. This date compares remarkably well with the final Atlantean catastrophe that occurred around the turn of the twelfth century B.C.E. Of course, O'Brien, who wrote in 1834, knew nothing about the untranslated wall texts at Egypt's Medinet Habu or late-twentieth-century oceanography and astrophysics supporting the ultimate destruction of Atlantis precisely in the same period he determined entirely from Irish folk tradition. His conclusions were reinforced in the next century by a fellow countryman, Mike Baillie, a leading dendrochronologist whose investigation of Irish peat bogs revealed that a major climate change with disastrous ecological consequences took place around 1200 B.C.E. Baillie's research contributed significantly to scientific understanding of the worldwide cataclysm that brought down the curtain on Bronze Age civilization. O'Brien believed that the strange obelisk-like towers still found in Ireland were erected by the Tuatha de Danann, citing the tenth-century *Book of Leccan*, which tells of "the Tuathan tower." Ruins of several such towers are found, appropriately enough, in County Roscommon, at Moy-tura, where the Tuatha de Danann decisively defeated their immediate enemies. Known more correctly as Moyetureadh, the battle area is translated as Field of Towers.

Hostilities among the various Atlantean groups in the midst of their disasters might in part be explained by their different origins, however they were related. The Tuatha de Danann told of four great cities—Findias, Gorias, Murias, and Falas—all simultaneously overtaken by a natural catastrophe and dragged to the bottom of the sea. They appear to have been located on separate islands in the Atlanean empire, from which various groups contested each other for control of Ireland. Gorias, for example, was probably in the Gorgon Isles, now associated with the Canary Islands.

The sixteenth-century scholar William O'Flaherty recorded that the Milesians, the last of the pre-Celtic invaders, arrived before 1000 B.C.E. His general time parameter also coincides with a Late Bronze Age Atlantis. The Milesians' leader was Eremon, whose name refers to all of Ireland and appears to be a linguistic inflection on Euaemon, the name of the fourth king of Atlantis in Plato's *Critias*. The *Book of Invasions* tells how Eremon established Tara as the capital of his new kingdom. Originally known as Tea-mhair, it was renamed after his wife, Tea. Together with her sister, Tephi, Queen Tea made Tara the spiritual center of ancient Ireland. The women are described as daughters of the royal house in the Blessed Isles lost beneath the sea.

The Milesians' chief deity, Macannan Mac Lir, was a worldwide wanderer from Annwn, famed throughout Celtic myth as Land under Wave, from the Brythonic *an* (abyss) and *dwfn* (world). Also known as the Revolving Castle (Caer Sidi), Annwn was a fortified island of great natural beauty with freshwater streams and a circular city surrounded by concentric walls lavishly decorated with gleaming sheets of precious metal. The central palace was called Emahin Ablach, "Emhain of the Apple Trees." Macannan Mac Lir's home away from home, however, was at the Isle of Man, where Reel Castle allegedly covers his gravesite.

Although a god and supposedly immortal, he preferred death to eternity when Ireland became Christian. Before then he traveled in a chariot as "the rider of the crested sea" and was the divine patron of sailors. He founded Llyr-cestre, modern Leicester, and was head of the "three Chief Holy Families of the Isle of Britain," known in Wales as the Children of Llyr. Today he is better remembered as the figure of tragic disillusionment in Shakespeare's *King Lear*.

Resemblances between Macannan Mac Lir and Poseidon, the Atlantean sea god, are unmistakable. Both crossed the waves in a chariot and were patrons of sailors and progenitors of royal families. Their islands were identically configured into concentric walls sheeted in decorative metal; and Emhain of the Apple Trees echoes Atlas's Garden of the Hesperides with its golden apple trees. The medieval *Fate of the*

Children of Tursun likewise describes an island called the Plain of Happiness, where trees bearing golden apples grew in the Garden of Hisberna. In surviving excerpts from the lost *Druidic Books of Pheryllt* and *Writings of Pridian,* Ynys Avallach, or Avallenau, was said to be "more ancient than the Flood, when all the rest of mankind had been overwhelmed."

Avallenau was also the name of a Celtic goddess of orchards, reaffirming the Hesperides' connection with Atlantis. Avalon was additionally referred to as Ynys-vitrius, the Island of Glass Towers, an isle of the dead and formerly the site of a great kingdom in the Atlantic Ocean. This is the same story embraced by Portuguese Gauls as their foundation myth. Another Irish memory of Atlantis preserved in *The Voyage of Maeldune,* presented below, mentions the Island of Apples. Britain's Geoffrey of Monmouth depicted an identically named place he additionally called "fortunate" in his twelfth-century *Vita Merlini.* Atlantis was often referred to by classical writers other than Plato (Strabo, Pliny, Aelian, etc.) as the Fortunate Isle.

Atlantis was remembered in several other Irish epics, such as *The Voyage of Bran,* which tells of

> . . . a distant isle, the plain on which the hosts hold games. Pillars of white bronze shine through eons of beauty. It is a lovely land through all the ages of the world, a silvery land on which dragon stone and crystal rain. Sweet music strikes the ear. The host races along Magh Mon, a beautiful sport. Coracle races against chariot. . . .

This portrayal of Bran's "isle" strongly resembles Plato's description of the island of Atlantis, from its vast plain to its horse races. "Pillars of white bronze" suggest orichalcum, the high-grade, gold alloy copper that Plato reports as the extraordinary product of Atlantean metallurgy. Orichalcum is mentioned again in other Irish accounts of Atlantis, such as the ninth-century *Travels of O'Corra,* which tells of a bright metal, *findrine,* unlike any other and found at Formigas. The island

> . . . had a wall of copper all around it. In the center stood a palace from which came a beautiful maiden wearing sandals of *findrine*

on her feet, a gold-colored jacket covered with bright, tinted metal, fastened at the neck with a brooch of pure gold. In one hand she held a pitcher of copper, and in the other a silver goblet.

Here again are encountered the central palace surrounded by walls adorned with precious metals, together with typical mineral opulence, especially copper, described in Plato's *Critias*.

The unique metal makes another appearance in *The Voyage of Maeldune,* where it is referred to as *bath*. The seafaring Maeldune lands on "a large, high island with terraces all around it, rising one behind one another; a shield-shaped island." As Maeldune explored the island, he found "a broad, green race course." But there were several other islands in the vicinity. The next one he visited was the Island of the Apples mentioned above. A third featured a city surrounded by a high wall, while a fourth was divided across its center by a massive wall of gleaming brass. The last island had no less than four concentric walls like rings encircling each other. The outer wall was decorated with gold, the second with silver, the third with copper, and the innermost wall with crystal.

It is clear in the body of his description that the four places Maeldune visits are not separate locations, but alternating rings of land and water on one large island—essentially, then, islands within islands, the same concentric arrangement Plato describes for Atlantis. Other tales recalled similar sites, such as Rath-cruachain, a circular stone fortification with walls 13 feet thick at the base and surrounded by five encircling ramparts. Its bronze, golden, and silver palace was the center of the fortresslike city, which one day vanished under the sea. Even the Atlantean sacred numeral occurs in Rath-cruachain's five walls.

If Eremon-Euaemon was the Atlantean-Milesian monarch of Ireland, Late Bronze Age Britain was ruled by the eighth refugee king mentioned in Plato's account of Atlantis. Mestor, whose name meant "counselor," may have been associated with Europe's most famous megalithic site, which gave counsel, as it were, regarding the movements of the heavens. According to archaeoastronomers, Stonehenge (see fig. 11.1) was a kind of astronomical computer primarily oriented to the positions and phases of the moon. Indeed, it resembles the concentric plan of Atlantis itself, even to the inclusion of the Atlantean

Fig. 11.1. An artist's rendition of Stonehenge as it appeared around 1200 B.C.E. Parallels with Atlantis are apparent in the concentric design and incorporation of sacred numerals. (Illustration courtesy of the National Trust of Britain)

sacred numerals, 5 and 6, which are repeated throughout its design.

Archaeologists believe the structure was first laid out by 3000 B.C.E., began to reach the apex of its construction 1,400 years later, and was suddenly abandoned around 1200 B.C.E. Its development, use, and abandonment parallel Atlantean immigration at the close of the fourth millennium B.C.E., the zenith of Atlantis as the foremost Bronze Age civilization, and its final destruction in 1198 B.C.E. Not coincidentally, Atlas was depicted in Greek myth as the founder of astronomy, hence his representation as a Titan supporting the sphere of the heavens on his shoulders. He therefore signified the birth and florescence of astronomy at the city named after him—Atlantis.

The impact of Atlantis on Britain was no less dramatic than on Ireland, as suggested by native folk memories of foreigners arriving from an oceanic catastrophe during the deep past. The Irish versions and their Welsh counterparts are often very close, suggesting a common event that was experienced independently by two different peoples. For example, Murias, the Tuatha de Danann's sunken homeland, was known in Wales by a very similar name, Morvo. British renditions of the story of Atlantis, however, throw new light on the fate of its survivors.

Llyon Llion was the "Lake of Waves" that overflowed its banks to inundate the entire earth. Before this former kingdom was drowned, the great shipwright Nefyed Nav Nevion completed a vessel just in time to ride out the cataclysm. He was joined in it by twin brothers, Dwyvan and Dwyvach, who, landing safely on the coast of Wales, became the first Welsh kings. This myth is less the slight degeneration of an obviously earlier tradition than it is an example of the Celtic inclination toward whimsical exaggeration, making a mere lake responsible for a world flood. In all other respects, it conforms to other Atlantean Deluge accounts, wherein surviving twins, such as those listed in Plato's Atlantis story, become the founding fathers of a new civilization.

Hu-Gadarn is mentioned in *Hanes Taliesan,* the "Tale of Taliesan," where he is known as Little Gwion. If this affectionate diminutive seems derivative of the Trojan capital, Ilios (Wilion in Hittite and perhaps in the Trojan language as well), the impression is deepened when Hu-Gadarn says, "I am now come here to the remnant of Troia." Troy was allied with Atlantis through common blood ties.

Hu-Gadarn is regarded as the first ancestor of the Cymry, the Welsh people, and his Atlantean identity is no less apparent: "I have been fostered in the Ark," he confesses. *Hanes Taliesan* reports, "He had been fostered between the knees of Dylan and the Deluge," arriving in Wales after a worldwide flood whipped up by a monstrous serpent.

Llys Helig, a stony patch on the floor of Conway Bay that is sometimes visible from the shore when the waters are clear, is still locally regarded as the site of a kingdom formerly ruled by Helig ap Glannawg, who is said to have perished with Llys Helig when it abruptly sank to the bottom of the sea. The stones taken for the ruins of his drowned palace are part of a suggestive natural formation that recalls one of several Welsh versions of the Atlantis disaster. Others speak similarly of Llyn Llynclys, a large, dark pool of fathomless water in the town of Radnorshire that is supposed to have swallowed an ancient castle known as Lyngwyn.

In the *Preiddu Annwn,* "The Spoils of Annwn," King Arthur and his men escape from Caer Wydyr, the Fortress of Glass, which sinks beneath the waves soon after. A "Tower of Glass" appears in the

Historium Britanum of medieval chronicler Nennius. Standing majestically in the midst of the sea and seemingly utterly abandoned (a Celtic device symbolizing death), Turris Vitrea echoes only the voices of outsiders. Similar Welsh tales are told of Caer Feddwid, the "Court of Carousal," and Caer Siddi, both opulent island kingdoms featuring fountains and curative freshwater springs, as similarly described in Plato's Atlantis dialogue.

The Tale of the Lowland Hundred tells of Cantref y Gwaelod, an island 40 miles long and 20 miles across. It was filled with fruit trees, natural hot springs, and forests and was ringed by a great range of mountains. A system of sluices created alternating rings of land embankments and moats with canals bridged by connecting walkways. The island had a capital, Caer Gwyddno, which extended political control over sixteen neighboring islands and cities. But a disaster overtook the city and it sank beneath the ocean, drowning most of its inhabitants. King Gwyddno Garanhir, along with a party of survivors, landed on the Welsh coast and eventually became the first royal family of Wales. A rocky ridge running some 7 or 8 miles out to sea before its disappearance underwater was said to mark the direction in which Caer Gwyddno lay at the bottom of the Atlantic.

Remembered in some parts of Wales as Llyn Syfaddon, Llyn Savathan was the extensive kingdom of Helig Voel ap Glannog, whose great possessions, which extended far into the waters from Priestholm, had been suddenly overwhelmed by the sea. His name is remarkable because it contains the *og* derivative of Atlantean Deluge heroes in other parts of the world. Another Welsh flood tradition, that of Llys Elisap Clynog, not only repeats the *og* theme but seems to include Plato's second king of Atlantis, Elasippos.

Many similar accounts deeply rooted in the folk consciousness of both Ireland and Wales were never regarded by their peoples as mere fables, but instead were revered as sacred traditions of ancestral beginnings. Myths such as these may not yield their truths to the archaeologist's spade, but the tales can disclose their authenticity to any honest mind, as they were intended to do.

12

HOW THE BAD DAYS CAME

Atland disappeared and the wild water rose so high over hill and valley that everything was buried under the sea.

FROM THE *OERA LINDA BOK*
(THE BOOK OF WHAT HAPPENED IN THE OLD TIME)

Olof Rudbeck was the Swedish Leonardo da Vinci. His seventeenth-century achievements in various fields were not only innovative but enduring, including the discovery of lymph glands, the invention of the anatomical theater dome, and the launching of modern botany. He was his country's first modern historian, a pioneer archaeologist, and designer of the first university gardens at Uppsala, where he was professor of medicine. Rudbeck instituted Latin as the lingua franca of the international scientific community; wrote fluently in Latin, Greek, and Hebrew; and possessed a grasp of classical literature nothing short of encyclopedic.

Combining his vast knowledge of the ancient world with personal archaeological research, he concluded during an intense period of investigation from 1651 to 1698 that Atlantis was fact, not fiction, and that it had been the fountainhead of civilization. He believed that Norse myths and some physical evidence among Sweden's megalithic ruins showed the impact Atlantean survivors may have had on northern Europe, contributing to its cultural development and laying the foundation (particularly in ship construction) for what would much later be remembered as the Viking Age from the ninth to twelfth centuries C.E.

159

Rudbeck's comparison of Norse ship design to Atlantean precursors was reaffirmed by his Scandinavian colleague A. E. Brogger, Norway's preeminent archaeologist in the 1950s. Brogger cited close resemblances between Viking dragon ships and similar vessels manned by an Atlantean tribe or clan, one of the Sea Peoples known as the Venetii. After the final destruction of Atlantis, Brogger maintained, they founded a city, their capital, Ateste, in northern Italy. Many centuries later, it was renamed Venice after its Venetii founders. The Atlantean provenance of Ateste is self-evident.

Brogger was seconded by another prominent scholar of the early twentieth century, Oswald Spengler. In his famous *Decline of the West* he observed that ships depicted at Ramses III's victory temple "differ completely from those used by the Egyptians and the Phoenicians, but they resemble those which Caesar found among the Venetii of Brittany" (Spengler 1962, 162). The early-twelfth-century B.C.E. monument was built to celebrate Pharaoh's triumph over the Sea People, identified with invaders from Atlantis. Their connection with these oceanic aggressors is underscored by Homer in the *Odyssey*. He includes the Venetii among the Trojan allies who went on after the fall of Ilios to found Patavium (the modern Padua) and Venice, which took its name from them.

The Caesar mentioned by Spengler was Julius, who admired the Venetii's long-distance trade with Britain and considered them the most skillful maritime people of his era. He wrote that their ships were "capable of facing the seas which rolled in from the Atlantic, flat-bottomed, with high prow and stern, built solidly of oak." The same craft are illustrated on a boulder at Tjaenguide, on the Baltic island of Gothland, where Rudbeck discerned connections between Atlantis and Scandinavia. Indeed, Caesar's portrayal of the Venetii he encountered during his campaign in Gaul matched descriptions of the Vikings' long-ships. Alice Kehoe, professor of anthropology at Marquette University, convincingly traced their Late Bronze Age lineage to the same Sea People vessels Spengler cites as depicted on the walls of Ramses III's victory temple.

After the final destruction of Atlantis, Venetii who refused to abide by the commands of their fellow survivors in Ateste relocated to territories off the French coast, north of the mouth of the Loire. These were subsequently known as the Veneti Islands, and it is here, appropriately enough, that traditions of a deluge followed by the arrival of Atlantean survivors are most abundant. An illustrative example is the story of Ker-is, also known as Ys. Famous throughout Brittany, it was even the subject of an evocative tone poem for piano, *La Cathédrale engloutie* (The Sunken Cathedral) by Claude Debussy, later scored for full orchestra by the renowned twentieth-century conductor Leopold Stokowski. Another French composer, Eduard Lalo, turned the legend into a grand opera, *Le Roi d'Ys* (The King of Ys).

Ys was an island kingdom in the North Atlantic ruled by Gradlon Meur (Meur is Celtic for "great"). His capital was an ingenious arrangement of interconnected canals constructed around an immense basin similar if not identical to the alternating rings of concentric land and water Plato describes as the city plan of Atlantis. A central palace was resplendent with marble floors, cedar roofs, and gold-sheeted walls, again recalling Plato's opulent sunken city.

The legend tells of a monarch who alone possesses a silver key, suspended by a chain around his neck, that could be used to open and close the great basin's sluice gates to accommodate the rhythm of the tides. One night, however, his sinful daughter, Dahut, steals the key from her father while he sleeps and tries to open the sea doors for one of her numerous lovers. The tale describes her as having "made a crown of her vices and taken for her pages the seven deadly sins." Unskilled in the gates' operation, Dahut inadvertently springs open the city's entire canal system, unleashing a huge inundation. Awakened by an admonishing vision of Saint Gwennole, King Gradlon swings onto his horse and gallops down one of the interconnecting causeways, the swiftly rising torrent close behind. He alone escapes, for Ys with all its inhabitants, including Dahut, disappears beneath the ocean.

His horse swims to coastal France, where Gradlon Meur finally arrives at Quimper. A very old statue of him once stood between two towers belonging to the cathedral. (In 1793 the monument's head was violently removed as part of the anti-aristocracy hysteria sweeping France. Sixty-six years later the head was restored.) Like the Greek flood hero Deucalion, Gradlon is said to have introduced wine to Europe. During the Middle Ages, the story of Gradlon was reenacted every Saint Cecilia's Day as a chorus sang of lost Ys. While the chorus was engaged in its narrative, an actor climbed onto Gradlon's statue to offer the antediluvian king a golden cup of wine. This done, he wiped the statue's mustache with a napkin, drank the wine himself, then tossed the empty cup into the crowd. Whoever caught it before it struck the ground and returned it to the acting company received a prize of two hundred crowns. Dahut still did mischief, but as a mermaid who tempted unwary fishermen, dragging them into the waters covering the city where she had drowned. The Ys myth describes her as "the white daughter of the sea," recalling the first lady of Atlantis in Plato's account—Leukippe, the "White Mare," and evoking the sea's foaming waves.

Although famous along the Normandy coast, Ys's pre-Christian origins appear in the Welsh place name Ynys Avallach and in England as Ynys-vitrius. Likewise, Avalon is a town in Burgundy named after the sunken island-city. The prominent Scottish mythologist Lewis Spence declared, "If the legend of Ys is not a variant of that of Atlantis, I am greatly mistaken" (Spence 1958, 152).

The story of Ys, however, is not the only such legend in France. Another tells of Sequana, a princess who sailed to the Burgundian highlands directly from the Great Flood that had drowned her distant island kingdom. Its name, Morois, is similar to Murias, the sunken city from which the Tuatha de Danann arrived in Ireland. Traveling up the Seine, Sequana erects a stone temple near Dijon. In it she stores a sumptuous treasure—loot from lost Atlantis?—in many secret chambers. After her death, she becomes a jealous river goddess. Near Dijon, in fact, there is a megalithic center made up of subterranean passageways that are still sometimes searched for ancient treasure. Sequana was reborn in the Sequani, a Celtic people who occupied territory between the Rhine, Rhône, and Saône Rivers. The Romans referred to the area as Maxima Sequanorum, known earlier as Sequana.

Similar traditions spread north with the migration of Atlantean culture bearers along the shores of the North Sea. Some were preserved in the *Voelupsa Saga,* the earliest account in Germanic myth. Although it was composed as late as the eighth or ninth centuries C.E., the folk material it contains undoubtedly reflects a far more ancient folk tradition. Voelupsa is a narrating sibyl who claims she is old enough to remember the ice giants, the first living creatures. One of them, Ymir, inundated the whole world with his spilled blood—actually with salt water, because he was a frost giant in whose veins the ocean flowed.

The only other survivors of his kind were Bergelmir and his wife, who packed their livestock in a ship and rode out the deluge. They drifted to the ends of the earth, finally landing at Joertunheim, where they sired a new race, the Jotnar. Just three mortal humans sailed away from the cataclysm in the *Naglfar,* a splendid vessel captained by Hrim Thursar (Hoar Frost) and bearing his parents, Lifthraser and Lif. In the Viking Age, all Norse traced their lineage from Hrim Thursar.

A thirteenth-century Scandinavian saga preserves oral traditions going back 1,500 years earlier to the Late Bronze Age. The *Atlakvith* (literally, The Punishment of Atla[ntis]) poetically describes the Atlantean cataclysm in terms of Norse myth, with special emphasis on the celestial role played in the catastrophe by "warring comets." Like the *Atlakvith,* the *Atlamal* (Twilight of the Gods) tells of the final destruction of the world order through celestial conflagrations, war, and flood. *Atlamal* literally means "The Story of Atla(ntis)."

Another tale, *Ragnarok* (The Breaking of the Gods), portrays the destruction of the world that was and will be again, over and over, as part of nature's eternal cycle. With its vivid descriptions of fiery skies and sinking land masses, *Ragnarok* surely reflects folk memories of Atlantis. It reads in part, "Already the stars were coming adrift from the sky and falling into the gaping void. They were like swallows, weary from too long a voyage, who drop and sink into the waves." A cosmic wolf, Fenrir, swallowed the sun at the time of the Great Flood, thereby spreading darkness over the whole world. His myth is a vivid metaphor for the phenomenal clouds of ash and dust that the Atlantean cataclysm raised that obscured daylight and plunged the earth into temporary but universal darkness.

Whenever the monstrous sea serpent Jormungandr tightened his coils about the world, earthquakes and tempests lashed out. In the *Ragnarok,* his agonies cause a worldwide flood. After this cataclysmic event, Frija, the queen of heaven, goes to dwell in her submerged palace, Fensalir (Halls of the Sea). The Midgaard Serpent, a monstrous snake coiled around the world, symbolizes geologic violence, particularly as it applies to the seismically unstable Mid-Atlantic Ridge that snakes its way down through the center of the ocean bottom almost from the Arctic Circle to the Antarctic. So too Fensalir may pass for the Norse version of sunken Atlantis.

According to the respected scholar of ancient Northern tradition H. R. Ellis Davidson, these myths may be traced back to the late seventeenth century B.C.E., a period corresponding to the third Atlantean deluge in 1629 B.C.E. But it is the second catastrophe that is more specifically documented in Northern literature.

The *Oera Linda Bok* (The Book of What Happened in the Old Time) is a compilation of ancient Frisian oral histories transcribed for the first time in 1256 C.E. by an anonymous author and finally published in Holland in 1871. The Frisians are a Germanic people of uncertain origins. All that is known of their earliest history is that they ousted the resident Celts from what is now a northern province of the Netherlands, today's Frisia and the Frisian Islands. They also live in Nordfriesland and Ostfriesland, in Germany. Their language is closely related to English. As late as the mideleventh century C.E. the Frisians sailed Venetii-like ships known as *kogge*s from their homeland on the Weser all the way to Greenland.

Branded as a fake from the moment of its discovery, the *Oera Linda Bok* has languished ever since in almost total obscurity. Allegedly composed as a hoax, it was actually a family heirloom passed down though many generations and unknown to the outside world until a descendant into whose keeping it fell decided to make it public. Just then, late-nineteenth-century scholars who were endeavoring to develop a scientific approach to understanding the past separated legend and religion from history to determine a more credible view of early events. To them the *Oera Linda Bok* represented just the kind of fantasy they believed obscured the facts, primarily because it offered a picture of preclassical times that ran contrary to everything they assumed about early civilization.

But the manuscript had its supporters too. William Barnes, a contemporary authority on Anglo-Saxon antiquities, declared in London's *MacMillan Magazine* that it featured far too many verifiable historical details for anyone but a university-trained expert to have included. As internal evidence he cited some convincing parallels from the *Germanicus* of Tacitus. More recently, investigator Warren Smith showed that no one ever profited from publication of the *Oera Linda Bok*. Nor has its allegedly modern author been identified in the more than 130 years since its release. A hoaxer usually seeks money and fame for his efforts, but no such person has ever been associated with the work.

The narration is not sensational but straightforward, presented in the unassuming style of a family chronicle. Its opening section, *He Alge tid Kem*, "How the Bad Days Came," begins with a description of the goddess Frya. She was the snow-white Eremoeder (Earth Mother) of the Frisian people, born on the sacred island of Atland. Like Plato's Atlantis, Atland is portrayed as a large island in the mid-Atlantic Ocean, the center of a powerful kingdom ruled by its magnificent capital city. But after many generations of peace and accomplishment, the Frisian homeland was overwhelmed by calamity.

He Alge tid Kem reports that during a summer long ago,

> the Earth began to tremble, as if she were dying. The mountains vomited fire and flames. Some sank into the bosom of the Earth, and in other places mountains rose out of the plains. The Earth trembled, the bottom of the isle of Textla sank, the heavens grew dark, and there were heavy explosions and reverberations of thunder. Aldland, called by the seafaring people, Atland, disappeared, and the wild water rose so high over hill and valley that everything was buried under the sea. Many people were swallowed up by the Earth, and others who had escaped death by fire, perished in the water.

In the aftermath

> . . . bands of Finda's people [ancestors of the Frisians] came and settled in the empty lands. When Atland sank, there was on the shores of the Middle Sea much suffering, on which account many of Finda's people, the Krekelanders and the people from Lyda's land, came to us. On the other hand, many of our people went to Lyda's land. So, the Krekelanders, far and wide, were lost to the control of the Mother.

In the confusion of migration, Inka, one of the Frisian chiefs still commanding a contingent of survivors, spoke up. "I have had enough of all these Finda's people," he declared. "I think that perhaps I might find some high land still above water, that is, some high-lying part of old Atland. If there be such an island in the ocean, I and my people may live on it in peace." He was joined by a cousin, Teunis, another chief, and the two, accompanied by their followers, sailed to Kadik (Cádiz) in Spain. There the cousins could not agree which way to travel, so they stood apart under their respective flags and offered their people a choice. Some willing to join Inka's proposed westward transatlantic voyage gathered around his blue standard. But somewhat more than half of the survivors rallied to the red banner of Teunis, who wanted to settle behind the narrow straits of the Middle Sea, just south and east of Kadik. The two chiefs and their followers separated amicably. Inka disappeared with his companions over the Atlantic Ocean toward the sunset, while Teunis and his two hundred ships sailed across the Middle Sea.

Landing in western Italy, Teunis and his followers reestablished their worship of the Earth Mother, lighting her perpetual flame at the Roman Temple of Vesta. Voyaging farther eastward, a princess from Atland, Min-erva, founded Athens and was worshipped after her death as the Greek goddess Minerva.

The Atlantis in the *Oera Linda Bok* demonstrates details comparable to those in other sources while throwing new light on the fate of its survivors. Frya, the snow-white Earth Mother of Atland, resembles White Mare—Leukippe, Poseidon's mother-in-law in Plato's account. The Frisian goddess was particularly revered throughout medieval Scandinavia, sometimes as Mardal-Frya, from *marr*, "sea." Among her gifts to humankind was a mystery cult known as Sejdr (pronounced *Say-their*). The cult practiced an early form of tantric yoga, evoking altered states of consciousness through sex magic, a technique of ecstasy used to achieve spiritual illumination and union with the god power. *Sejdr* means "heating" or "boiling" with sensual fervor. The cult's mortal representative was a *voelva*, less a priestess drilled in the performance of ritual than a seeress naturally gifted with psychic power. The *Voelupsa Saga* refers to Frya's earthly *voelva*, who told of the Great Deluge.

In Viking Age northern Europe, Friday was named after Frya. Appropriately, the *Oera Linda Bok* relates that Atland was overwhelmed on a Friday. It also claims that the catastrophe occurred in the summer of 2193 B.C.E. Choice of such a precise date seems peculiar, but the text insists that the specific year cited is the correct one. In fact, it coincides with a worldwide cataclysm that science now acknowledges to have taken place during the late third millennium B.C.E. This was the second Atlantean disaster described in Greek myth as the Flood of Ogyges and in the *Book of Invasions* as the cause of Partholon's arrival in Ireland with his "family."

The *Book of Invasions* mentions other discernibly Atlantean new-comers—the Fir Gailion and Fir Bolg—the People of Ilion and the Leather People (a reference to their boats of stretched leather). In similar language, the *Oera Linda Bok* tells of Finda's People. Its description of Atland's destruction is unlike Plato's version, however. Mountains rise and fall, and other islands are involved: "The bottom of the isle of Textla sank." The Frisian account claims that some survivors escaped to Britain, bringing with them the *Tex,* the legal structure of Atland, which, in subsequent generations, came to be known as Old English common law. One of the Frisian Islands is today still known as Texel. Textla was probably another island not far from Atland that suffered a similar annihilation. Aldland, as it was originally known, perhaps meant Alt Land, or "Old Land." The Hopi Indians of the American Southwest still refer to the Atlantis-like homeland of their ancestors as the Old Red Land.

American connections to the *Oera Linda Bok* are intriguingly suggested in the person of Inka, the Frisian chief who led followers under his blue banner westward across the sea, never to be heard from again. The leading Andean myth describes a great flood followed by the arrival of a bearded, fair-haired man from the east. Kon-tiki-Viracocha (Sea Foam) was regarded throughout Peru and Bolivia as the founding father of pre-Columbian civilization in South America. Could the Frisian Inka, fleeing with "Finda's people" from the deluge that over-whelmed Atland, have been the same Sea Foam who gave his name to the Incas?

Inka's cousin, Teunis, appears to have been no less influential a cul-ture bearer. His passage into the Middle Sea and the depositing of sur-vivors along the coast of Libya indicates an entrance into the Mediterranean Sea, where he founded a city named after himself in Lybia (synonymous in preclassical times for all of North Africa, minus

Egypt): Tunis. Teunis and Inka arrived in the Spanish city of Kadik to plan their migration strategy. This city was none other than Cádiz, the former Atlantean capital in Iberia, then known as Gades. From there Teunis and his people sailed to another Atlantean stronghold, this time in western Italy, cited by Plato as the farthest extent of occupation forces from Atlantis in continental Europe.

Finda was the Frisian version of Fand (Pearl of Beauty), wife of the Irish Poseidon, Macannan Mac Lyr. They dwelled on Land under Wave, an island in the west whose concentric walls were lavishly decorated with gleaming sheets of precious metal virtually identical to those in Plato's description of Atlantis. Their kingdom was also called Lir Sorcha, "Shining Land," reminiscent of the "Shining One," or Diaprepes, the tenth and last king listed in Plato's account of Atlantis. Diaprepes ruled the Canary Islands, specifically the large island of Tenerife, with its "shining" volcano, Mount Teide.

The Krekelanders are less certainly identified, but they appear to have been a related people, perhaps the Guanche, or Canary Islanders. In any case, the Atlantean catastrophe seems to have killed most of them and dispersed their survivors "far and wide," where they were "lost to the control of the Mother."

Some conception of the magnitude of the Atlantean disaster may be gleaned from the *Oera Linda Bok*'s description of post-Deluge conditions in Frisia. The country suffered from severe overcrowding, and the swollen population was in perpetual dissension for more than a century. Strain on the land's agricultural base was serious, and many survivors sought out alternative places of refuge: "Bands of Finda's people came and settled in the empty lands. When Atland sank, there was on the shores of the Middle Sea much suffering." Following a volcanic event of the scope described, it seems that at least one major seaquake would have been inevitable, and its effect along the coastal areas of western Europe and northwest Africa would have been devastating. The 100-foot-high, 300-mile-per-hour waves generated by Krakatau's eruption in 1883 killed thirty-six thousand people throughout the Sumatra Straits.

The *Oera Linda Bok* does not stand alone in its description of an Atlantean catastrophe, which also appears throughout the sagas of northern Europe. Its unique status among all other source materials for that cataclysm rests in its identity as one family's legacy from a natural disaster that long ago touched all humanity. Moreover, its specification of 2193 B.C.E. as the precise year for that calamity identifies the second geologic episode that wracked the island of Atlas, sending its refugees across the world as the instigators of new civilizations.

13

NATIVE AMERICANS REMEMBER ATLANTIS

Down on the bottom of the seas lie all the proud cities and the worldly treasures corrupted with evil, and those people who found no time to sing praises to the Creator from the top of their hills.

FROM THE HOPI INDIAN *SONG OF THE FLOOD*

For a people who, according to conventional anthropologists, arrived in North America from Siberia over a former land bridge spanning the Bering Straits only about twelve thousand years ago, the various American Indian tribes present a bewildering diversity of physical types that cannot be entirely explained by localized development. True, many Native Americans, such as the Apaches or Pimas, still evidence their Asian origins. But others, including the Mandans and Cherokees, often exhibit traits unusual in those of Asian ancestry, such as gray eyes, auburn hair, and lighter complexions.

What is the origin of these atypical characteristics long in evidence before the arrival of modern Europeans? Can they be the genetic remnants of connections between indigenous peoples and overseas visitors during pre-Columbian times? Although mainstream scholars strongly deny any such relationships ever existed, American Indian oral tradition is rich in reports of contacts with foreigners from lands far across the ocean who were often survivors from a great flood. When we consider the profound ethnic, cultural, and linguistic differences among the

Indian tribes; their separation by vast distances of the North American continent; and the animosities that pitted them against each other in perennial warfare, their common memory of a world-wrecking deluge seems most remarkable.

True, each tribe has its own version of the event and usually claims direct descent from a hero or god who survived. But the more-than-fundamental similarity and consistency of these renditions, when viewed in the aggregate, strongly suggests that they preserve the spoken account of an actual cataclysm separately witnessed or experienced by tribal ancestors. For so many variants to have endured across unknown generations of speakers and listeners at once implies the broad magnitude of the disaster and its persistent importance in Native American tradition.

No less remarkably, on closer examination many Indian flood stories feature striking resemblances to Plato's description of Atlantis. In cross-referencing each other, their often close parallels to details in *Timaeus* and *Critias* simultaneously bear out the authenticity of both indigenous traditions and his dialogues. The native tales are yet more valuable because they sometimes carry the classical Platonic version, which ends with the Atlantean destruction, beyond its fourth-century B.C.E. parameters to tell us what became of its survivors.

An example appears in Creek Indian cosmology. The Creeks believed the world began when the first mountain emerged from a sea known as Nunne Chaha, after which the mountain was named. This was the dwelling place of the Master of Breath, Esaugetuh Emissee. He divided his mountain island into alternating rings of land and water interconnected by a series of canals and surrounded by a high wall. In the center of the island he built a great stone house bounded by fruitful gardens. At Nunne Chaha Esaugetuh Emissee formed the first humans out of clay, gave them the sun to worship, and quartered the four cardinal directions from its center, assigning each one its own symbolic color.

There his creations lived in peace for many years, until they grew tired of their virtue and warred among themselves for selfish reasons. But the Master of Breath punished them for their ingratitude by destroying Nunne Chaha in a terrible flood. A few survivors crossed the sea from the rising sun to become the first great chiefs of the Indian peoples.

The Creeks shared this version of the Deluge with the Seminoles, Chortans, Cherokees, Chickasaws, Atakapas—in fact, with every other southern tribe dwelling near the Gulf of Mexico or the Atlantic Ocean. Their indigenous oral tradition contains all the leading features of Plato's account as well as some additional details. Similar to Mount Atlas on Atlantis, which lent its name to the Atlantic Ocean, Nunne Chaha gave its name to the sea it dominated. Both the Greek Poseidon and Creek Esaugetuh Emissee took the unusual step of dividing the land into concentric rings of alternating land and water and intersecting them with canals. The former's central temple with its lush gardens is mirrored by the Master of Breath's stone house and surroundings.

Unlike Plato's Atlantis, but found among other accounts of Atlantis described in this book's chapters on Mexico and South America, human beings originated at Nunne Chaha, where they engaged in solar worship. In both the American Indian and Platonic renditions, however, it was the moral corruption of these first men and women that brought about the catastrophe. What Plato could not have known about was the arrival of a few survivors in North America, where they are still revered as the progenitors of the Creek tribe. Another element in the native version that is less Platonic than Atlantean is the name Nunne Chaha itself. Ancient Egyptian cosmology as presented at the sacred "sun city" of Heliopolis described a Primal Mound or island home that emerged from the sea to serve as the place where humans first appeared. This island birthplace was known as Nun.

The Iroquois recalled "a land in the far east on the borders of the great water, where the sun comes up." It was there that "a white man sank the world" by digging too deeply into the soil, drowning an entire people save one survivor, who escaped with some animals in a large boat. After days lost at sea he sent out a dove, which returned from the region of the setting sun with a willow branch in its beak. He sailed westward, finally landing among the Iroquois to become their first and greatest chief. Hence the Indians conducted their spring festival—which prominently featured the dove—as soon as the willow bloomed.

The Iroquois legend and ceremony, known long before contact with Christian missionaries in the modern era, was shared by the Sioux, Chickasaw, Pima, Okanogan, and Mandan. This last tribe went even further to commemorate the flood hero's arrival in a spring ritual that called for a lone actor to walk in a stately manner "from far away." His face was painted white, and all chiefs bowed at his approach. This Nu-mohk-muck-a-nah, or the "First One," paused before the entrance of each lodge, where he chanted his mournful tale of the great deluge that had consumed his homeland, and how he, as "the only man," survived in "a big canoe."

George Catlin, the early chronicler of Native America in paintings and eyewitness reports, observed this Mandan ceremony in the first years of the nineteenth century. He described a 9-foot-tall hollow cylinder built of wood and set up at the center of the Indian village, where dancers and "speakers" sacrificed edged tools used for its construction as prevention against any recurrence of the Great Flood. This large object symbolized the big canoe that saved the First One. According to Catlin, the Mandan believed "that the omission of this annual ceremony, with its sacrifices made to the waters, would bring upon them a repetition of the calamity which their tradition says once befell them, destroying the whole human race, excepting one man from his canoe on a high mountain in the west" (Catlin 1970, 143).

The name of this ceremony, the O-kee-pa, or Bull Dance, referred, as the Mandan told Catlin, to the bull's-hide-covered tortoise drums in which was preserved water from the original Deluge. The Mandan speakers stunned him with the O-kee-pa's often close resemblances to the biblical version of the Flood. Their ceremony was not allowed to begin until the willow leaves were fully grown because, as the chief informed him, "The twig which the bird [mourning dove] brought into the Big Canoe was a willow bough, and had full-grown leaves on it." The Mandan also believed the Deluge covered the earth for forty days, the same number found in Genesis. The central rite of the Bull Dance was the Mee-ne-ro-ka-ha-sha, the "settling down of the waters," which was formally concluded when the dancers tossed the arklike structure's edged tools into a nearby river.

As Catlin continued his investigation of the Deluge story among the Plains Indians, he was amazed to find it so widespread among tribes that were different from each other in language and culture:

> This tradition . . . was not peculiar to the Mandan, for amongst 120 different tribes that I have visited in North, South and Central America, not a tribe exists that has not related to me directly . . .

such a calamity, in which 1 or 3 or 8 persons were saved above the waters on the top of a high mountain. Some of these at the base of the Rocky Mountains and in the plains of Venezuela and in the Pampa del Sacramento, in South America, make annual pilgrimages to the fancied summits where the antediluvian survivors were saved in canoes or otherwise, and under the regulations of their medicine men, tender their prayers and sacrifices to the Great Spirit, to ensure their exemption from a similar catastrophe. Indian traditions are generally conflicting and soon turn into fable. But how strong a proof is the unanimous tradition of the aboriginal races of the whole continent of such an event! (Catlin 1970, 141)

The Mandan's earliest known origins were in the Ohio Valley, site of the highly Atlantean Great Serpent Mound described in *The Destruction of Atlantis*. They occasionally exhibited racially mixed characteristics, which support their claim that white men met with their ancestors during the ancient past after the Great Flood. Catlin, who lived among the Mandan, observed:

In complexion, color of hair and eyes, they generally bore a family resemblance to the rest of the American tribes, but there were exceptions constituting perhaps 1/5 to 1/6 part of the tribe, eyes bright blue, their faces oval, devoid of salient angles so strongly characterizing all the other American tribes, and originating unquestionably to the influence of some foreign stock (Catlin 1970, 139).

The Apache Crown Dance calls for its performers to enter a chalk circle on the ground from the direction of the Lost Land under the Sunrise Sea. A singer stands in the middle of the circle with a trident, the emblem of Poseidon, the sea god and creator of Atlantis in Plato's account. When the dancers have finished, the singer turns his trident upside down, drives it poignantly into the ground before him, then begins his chant: "I remember the old red land of my forefathers and how it sank beneath the sea." In *Critias* Plato wrote that the island of Atlantis was rich in a red stone, tufa, common among volcanic islands.

The Lost Land under the Sunrise Sea referred to by the Apache speaker was also known as the Isle of Flame. He said it had a large port with an entrance of heavy masonry, where ships had to be guided in by pilots. One day, a Fire Dragon arose, forcing the residents to flee for their lives. They wandered for a long time, carrying with them seeds and fruit plants, before finally settling in the land of the Indians. The Egyptian *Book of the Dead* likewise speaks of an Isle of Flame surrounded by a high iron wall and located in the Distant West. Tefnut, the personification of destructive heat in Egyptian myth and the sister of Shu, the Egyptian Atlas, went to the Isle of Flame, where a terrific slaughter of humans took place.

Both the Apache and Egyptian versions appear to stem from a common source: the destruction of Atlantis so graphically portrayed as an Isle of Flame with its active volcano, Mount Atlas. The Cheyenne custom of offering food or tobacco to the ocean was meant to propitiate a dragon whose great fires had once erupted from the midst of the waters.

Kiowa Apaches conducted lakeside commemorations of "a sunken village" lost during the Deluge. American mythologists Alice Marriott and Carol Rachlin remark that the tale is similar to that of Brittany's *cathédrale engloutie,* "although it is highly unlikely that the informant who told the story knew anything of European folklore at the time of the telling. Possibly this is a fragment or combination of fragments of a longer and more complex story." (Marriott and Rachlin, 1968, 8). The closely related Navajo version of the Crown Dance tells how the gods "visited all parts of the world" after the Flood (Marriott and Rachlin 1968, 14).

California's Aschochimi remembered how a massive inundation wiped out almost all humankind before their tribe came into being. Even the Indians of the northwest coast around St. Michael still "tell a story about a flood that took place in the first days of the Earth" (Marriott and Rachlin, 1968, 9). The Comanche believed a white people existed before themselves, but that they all perished in a horrific flood. Only a few were transformed into white seagulls by the cataclysm.

Every American tribe had its own Deluge hero from whom ancestral descent was claimed. Among the Aschochimi, he was Atapasks, while the Delaware called him Powako. Many so-called totem poles, actually memorial or heraldic structures used as decorative houseposts to reflect their owners' wealth and lineage, were said to have been made "at the time of the flood," which they were supposed to commemorate. Ring dances around the base of these poles were performed as they were being erected, and a "sayer" recounted tribal history from earliest times, never without references to the cataclysm from which his ancestors escaped over the Great Water.

Native American Deluge stories often bear features remarkably similar to Plato's description of Atlantis, as we observed in the Creek story of Nunne Chaha. Like Poseidon, the Algonquian Manibozho "carved and shaped the land and the sea to his liking." The Walaam Olum is a collection of Algonquian tribal histories that tells of a cataclysmic deluge from which a few humans escaped to become the first chiefs. The same story is told by a Shawnee dance ceremoniously held in Oklahoma forest groves. Oklatabashih, Choctaw for "Survivor of the Great Flood," is considered to be the tribe's ancestor. The chief who led the refugees to safety was called Tiamuni. The name resembles that of Tiamut, a Babylonian personification of the ocean, which derived from an even older Sumerian version.

Algonquian tradition told of the Father of the Tribes who came "from the rising sun," from the land of the Abenaki, "our white ancestors in the east," after he was forewarned in a dream that the gods would sink his land beneath the sea. In haste he built "a great reed raft" (shades of Thor Heyerdahl's Ra expeditions!) on which he sailed away with his family and a number of animals. In those days beasts could speak, but because they grew impatient, ridiculed the Father, and were on the verge of mutiny when land was finally sighted, the gods deprived them of this ability—though they all walked safely ashore. The Hopi version of this tale is identical.

Plato's Kleito, the princess who dwelled on a hill in Atlantis, and the Egyptian Nun of the Primal Mound are vividly recalled in the Hopi story of Childbirth Water Woman, Tuwa-bontumsi: "A very long time ago there was nothing in the world but water. But where Tuwa-bontumsi lived there was a small piece of land. She lived in a hill called Talaschomo, a mound created when it rose out of the primal sea."

The migration myth of the Patki Indians also includes a woman on an island far away at sea. Palatkwapi was the isle of a sorceress who was punished for her wickedness by a terrific inundation. When Palatkwapi sank beneath the waves, most humans were drowned in the resulting tsunami, but a few reached North American shores to become the ancestors of the Patki.

According to Delaware tradition, "at this time [of the flood], Tula, that island, became the father of all mankind." This Song of Tula was known to the Sioux, Dakota, Pima, and Papago. Tula was also the Island in the Sunrise Sea, regarded by Mexico's Toltecs and Aztecs as the homeland of the Feathered Serpent, the white-skinned, yellow-bearded founding father of Mesoamerican civilization. When we consider the sometimes prodigious distances separating these tribes, their common knowledge of the "Song of Tula" underscores its fundamental importance to many of the continent's indigenous peoples.

Some Gulf Coast tribes knew of the Eagle Man, portrayed in regional artifacts as a bearded man emerging from a conch shell, very similar to Mesoamerican representations of the Feathered Serpent. When the Norse seafarer Thorfinn Karlsefni landed at Labrador in 1011 C.E., a pair of Indian boys told him that the Eagle Man was like himself: tall, red-bearded, and fair-skinned, with a home located east across the sea.

The Potawatami flood, like Plato's account, cites the immorality of the inhabitants living on a great island far out across the Big Water in the east. The Creator, Kitchemonedo, made their home a veritable paradise, but because humans eventually grew "perverse, ungrateful and wicked," he sank it along with most of its sinners. Only one man and his wife survived by fleeing in a big canoe, a tradition repeated across the continental spectrum of Native American myth.

The Okanogans of British Columbia had a great medicine woman for a progenitor, Scomalt, who once "ruled over a lost island" called Samatumi-whooah, literally "White Man's Island." It sank in the midst of a gigantic war, drowning all the combatants save a husband and wife who landed among the Okanogans. So too, Plato states, did the people of Atlantis perish while engaged in far-flung military operations.

Native tradition in Maryland held that white people belonged to a deeply ancient generation who, perishing in a world flood, were reborn and returned to claim their former lands. Henry Brinton, one of the mid-nineteenth century's outstanding mythologists, pointed out that "the Algonquians call their tribes living east, Abnakes, 'our white ancestors'" (Hennes 1963, 177). The Delaware account of their ancestors told how they came from "the first land beyond the great ocean." The oldest branch of the Algonquian family, they displayed Caucasian characteristics so pronounced that some of the early American settlers imagined they were descended from the Old Testament's lost tribe of Israel. In fact, the Delawares referred to themselves as the Leno-Lenape, the "unmixed men."

The Acoma likewise claim their ancestors were white people who appeared after a deluge destroyed their distant homeland. The Sioux described how "the tribes of Indians were formerly one, and all dwelt on an island toward the east, the sunrise." When their island sank under the weight of popular immorality, a few virtuous survivors departed in "huge canoes." After weeks of sailing, they reached the shores where the Sioux came to dwell.

The Iowa inflected the same story: "At first all men lived on an island, where the day star is born." The ancient Egyptians associated Venus, the "day star," with Osiris, the man-god intent on civilizing the world. Venus was the avatar of the Feathered Serpent, who came from over the sea bearing the gifts of civilization to Middle America.

Chief differences between various tribal versions of the Flood involve the number of survivors who landed in prehistoric America. Some claimed only a few arrived, while others insisted a larger migration occurred in big canoes. Still others, such as the Mandan, stated that one man made the perilous voyage. Inconsistency around this common theme does not invalidate these accounts; various survivors of the Atlantis catastrophe who fled for their lives as best they could probably arrived independently, some in larger or smaller groups, a few as lone individuals landing at different locations along eastern and southeastern shores. Thus all American Indian Deluge legends do not trace back to a common tradition, but instead reflect individual tribal experiences of similar, related events: the arrival of survivors at separate landfalls from destroyed Atlantis.

These numerous, highly suggestive Native American myths find their most obvious realization at a major archaeological site in northeastern Louisiana called Poverty Point. Here is truly Atlantis in America, a smaller-scale reproduction—although nonetheless imposing—of the vanished capital found in Plato's dialogues. (See figs. 13.1. and 13.2.) Three millennia before Columbus set sail for the New World, a city such as Plato describes thrived on the east bank of the Arkansas River. An arrangement of alternating land and water rings there was bisected by canals converging at the city center.

On its north end reared a large ceremonial mound 700 by 800 feet at its base and rising 70 feet above the surrounding plain. "It was an almost perfect cone," observed James Ford, an archaeologist who first worked the site during the mid-1950s (Ford and Webb 1956, 35). In *Critias* Plato writes that volcanic Mount Atlas likewise stood just north of Atlantis. To complete the simulation of a volcano at Poverty Point, cane fires were ignited at the cone's summit.

Plato states that 6, a sacred number in Atlantis, was incorporated into the capital's unique construction of concentric rings linked by canals cut across these concentric rings. Poverty Point also comprises six concentric mounds alternating with earthen embankments and circular watercourses that were crosscut by a network of canals.

Artifacts retrieved from Poverty Point are important clues to the origin of its civilizers. The small, worn figures with European facial features exhibit a non-Indian style of execution, particularly relative to the human torso. Soapstones are carved with the profile drawings of longships terminating in high prows, some in the shape of animal

Fig. 13.1. Aerial perspective shows the immensity of Poverty Point, with its alternating rings and moats patterned after Atlantis. (Photo courtesy of the Poverty Point Archaeological Museum, Louisiana)

heads, with low, sloping sterns like those seen in the depictions of Bronze Age ships sailed against Egypt by Atlantean crew members.

No less Atlantean is the vast scope of Poverty Point's grand design. Lacking local sources of stone, its city planners relied on building materials close at hand, much as modern construction engineers are forced to do. The ancient metropolis was built from more than half a million yards of soil, a mass thirty-five times greater than the cubic area of the Great Pyramid on the Giza Plateau. The city required twenty million fifty-pound basketloads of earth and more than three million man-hours to complete. Poverty Point could have been built only by a large, concentrated population. Ford explains:

> The few examples of chronological information that have been secured from excavation in various parts of the earthwork suggest that probably all of it was built and inhabited about the same time. This effort was obviously well-controlled. The geometrical design of the town is clearly the result of central planning and direction (Ford and Webb 1956, 37).

Poverty Point is, therefore, an anomaly among the "loosely organized societies" of the Plains Indians.

Like Atlantis, Louisiana's prehistoric metropolis was the hub of a far-flung commercial enterprise composed chiefly of water routes. Poverty Point was a true urban center of at least five thousand residents (revised estimates may expand that number by a factor of three) who imported quartz crystal from Hot Springs, Arkansas, 200 airline miles distant, and copper from Lake Superior, 1,100 airline miles away. Strangely, they traded for, in Ford's words, "enormous weights" of steatite, or soapstone, from Appalachia, more than 1,500 miles away by river (Ford and Webb 1956, 38). They also worked in iron (for plummets in fishing and, perhaps, surveying), red jasper (a crystalline quartz), hematite (a red iron ore), and translucent fluorite (another crystal). The value placed on decorative imports recalls Plato's account, wherein the Atlanteans are described as having gone to great lengths to adorn their massive walls and public buildings with precious construction materials.

Should there remain any doubt concerning the identity of the builders or original inhabitants of Poverty Point, reliable carbon dating has revealed that the Louisiana site is North America's oldest city. Thanks in large measure to an abundance of burned bone fragments recovered from its large ceremonial mound, archaeologists know that Poverty Point sprang into existence around 1600 B.C.E., coinciding with the third Atlantean flood. The entire continent's indigenous inhabitants, referred to as Paleo-Indians of the Archaic period, did not possess a material culture approaching the system of weights and measures, irrigation, astronomy, large-scale social organization, surveying, and city planning that went into the creation of Poverty Point. This, along with the city's abrupt appearance without any precursors, defines its prepackaged birth as the accomplishment of an outside people already skilled in urban construction and long-distance commerce.

The area had been occupied at least another 1,500 years before, but by a far less sophisticated culture unrelated to the master builders who appeared around the turn of the seventeenth century B.C.E. Some four hundred years later Poverty Point experienced a sudden population increase coincident with the addition of important astronomical alignments at the city center. It flourished for about another three hundred years, then collapsed when its inhabitants inexplicably abandoned the site and disappeared. It was never reoccupied and was discovered only in the 1950s during aerial surveys of the Arkansas River.

That Poverty Point was deliberately patterned after Atlantis seems inescapably clear. Their close physical resemblance and shared time frames leave little room for other interpretations. A third wave of migration from Atlantis occurred in 1628 B.C.E. with the penultimate Bronze Age cataclysm of that year, just when Poverty Point appeared at full flower in northeastern Louisiana. It was at this moment too that copper mining in the Upper Great Lakes region shifted into high gear. Poverty Point, where Great Lakes copper artifacts have been found, was very likely a mining town or clearinghouse for the mineral before it was freighted in great quantity to Atlantis, whose soaring wealth as the capital of the Bronze Age world depended on its North American sources. So too was 1200 B.C.E. a watershed date for both Poverty Point, whose population experienced an abrupt increase at that time, and Atlantis, which met with its final destruction in that year.

It appears that Atlanteans built Poverty Point for miners wintering from their excavations at Michigan's Upper Peninsula. Copper was collected and smelted into ingots for transportation down the Arkansas and Mississippi Rivers, out into the Gulf of Mexico, and back to Atlantis for sale and distribution to the kingdoms and civilizations of the Mediterranean and the Near East. When Atlantis was obliterated in the worldwide geologic upheavals that ended the Bronze Age, some of its survivors fled overseas to the well-known mining town in Louisiana, swelling its population with their numbers. This is the drama preserved down the generations in Indian myth and ceremony.

14

FEATHERED SERPENTS FROM SUNKEN CITIES

Ocean, from where the gods are sprung . . .

HOMER, THE ILIAD (BOOK XIV, 201)

W hen European ships appeared for the first time off the Mexican coast in 1519, thousands of ceremoniously dressed Indians crowded the beaches to welcome them with loud music and shouts of joy. Some swam out just to touch the bows of the great Spanish galleys. After the conquistadors set foot on shore amid almost hysterical jubilation, they were presented with gifts of rare feathers and a helmet full of gold dust. An entire empire, unbidden, prostrated itself before the strangers as they passed through a capital rivaling in size and splendor any European city. Finally, the visitors stood before the Aztec emperor. His ministers had welcomed the perplexed Spaniards "home," and it was up to Montezuma to explain why:

> Long time have we been informed by the writings of our ancestors that neither myself nor any of those who inhabit this land are natives to it, but [are] rather strangers who have come to it from foreign parts. We likewise know that from those parts our nation was led by a certain lord to whom all were subject, and who then went back to his native land, where he remained so long delaying his return that at his coming those whom he had left behind had married the women of the land, and had many children by them, and had built

themselves cities in which they lived, so that they would in no wise return to their own land, or acknowledge him as lord, upon which he left them. And we have always believed that among his descendants one would surely come to subject this land and us as rightful vassals. Now, seeing the regions from which you say you come, which is from where the sun rises, and the news you tell us of this great king and ruler who sent you hither, we believe and hold it certain that he is our natural lord (Forman 1968, 34–35).

It must all have been very complicated for the Spanish visitors, but they did not pause long to consider the mythic implications of their timely arrival. Within two years after Hernán Cortés dropped anchor off Veracruz, Montezuma was dead, his people enslaved, their empire dissolved, and their illusions dispelled by some of the most blood-stained acts of ingratitude in all history. The unfortunate Indians had mistaken the bearded Spaniards for the bearded Quetzalcoatl, who had promised to return someday. The future was now, but Cortés was not the Feathered Serpent.

The story of this dramatic figure was the central pillar of the Aztec's history, the inspiration of their religion, art, and astronomy. He exerted a dominant influence on all Mesoamerican cultures, including some that were separated from the Aztecs by many centuries and great distances. For tens of thousands of years, the Indian populations of Mesoamerica settled in huddled, scattered villages, where they made crude pottery and a few simple tools while scratching out a subsistence agriculture one step removed from their hunter-gatherer forebears. Then, before 1500 B.C.E., a literate, dynamically full-blown civilization suddenly erupted into existence at Veracruz—ironically, the same location where Cortés and his band of gold-greedy adventurers landed after 1500 C.E.

Archaeologists call Mexico's seminal civilization the Olmec, but how its own people referred to themselves is unknown. The literate ancient culture bearers built monumental ceremonial centers, where they raised massive stonework; instituted a transformational religion; and practiced the arts of medicine, astronomy, and astrology. Their civilization spread along and beyond the Gulf Coast region, but before 600 B.C.E. a decline set in, and they were superseded by the west-central Oaxaca, who adapted the patterns for Mesoamerican civilization set by the Olmec until 200 B.C.E. Those patterns were further preserved and expanded by the Maya, particularly in the fields of astronomy and literature. The tenth century witnessed their passing when Mesoamerica's legacy was inherited by the Toltecs. The final phase of Mexico's pre-Columbian world belonged to the Aztecs, foreigners from the north, who attempted a synthesis of previous phases in an imperialist enterprise.

Each people relied on the figure of the Feathered Serpent as the single most important personality in their religion and history. To the Maya he was Kukulcan. The Quiché knew him as Votan. The Toltec, Mixtec, and Aztec remembered him as Quetzalcoatl. His legend was even known and revered in parts of pre-Conquest America never visited by the Maya or Aztec. In Brazil he was called Tupi or Same by tribes totally unrelated to each other and those of Mexico. Among the Indians of Colombia he was Bochica or Zuhe. In fact, the Colombian natives first greeted each Spaniard as "Zuhe." The Feathered Serpent was Condoy to the Zoques in southern Guatemala, and the Venezuelan Cunas knew him as Tsuma. He was known as Tamandare among the indigenous populations of Argentina and Paraguay.

It is astonishing that his legend underwent only minor local inflections and variations among peoples of widely diverse cultures over at least three thousand years, a fact suggesting that all the societies that preserved his story had indeed been visited by a beneficent traveler from over the Sunrise Sea. The Feathered Serpent was said to have arrived at Veracruz with a flotilla of "water houses," the same term a Guanche prophet, Yone, used to describe the ships of the Canary Islands god Eraoranhan, who also came from across the sea.

Kukulcan's home was "the Red and Black Land over the water, where the sun rises." Along with his fellow visitors—poets, artists, doctors, priests, astronomers, architects, and sculptors—he introduced the benefits of civilization. He was remembered by the Indians as a tall man with long yellow hair and beard and light eyes. He was dressed in a flowing robe of white designed with red crosses, and in his hand he held either a bunch of flowers or a sickle. Interestingly, the sickle was also the symbol of the Old World Kronos, the Titan associated with the Atlantic Ocean. The Feathered Serpent sought to suppress human sacrifice among indigenous Americans, but his failure led to difficulties

with the native priests. They were joined by some of his own followers who had turned against him, so he sailed away before they could
do him violence.

The Feathered Serpent's departure was mourned by the rest of the
people, but as he stepped aboard his "raft of serpents" (a reed boat
with its sinuous hull?), he promised that either he himself or his descendants would come back someday to rule the land. The people were to
preserve it in safekeeping until his return. With that, he floated away
over the same sea that brought him to Mexico, toward his island kingdom, the Red and Black Land of Tollan, or the White Island, Aztlan.

One of the few poems to have survived the fires of religious bigotry
that consumed the great body of Aztec literature is *The Prophet,* which
includes perhaps the most specific description of the Feathered Serpent:
"See, exceedingly long is his beard. Yellow as straw is his beard." The
culture hero's portrait in stone appears at Chichén Itzá's ziggurat-like
Temple of Kukulcan, ornamented with several sculpted heads display-
ing pointed beards and facial features that are not Indian. The wall
paintings at Cacxtla represented his birth from a conch shell, the symbol of the sea. He was elsewhere depicted wearing a conch shell around
his neck. Known as the Wind Jewel, the shell stood for the hurricane
that preceded his arrival. This pectoral is but one link, the first of many,
to the Feathered Serpent's Atlantean identity.

For example, Teuhtile, Emperor Montezuma's first representative
to face the newly arrived Spaniards, told Hernán Cortés that his helmet,
being finely crafted of a shining metal unknown to the Aztecs, reminded
him of Quetzalcoatl's headgear, as graphically described in oral tradition. The Aztec, in fact, referred to Cortés and his men individually as
Calion, an honorific title alluding to one of Mesoamerica's flood heroes
and ultimately derived, it would seem, from the Greco-Atlantean
Deluge figure Deucalion. His uncle was, after all, no less than Atlas
himself.

Plato tells how the kings of Atlantis were twins. So too,
Quetzalcoatl's title was Precious Twin, a reference to his brother,
Xolotl. Like Atlas, the Feathered Serpent was an astrologer, and both
were represented as anthropomorphic figures upholding the sky
(Brundage 1960, 105). But the similarities do not stop there. Atlas's
seven daughters, the Pleiades, became stars after their deaths;

Quetzalcoatl carried a ceremonial baton studded with seven jewels signifying the Pleiades, which were especially revered throughout pre-Columbian America. Quetzalcoatl was said to have come from Michatlauhco, or the Fish Deeps, the Atlantic Ocean. Even the names Atlantic and Mich*atlauhc*o are so much alike that they suggest some common origin. Quetzalcoatl's island birthplace was sometimes called Tlapallan, regarded by Brundage as "an actual, geographical location somewhere in the east" (Brundage 1960, 105). Indeed, in his incarnation *(ixiptla)* as Yohualli Ehecatl, the Feathered Serpent was said to have led the first settlers to Mesoamerica from the east. When he sailed away he passed eastward along the Gulf Coast to Campeche, then beyond to Tlapallan, whose name also echoes that of Atlantis: Tl*apallan*.

In *Critias* Plato tells of a pillar at the very center of Atlantis in the Temple of Poseidon, where stood a statue of Atlas, the Upholder of the Heavens. Alternating every fifth and sixth year, the kings of the Atlantean empire gathered around this column and made a bloody sacrifice over its top as part of their royalty-cult worship. In Tenochtitlán, the Aztec capital, a freestanding column known as In the Midst of the Heavens was the center of a pillar cult involving bloody sacrifices to the Feathered Serpent. The comparison draws still closer when we realize that Quetzalcoatl was venerated as Atlahua "in a temple on the legendary island of Aztlan" (Brundage 1960, 105). Aztlan is undoubtedly Atlantis, just as Atlahua is unmistakably Atlas. The Aztecs themselves drew their own name from Aztecatl, or Man of Watery Aztlan. In their Nahuatl dialect the Aztecs called themselves Tenoches.

Aztlan literally means "field of reeds," a metaphor for great wisdom because reeds were writing instruments used only by literate scholars. The Egyptians' Sekhet-Aaru was a kingdom in the Distant West from which, before it sank, their ancestors fled to the Nile Delta. Sekhet-Aaru likewise means Field of Reeds, connoting the same place of high learning. In fact, Egyptian temple art sometimes depicts a king making offerings to Thaut, the divine patron of literature, in the hieroglyphs of a scribe's palette with a bunch of reed pens. Thaut was usually portrayed as a man with the feathered head of an ibis, and was said to have come to Egypt with the rest of the gods from Sekhet-Aaru. So too the Aztecs remembered Quetzalcoatl as the Feathered Serpent who arrived from Aztlan, which was depicted in temple art as a volcanic island in the eastern ocean. A cultural coincidence of this magnitude is difficult to accept, especially when we realize that the calendric name of Quetzalcoatl was Reed One, signifying his position as the first among literate men.

Together with the ibis-headed Thaut, the closest physical resemblance to the Feathered Serpent in Egypt may have been Wadjet. As the protector of the Lower Nile, she was among the most ancient of deities, apparently known even before dynastic times. Sometimes Wadjet was shown in the form of a winged cobra—a feathered serpent. As such she was the standard device on each pharaoh's crown, an emblem that epitomized his supreme spiritual and temporal power. Seeing Wadjet prominently worn on the headgear of a visiting culture bearer, the American Indians may have named him after his impressive badge of authority. In a variation of her name, Wadjet bears some phonetic similarity to Quetzalcoatl: Ur-Uatchti.

Another predynastic deity was Amen, portrayed in temple art as a bearded man wearing a headdress of double plumes alternating with red and green or red and blue feathers—another vision that suggests the Feathered Serpent. Ahmen, meaning He Who Knows, was a title of the highest honor that the Maya bestowed on their doctors, sorcerers, astronomers, and the most distinguished members of their intellectual classes.

Also revered as He Who Divides the Waters and Inventor of the Trident (the emblem of Poseidon, the sea god and creator of Atlantis, according to Plato), Quetzalcoatl bore the title of Amimitl, the Harpoon. It seems remarkable that more than five thousand years ago on the other side of the world the first bringers of civilization to the Nile Delta were remembered as Harpooners, the Mesentiu, who arrived in their ships from the Distant West. Here, as before, there is something of a philological resemblance between the Aztec name Amimitl and the Egyptian name Mesentiu.

The Feathered Serpent's fabled landing at Veracruz is borne out by oceanographic evidence pointing to the origins of Olmec civilization there five thousand years ago. Running from the northwest coast of Africa, the Canary Island current ends in Veracruz, specifically at La Venta, the first and most important Olmec site. It was this current that

Dr. Thor Heyerdahl took for his Ra expeditions, proving that transatlantic travel by classical and preclassical mariners was at least possible. If prehistoric mariners did venture out into the open sea, they would have eventually landed at the very spot where the Feathered Serpent was said to have arrived and, in fact, where Mesoamerican civilization arose.

Recorded testimony of the Mayan priests as set down in the reports of the Crown historian Father Sahagun quoted them as saying, "They [the Maya's ancestors] came from across the water and landed near Veracruz, the wise men who had all the writings, the books, the paintings." Following the same Canary Island current, Cortés also arrived off Veracruz. The Maya called Veracruz "Panco, where those who crossed the water arrived."

The Olmec, as portrayed in stone carvings at Monte Albán, were a relatively tall, occasionally bearded people ruling the short, beardless Indians. Although they were familiar with the Feathered Serpent, too little information about this pioneering race survives, so we can begin his story only with the later, better understood Maya. They knew him as Kukulcan, the Master of Breath, precisely the same title used by the Creek, Chortan, and Seminole Indians of North America to describe their founding father, Esaugetuh Emissee.

Itzamna (fig. 14.1), an even earlier flood hero, was installed as the chief Mayan god, the Lord of Heaven, inventor of "sacred writing" (hieroglyphs) and astronomy-astrology. He was the founder of Mayapán and Chichén Itzá, where twelve high priests met annually, their bodies dyed deep blue. These were the Ah-Kin, or diviners (from *kinya,* "to divine"), recalling the Atlantean kings described by Plato as first priests and augurs who dressed in dark blue robes and convened in the Temple of Poseidon. Itzamna gave his name to a Maya people, the Itzas, referred to as Ah-Auab or "foreigners to the land," but whose name literally meant "white men." Among their other titles were Lords, True Men, or Halach-Unicob (Lineage of the Land), and sometimes the Great Men or the Priest-Rulers.

They were portrayed on the twenty-seventh stele at Yaxchilan, the eleventh stele at Piedras Negras, and the Temple of the Warriors at Chichén Itzá as bearded, with long, thin noses and European facial features. The Halach-Unicob were said to have come from Tutulxiu, the

Fig. 14.1. These Atlas figures, each representing Itzamna, support stone slabs emblazoned with the hieroglyph for *heaven* at the Temple of the Warriors in the ceremonial center Chichén Itzá. After surviving a disastrous flood, Itzamna and his wife, Ixchel, were said to have brought civilization to the Maya.

Land of Abundance, or the Bountiful, far across the sea "where the sun rises." Kukulcan's father was Citallatonali, whose name was preserved in the Capactli hieroglyph, representing a dragon slashing the ocean and reminiscent of the Atlanto-Greek Ladon (a great serpent guarding Atlas's Tree of Life) or the Norse Midgaard Serpent, both associated with the Atlantic Ocean.

In Mesoamerican art the Feathered Serpent was commonly shown emerging from between the jaws of a monstrous snake, precisely the same image repeated by Greek vase painters when they depicted Pelasgus (fig. 14.2), leader of the pre-Hellenic Pelasgians, or Sea People, who brought civilization to the Peloponnese after the Great Flood. As the prominent folk scholar J. H. Baecker observed, "The snake-race was that of the first primeval seafarers. The faring-wise serpent races became rulers and civilizers" (Boswick 1924, 186).

A stone relief at Chichén Itzá portrayed the Feathered Serpent holding up the sky. He is represented as a bearded man with a non-Indian profile, a depiction that prompted an early-twentieth-century leading

Fig. 14.2. The interior of a fifth-century B.C.E. bowl depicts Pelasgus, leader of the Pelasgian Sea People, being disgorged from the ocean onto Greek shores. Waiting for him is Athena, the divine personification of civilization. (National Museum of Athens, Greece)

authority on Mayan civilization, J. H. Spinden, to describe him as Atlantean. Similar atlantes at Porrero Nuevo support the glyph for sky. The Maya's four Bacab gods, also represented as atlantes, were believed to have come to Chichén Itzá just after a world-class deluge destroyed their capital across the sea. Their homeland was described as the Red and Black Land, recalling Plato's description of the red (tufa) and black (lava) natural formations on the island of Atlantis. Indeed, Mexico's Teotihuacán Temple of the Feathered Serpent features a sculpted relief of Quetzalcoatl literally swimming to shore.

Most Mayan literature was incinerated by Spanish friars, but enough survived to tell the story of a natural catastrophe that immediately preceded the Feathered Serpent migrations to Middle America. The Chilam Balam tells of life in the Red and Black Land as ideal for many centuries. But one day "a fiery rain fell, ashes fell, rocks and trees crashed to the ground. Then the waters rose in a terrible flood. The sky fell in, and the dry land sank into the sea." (See fig. 14.3.)

The Haiyococab, an event recounted in the Dresden Codex, was the

Fig. 14.3. Quetzalcoatl, the Feathered Serpent, who brought civilization to Mesoamerica, emerges from the jaws of a serpent, signifying his arrival by sea. The Greek Pelasgus and Mexican Quetzalcoatl were said to have arrived at opposite ends of the world following a catastrophic flood. (Field Museum, Chicago)

Water over the Earth from which the "Earth-upholding gods escaped when the world was destroyed by the deluge." The Chimalpopca Codex parallels Plato's account of the Atlantis cataclysm "in a single day and night." It tells of the world coming to an end "in one day of deluge. Even the mountains sank into the water." In "The Legend of the Four Suns," "It rained fire upon them. They were swallowed by the waters." Sailing from disaster, the survivors, from whom successive generations of ruling aristocrats traced their descent, settled in Mayaland. The destruction of Atlantis seems to be clearly reflected in these fragmentary accounts, as is the recurring theme of an Atlas-like figure.

Literary traditions of a doomed city were somewhat better preserved among the Quiché, a people living in the midwestern highlands of Guatemala, and therefore partially removed from the mainstream of Mayan civilization, although their cultural achievements were no less impressive. In the Chakchiquel Manuscript, Quiché origins are described:

> The wise men, the chiefs and captains of three great peoples and others which were assembled, called *Umamae,* extending their vision through the four quarters of the world and under all that which is beneath the sky, and encountering no obstacle, came from the other side of the ocean, from where the sun rises, from the place called *Tulan pa Civan* [Sunrise of the Depths]. These divisions came together from the other side of the Sea of the East, from Tulan of one language and the same customs.

The Popul Vuh, which contains Quiché cosmogony and early semi-mythic history, describes what became of Tulan:

> A resinous thickness descended from heaven. The face of the Earth was obscured, and a heavy, darkening rain commenced; rain by day, and rain by night. There was heard a great noise above their heads, as if produced by fire. Then were seen men running, pushing each other, filled with despair. They wished to climb upon their houses. And the houses, tumbling down, fell to the ground. They wished to climb upon the trees, and the trees shook them off. They wished to enter into the grottoes, and the grottoes closed before them. Water and fire contributed to the universal ruin at that time of the last great cataclysm which preceded the Fourth Creation.

Out of these violent upheavals the last migrations arrived in Guatemala:

> Those who gazed at the rising of the sun had but one language. This occurred after they had arrived at New Tulan, before going west. Here the language of the tribes had changed. Then speech became different. All that they had heard or understood when departing from [Old] Tulan had become incomprehensible to them.

Tulan was apparently a name used by the Quiché for both Atlantis and Mexico, in the same way British settlers from "merry Old England" during the seventeenth century named their part of America *New England*. This analogy is borne out by the Cakchiquel Manuscript in which four different Tulans are mentioned: "It is where the sun set that we came to [New] Tulan from the other side of the sea, and it is there that we were conceived and begotten by our mothers and fathers."

As the first Spanish chroniclers reported, "Some of the old people of Yucatan say that they have heard from their ancestors that this land was occupied by a race of people who came from the east, and who God had delivered by opening twelve paths through the sea." Similarly, the Toltecs claimed that their forefathers came from a city in the ocean, Tollan, after its people grew decadent, and its red and black walls "melted." Xelhua, a white-skinned giant, led the survivors to Cholula, where he built a "flood tower" in case the waters should ever again rise to threaten the world. The Deluge theme grows in the Quiché Maya version of Tollan: Tulum, from *tu* (around) and *tul-nah,* (to be too full; to overflow; high tide) (Nuttall 1900, 88, 89) are descriptive of a circular place drowned by a flood.

The Aztec prose poem *The Prophet* extols Quetzalcoatl's people and their overseas homeland:

> And his people, they the Toltecs, wondrous skilled in all the trades were, all the arts and artifices. And as master craftsmen worked they. And in Quetzalcoatl all these arts and crafts had their beginning. He the master workman taught them. Nothing pleasing to the palate, nothing helpful to the body, ever lacked they there in Tula. Masters they of wealth uncounted. Every need was satisfied them. In the days of ancient Tula, there in grandeur rose his temple, reared aloft its mighty ramparts, reaching upward to the heavens.

Mazatl, the second day-sign in the Aztec calendar, represented the Mixtec deer god and goddess, who "raised a great mountain" called Place Where the Heaven Stood in the middle of the Atlantic Ocean. Their offspring were pairs of twin sons, builders of glittering palaces and shrines until they were mostly killed by a massive flood that sank the mountain to the bottom of the sea. One pair of royal deer twins survived the cataclysm, however, by sailing to the shores of Mesoamerica after the catastrophe, where they built the first kingdom. Strangely, this Mixtec memory of Atlantis found an Old World correspondence in North Africa. Jakob Ben Chaim, a sixteenth-century rabbi in Fez, Morocco, quoted a fragment from the Sibyl of Erythraea on a descendant people who "had their original dwelling in Atlantis, and are half deer" (Borges 1980, 81). Deer are sometimes regarded as symbols of regeneration for their antlers' ability to regenerate. They therefore appropriately signify the rebirth of Atlantean civilization on both sides of the ocean.

Bochica, the chief god of Colombia's Muyscas Indians, supported the sky on his shoulders from a mountaintop far out at sea. Whenever he shifted his weight, the earth quaked, recalling not only Atlas, but the creator of Atlantis, Poseidon, who also created earthquakes. The Chibcha of Colombia had a different version of the story: Chibchacun, a storm god whom Bochica punished by making him hold up the heavens, caused a flood that drowned the world. It was from Chibchacun, the Atlas figure, that the Chibcha, like the Atlanteans, traced their descent.

The Portuguese royal historian Francisco Lopez recorded his account of an oceanic capital that once sent "visitors" to the Brazilian natives:

> Manoa is on an island in a great salt lake. Its walls and roof are made of gold and [are] reflected in a gold-tiled lake. All the serving dishes for the palace are made of pure gold and silver, and even the most insignificant things are made of silver and copper. In the middle of the island stands a temple dedicated to the sun. Around the building, there are statues of gold, which represent giants. There are also trees made of gold and silver on the island, and the statue of a prince covered entirely with gold dust.

Manoa's resemblance to Plato's opulent Atlantis, with its titans and oceanic location ("on an island in a great salt lake"), is apparent.

The Ge-speaking Indians of Brazil still conduct a "sun pole" ceremony that recounts the story of Mai-Ra, king of "the land without evil." The inhabitants did not live up to his high standards, however, so he set the island on fire, then sank it under the sea. Taking a few virtuous survivors with him, Mai-Ra voyaged to the shores of Brazil, where the Indians still remember him as the Walker, or the Maker.

Until destroyed as idolatrous by Christian missionaries, a large natural rock sculpted in the form of a bearded human head wearing a conical helmet was revered by the natives as "the great Atlas."

The Antis Indians believed the earth was destroyed by an exploding volcano, which plunged into the sea, causing a worldwide deluge. The few survivors, such as the Greek Deucalion and Pyrrha, repopulated the planet by tossing stones over their shoulders; as the stones struck the ground, men and women sprang up in their places.

The Aztec legend of Tlaloc told how the god of water raised a great mountain out of the primeval sea. His Quaitleloa Festival commemorated the destruction of the world by flood: "Men had been given up to vice, on which account, it [the world] had been destroyed." Tlaloc's wife, Chalchihuitlicue, was represented as a torrent carrying away a man, a woman, and a treasure chest, which was intended to portray *otocoa*, "the loss of property." As though to emphasize the Atlantean identity of Tlaloc, the Quaitleloa Festival took place in the vicinity of Mount Tlalocan, or Place of Tlaloc, in nothing less than a ritualized recreation of the final destruction of Atlantis.

Duran, a Spanish priest who lived and worked among the native Mexicans only sixty years after the conquest, described the event that occurred every spring. On the summit was the god's temple in which his statue was surrounded by a circle of lesser deities. Numerous celebrants, including the Great Speaker, or emperor, with his nobles, peasants, and aristocrats, high-born and low, arrived in elaborately festooned boats across a sacred lake that lapped at the foot of the mountain. Solemn songs were intoned on behalf of a young woman selected for her beauty and dressed as a princess. She wore a royal blue robe, "representing," as Duran reported, "the Great Water," or Atlantic Ocean.

Taken first to the temple, she was honorably dedicated to Tlaloc, then brought back down to the shore, where the multitudes gathered, humming a dirgelike melody. The woman was escorted into a gaily decorated skiff oared by high priests. They rowed her out to a spot in the center of the holy lake called Pantitlan, where they waited until a powerful whirlpool began to form. When it reached the zenith of its power, the Daughter of Tlaloc was thrown into its vortex, weighted down with jewels, precious stones, gold necklaces, gilt bracelets, and other personal treasures. "It was said that Pantitlan swallows her so that she was never seen again," Duran wrote. The whirlpool eventually dissipated, and "in silence all returned to the city." In a striking parallel with the Old World, Lambert pointed out, "There was another [pre-Dynastic Egyptian] tradition of a gaily dressed young virgin being thrown to the river as its bride to secure a plentiful inundation."

The female sacrifice's identification with Atlantis is apparent in her blue robe (like those worn by the Atlantean royalty in Plato's description); her total and symbolic disappearance into the depths; the Atlas-like mountain she visits prior to her death; and the very name of the month in which the ceremony takes place: Atlcaualo. More resonant is the Aztec name of the Daughter of Tlaloc impersonated by the drowned virgin: Atlatonan (Frazer 1922, 181). The similarity between the Daughter of Atlas and Atlantis and Atlatonan, the Daughter of Tlaloc, the Aztec Atlas, is self-evident.

In the Codex Telleriano-Temensis, Chalchihuitlicue is called "the woman who saved herself from the deluge." A bearded European head from the Zapotec site at Oaxaca, in west-coastal Mexico, has been identified by an accompanying hieroglyph that translates as Number One, or First of the First.

The city of Utatlan was in Guatemala, as was Atitlan, encircled by the Fire Mountains. The Toltec city of Tolan was named after their ancestral homeland. Atla was a pre-Columbian coastal city, and the Parian tribesmen of Venezuela told their Spanish conquerors that their city of Atlan was founded by "white Indians" from a "drowned land." In these place names, extending all along the eastern coasts of Mexico and upper South America, is clearly revealed the powerful historical impact made on pre-Columbian America by the vanished city of Atlantis, whose survivors were the founding fathers of new civilizations in this region of the world.

The Feathered Serpent is the most universally famous figure in Mesoamerica. Yet his identity has been a mystery to conventional archaeologists and a source of almost unlimited speculation among cultural diffusionists, who have garbed him in the robes of every foreign land from Israel to Ireland. But a close examination of his story, remarkable in its essential consistency throughout the tribes and cultures of Mesoamerica, reveals all the leading details of the Red and Black Land from which he came. The Feathered Serpent was Atlantean.

15

THE GREATER ARRIVAL
FROM ATLANTIS

And after Osiris banished barbarism from Egypt, he planted the lotus of wisdom there, and then left on his long journey to civilize the rest of the world.

MANETHO, FOURTH CENTURY B.C.E. EGYPTIAN PRIEST-HISTORIAN

The Maya told of two major waves of foreign immigration that washed ashore in Mesoamerica. Separated in time by many generations, the Greater and Lesser Arrivals constituted the seminal events in their history. Both coincided with transformational happenings in the outside world and paralleled the major geologic upheavals that forced mass evacuations from Atlantis.

According to the Mayan calendar a new world age began on 4 Ahu 2 Cimhu, or August 12, 3113 B.C.E. This date conforms remarkably well to archaeological time scales for Mexico's first civilizers, the Olmecs. Originally scholars believed they appeared in 1200 B.C.E., until additional evidence for a period three hundred years earlier came to light. More recently, a date in the late fourth millennium B.C.E. has been confirmed. In the early 1980s astronaut Gordon Cooper, still employed by NASA and accompanied by a *National Geographic* photographer, recovered carbon-datable Olmec pottery shards from an offshore island in the Gulf of Mexico. Analysis at Texas A & M University established that the materials were five thousand years old. The discovery prompted Dr. Pablo Bush

Romero, head of Mexico City University's National Archaeology Department, to personally investigate the island. He and his colleagues confirmed the older date, which was thereafter officially indicated at the Jalapa Museum (State of Veracruz) specializing in Olmec culture. Interestingly, the two previously theorized time horizons (1500 and 1200 B.C.E.) for the abrupt beginnings of Mesoamerican civilization reflect, respectively, the second series of geologic upheavals and final destruction of Atlantis. Both cataclysms sparked different migrations that created the two later cultural levels of Olmec civilization.

The date of 3113 B.C.E. for the founding of the Mayan civilization is still more remarkable, for it is the same year in which dynastic civilization began in Egypt. These two formative events, separated by half a world but united in time, were not coincidental. Their commonality is demonstrated in a remarkable comparison of artifacts. Hierakonopolis's famous Narmer Palette, named after the first pharaoh of the First Dynasty, and an illustration of the first Aztec monarch, Montezuma I, in Mexico's Codex Mendoza, show identical depictions of men grabbing the hair of a defeated enemy with one hand while raising a war club in the other. In both illustrations a male figure appearing to the left of the scene in the guise of a bird, apparently emblematic of royalty, attacks another enemy. This extraordinary parallel could not possibly have been the result of chance creation. The specific, highly individualized details of both images reflect a common inspiration reproduced nowhere else in the ancient world.

Combined with the identical foundation dates for the Valley of Mexico and Nile Valley civilizations, plus the representation of both cultures' first monarchs in both artifacts, a fundamental relationship between Mesoamerica and pharaonic Egypt is beyond question. There are no Egyptian traditions suggesting direct overseas contacts in Mexico, however, much less indications of Aztec or Mayan connections with Egypt. Yet both Mesoamerica and ancient Egypt shared remarkably similar accounts of powerful culture bearers who arrived to institute civilization in their own respective lands from across the Atlantic Ocean. To the Egyptians their founding fathers came from the west; to the Maya, they arrived from the east. Both cultures told essentially the same story because they were recipients of a common Atlantean heritage.

The imported features of dynastic Egypt are fundamentally the same details introduced into Mesoamerica. Both civilizations appeared full-blown in history, without the long-term, painstaking progression of development observed in other complex organized societies. If the Egyptians had planted their culture in Mesoamerica, the two civilizations would appear virtually identical, the one having been little more than a colonial extension of the other, but this is certainly not the case among any of the uniquely identifiable societies of Mesoamerica. For example, that both the Maya and Egyptians, isolated from each other by a vast ocean, used hieroglyphs suggests that both peoples received them from the same source. Neither written language translates the other because both systems evolved separately over many centuries.

Differences separating Egyptian from Mesoamerican civilizations stem from the particular reaction of immigrating Atlantean culture bearers to the local environments they found in two different lands. There were enough similarities, however, to show they sprouted from the same Atlantean seed. In other words, Mesoamerica and dynastic Egypt were local inflections of the Atlantean theme common to both. The mythic and historical heritages of these societies do not speak of Egyptian but rather Atlantean origins. Indeed, civilizing influences reached Mexico at the same time they appeared in the Nile Delta. The Maya foundation date of August 12, 3113 B.C.E., must have been the day that Atlantean refugees landed at Veracruz. Sailing in their reed boats, they fled the first of the serious geologic upheavals that troubled but did not yet destroy their oceanic homeland.

The Narmer Palette/Codex Mendoza images and shared foundation date in the late fourth millennium B.C.E. are not the only similarities between the two cultures. Fundamental connections between Mexico and Egypt through Atlantis are apparent in abundant cross-cultural illustrations. For example, Mesoamerican pyramids bear strong resemblances to Sumerian ziggurats and especially early Egyptian step pyramids. The most famous step pyramid in the New World is Yucatán's Pyramid of Kukulcan, the Feathered Serpent (fig. 15.1). After dawn on the vernal equinox the lower portion of the west face of both this Mayan structure and Egypt's Great Pyramid are in shadow. As the day progresses, the west face of each become increasingly illuminated as the rays of the sun move from the north, crossing the zenith at noon. This

Fig. 15.1. The ziggurat-like Pyramid of the Feathered Serpent is a memorial to Kukulcan, the Maya's founding father, who arrived on the shores of the Yucatán from his drowned capital across the sea.

phenomenon is unique and occurs only on the first day of spring. In view of the Great Pyramid's discernibly Atlantean influences, the features it shares with Mesoamerica's foremost Atlantean structure, including sculpted Atlas-like figures at the summit supporting the four cardinal directions, it is difficult to ignore the apparent cultural link connecting them through Atlantis.

Architects of Sumerian, Egyptian, and Mayan sacred structures preferred working with blue tiles and mosaics. The ziggurat of Ur (see fig. 15.2), dedicated to the sky god An, was originally faced with glistening blue tiles; the Aztecs referred to the sky as "that blue stone pyramid." The Third Dynasty Pharaoh Zoser built his Saqqara pyramid (fig. 15.3) about 2650 B.C.E., some three thousand years before the Mayan pyramid at Palenque was constructed, yet the two are strikingly similar in numerous details. Beyond their obvious outward resemblance as step pyramids, both contain subterranean chambers with descending corridors.

The Palenque pyramid contained the body of a Mayan monarch known as Pacal. The funeral practices and beliefs that pertained to him

Fig. 15.2. A model reconstruction of Sumer's ziggurat at Ur, built in imitation of the sacred mountain associated with the flood survivor Utnashpitim

were remarkably similar to those known in the Old World. Noted researcher R. A. Jairazbhoy showed that the eight degrees the king's soul was expected to pass on its way through the Underworld were virtually identical in Mesoamerican and Egyptian belief systems. In the latter tradition the third degree was overseen by a crocodile, *Sebek* (see fig. 15.4 on page 204), while *cipak* is Nahuatl for the Aztecs' sacred alligator boat. (See fig. 15.4.) The human soul was conceived identically in Egyptian and Mesoamerican thought. Temple art across the Nile Valley portrayed the ba as a human-headed bird often soaring through a hole in a tomb. A Mayan temple relief at Izapa similarly depicted a man-headed bird flying out of a sepulchral cave.

Wall paintings at Palenque are strikingly reminiscent of the Egyptian technique. Mayan figures, like their Egyptian counterparts, are arrayed in rows, while the feet and heads of most of the nobles are portrayed in flat profile. In funeral refinement scarcely different from a pharaoh's,

15.3. With no small resemblance to Sumer's ziggurat or the Yucatán's pyramid, Zoser's Pyramid towers over the sands of Egypt. Dynastic Egyptians claimed the technology to raise such a colossal structure arrived with culture bearers from a kingdom that was sinking in the western ocean.

Pacal's sarcophagus and earrings were decorated with hieroglyphs, and he wore a beaded necklace whose design, with precious stones cut in the forms of flowers and fruits, could nearly have passed for Nile workmanship. But Pacal's Egyptian parallels do not stop there. Mirroring the pharaohs, he was fitted with a death mask. The bottom end of his sarcophagus, like Pharaoh Zoser's, was made so that the entire enclosure could be stood upright on a base. Pacal also wore a false chin-beard, as did all the pharaohs, even Queen Hatshepsut.

American surveyor Hugh Harleston Jr. discovered in 1974 that Palenque's Temple of the Inscriptions did not fit standard units of 1.059 meters in the Maya's *hunab*. He did find, however, that the structure was laid out perfectly in Egyptian "royal cubits" (Corliss 2001, 162). It contained a large room 23 feet high with a floor space of 13 by 29 feet. "This vault was roofed by huge stone beams somewhat reminiscent of the King's Chamber in the Great Pyramid," according to Corliss (161).

Fig. 15.4. The crocodile-headed god, Sebek, associated with the power of the Nile River, presents Prince Amenhotep III. (Luxor Museum, Egypt)

Alberto Ruz Lhuillier, the Mexican archaeologist who discovered Pacal's resting place, admitted that "the sumptuous chamber brings us close to the Egyptian pyramids: evidently there was a similarity in the architectural function of the pyramid and in the spiritual attitude of the great leader-priest"(Corliss 2001, 162).

Corliss went on to conclude:

Within the Temple of Inscriptions, the style of architecture and the graphic artifacts are so similar to those in some of the Egyptian pyramids that ancient cultural diffusion is suggested. There are the same stones, the blocked passages, the ornateness of the vault. There is even a ventilation shaft analogous to those in the Great Pyramid. Stranger still was a long, sinuous clay tube that led out of the sarcophagus, up the stairway to a vertical stone slab that blocked the passageway. Was this tube the escape pathway for the

Fig. 15.5. The human figure with an alligator is Cipak, the Aztec personification of a sacred boat and a mythic carryover from Mayan precursors. Similar in name, appearance, and function, the Egyptian Sebek and Aztec Cipak were derived from a common source. (Bonampak Murals, Chiapas, Mexico)

soul of the buried king? Who knows, but how like a concept out of ancient Egypt! (160–62).

Around Pacal's elaborately carved stone sarcophagus were placed jade statuettes of Kinich-Ahau (Lord of the Eye of the Sun), no different than the Egyptian *ushabti* (answerers), small statues made of faience that were included in royal burials. Significantly, the Egyptian Horus was also known as Lord of the Eye of the Sun and was revered as the deified embodiment of kingship.

Jade was the most important ceremonial stone in Mesoamerica because its color symbolized the Atlantic waters across which the Feathered Serpent and his followers traveled to arrive in Mesoamerica. In the Aztec version of the Flood, one among his company was the Princess Chalchuitl, with whom jade was personally identified. Pacal's jade statuettes were, in fact, known as *chalchuitls*.

Chalchiuhtlicue was an Aztec goddess who changed victims of the Great Flood into fish. The same transformation appears in the Deluge myths of the Babylonians and the American Lakota Sioux. She was honored during an annual ceremony in which priests collected reeds, dried them out, then placed them inside her shrine. The reeds symbolized both wisdom (as writing utensils) and the Place of Reeds, Aztlan, her overseas homeland. Temple art represented Chalchiuhtlicue seated on a throne around which men and women were shown drowning in huge whirlpools. Her name, Our Lady of the Jade Skirt, refers to the feminine Atlantis (Daughter of Atlas) in the midst of the sea. Jade was a colorful metaphor for the blue-green Atlantic Ocean. Her myth is a self-evident recollection of the Atlantean catastrophe.

The Feathered Serpent's vassals were the Tlanquacemilhitime, named after the mountain on which he addressed them. To commemorate his title, Heart of the Sea, they worked in jade stones called *chalchiuites*. Millennia earlier the Olmec were skillful jade craftsmen. Jade was the "heart" of the Maya's Tree of Life, the Imix Tree, a symbol of the Flood, much as lapis lazuli was the "fruit" of the Tree of Life sought by the Sumerian hero Gilgamesh after his encounter with Utnashpitim, the Deluge survivor. The Maya's Atlantean founding father, Itzamna, Lord of Heaven, possessed the Imix Tree, which was depicted in temple art as growing from a vase overflowing with water. In Egyptian symbolism, a water-filled vase represented the primeval sea from which the first gods and humans came to the Nile Delta.

Another ancient Egyptian ceremonial practice known in Mesoamerica was the ritual shooting of arrows in the four cardinal directions. It was undertaken by each pharaoh as part of his kingship initiation and simultaneous assumption of divinity after having reigned for thirty years. Thereafter he celebrated it every three years. Interestingly, this Sed Festival ritual seems to have been described in an Aztec Nahuatl poem, which tells of a mortal archer who assumes godhood in identical fashion.

Parallels between Egypt and Mesoamerica are not only confined to comparative ceremonial practices or massive architecture, but also find correspondences in humbler artifacts. Mexico's Jalapa Museum displays a small sculpted Olmec figure in a squatting position with two twisted ropes emerging from its mouth. The significance of this statuette is unknown, but Pharaoh Ramses IV's *Book of Gates* describes a double-twisted rope coming out of Akhen's mouth. Akhen was a guardian of the Underworld through which the supreme sun god, Ra (or Re), passed in his solar boat. Another Olmec figurine with solar significance represents a seated baby with its thumb in its mouth, symbolic of sunrise, "the beautiful child." Egyptian temple art similarly portrayed the dawning sun god as "Herupkhart, Infant Horus, the babe with the finger in his mouth" (*Book of the Dead,* chapter 171).

Smoking Mirror was the name of Tezcatlipoca, a Toltec-Aztec god, whose *nagual,* or animal disguise, was the jaguar. Its spotted skin represented the starry heaven. Also known as Hurakan (from which our *hurricane* is derived), he ruled over the Ocelotonatiuh, or Jaguar Sun, the first of four "worlds" (ages or epochs) destroyed before the present one. In his mirror Tezcatlipoca saw everything—past, present, and future. The Atlantean features of this deity are clear from his sovereignty over a world cataclysm to his identification with the heavenly bodies, signifying his astrological character, as emphasized by his prophetic mirror. Tezcatlipoca's Old World correspondent may be seen at Turin's Egyptian Museum, which houses a statue of the astrologer Anen wearing a cheetah skin. Its spots have been reworked into five-pointed stars. The hide is fastened by a gold mask representing a cheetah's face. Lindsay reproduces the drawing of a Dionysiac officiant wrapped in a lion skin spotted with stars as she appeals for an omen from Dionysus (Lindsay 1969, 129).

An additional celestial parallel appears in a large ceremonial disc (approximately 6 feet in diameter) from the Aztec capital of Tenochtitlán. It carries the relief sculpture of Coyolxauqui, a lunar goddess, appropriately executed in pale white stone. Her stiff arms and legs are bent at right angles to her straight torso along the rim of the disc, forming her dismembered body into a right-facing hooked cross. From the Far East, India, the Caucasus, and the Aegean, to the European continent and the British Isles, deeply prehistoric Indo-European tradition identified the moon as a goddess symbolized by the sauvastika, the inverse of the solar swastika. The identification is exemplified by the tiny sauvastikas appearing on the gown of Artemis, the Greek moon goddess. Her twin brother, the sun god Apollo, wore the swastika. That Coyolxauqui is the

New World counterpart of Artemis is made abundantly clear by her visual association with the same emblem shared by these lunar deities, the sauvastika.

Material comparisons between Mesoamerica and the Old World are underscored by shared ritual correspondences occurring on both sides of the Atlantic Ocean. Pharaoh Ramses III's libation ceremony in which two streams of water cross over each other is similarly featured in the Mexican Codex. At Medinet Habu, his victory temple complex in West Thebes, he is shown pitching incense pebbles in preparation for prayer. The same scene is repeated in the Codex Selden, even to the inclusion of the spoon-shaped censer. He mourned for the death of his son, who had gone to join "the excellent souls of Manu." This was a name or title for the Primal Mound of Atum that stood as an island in the western ocean, where gods and men once lived in harmony. Chapter 15 in the Egyptian *Book of the Dead* says of the sun, "You sink into the horizon of Manu." As Budge wrote, "Manu is a synonym of west" (Budge 1907, 135). Similarly, the Maya sometimes referred to their homeland as Mani, but it lay across the Sunrise Sea in the east.

Another striking parallel involving incense appears on an Olmec stone tablet at Mexico City's National Museum of Anthropology. It shows a man paying homage to a great serpent with a small pouch of powdered copal, a resinous, fragrant substance made from tree sap. In a Sumerian cylinder seal (circa 2350 B.C.E.) at the University of Chicago's Oriental Institute, a male figure officiates before a serpent king carrying a container of incense identical in form to the Olmec pouch.

The Maya's Itzamna, the first civilizer to set foot on the shores of the Yucatán, was a man-god who led the Greater Arrival, afterward founding the capital of Mayapán. His name means "Iguana House," and the iguana was one of the living symbols associated with the Feathered Serpent. Itzamna resembles the Egyptian *perhoe* for "pharaoh," which is translated as "Great House." Like the pharaohs, Itzamna wore a false chin-beard. An additional pharaonic detail is the Mayan word for priest, *ahkin,* or "he of the sun," which seems to reflect the Egyptian ankh, or cross of life, symbol of immortality. In fact, Gunnar Thompson illustrates a pre-Columbian vase prominently decorated with an ankh that was found in 1895 and is currently owned by Mexico City's Anthropological Museum (Thompson 1994, 82).

The life force symbolized by the ankh was said to have first manifested itself when a bird arose from the primeval sea. The creature's call brought forth existence on earth, personified in the Great Cackler, the Egyptian god Kenkenwer. A large Olmec water basin formed to resemble a duck portrays a seascape from which arises a bird, its mouth open as though calling. This very early Mesoamerican artifact was clearly meant to convey the same creation story enshrined in Egyptian belief.

The very name Guatemala appears to be an Indian version of the Egyptian Watemra, or "Way of Ra's Rest," seemingly corresponding to Guatemala's western location. Campeche Bay likewise transposes into Egyptian as *khampetche,* a curving body of water, which certainly describes Campeche Bay. A particularly revealing comparison is to be found between Nahuatl, the language of the Aztecs, and Guanche, spoken by the ancient inhabitants of the Canary Islands, which lie directly opposite Mexico on the other side of the Atlantic Ocean. Among both peoples the word for water was *atl,* the first three letters of Atlantis. It would appear that the lost civilization bequeathed this seminal word to both cultures, which are additionally rich in architecture, historical accounts, rituals, and mythic images describing the Atlantean experience.

Further, like nobility in Egypt and the Canary Islands, the Aztecs practiced head elongation, as did the Mayan elite, who were quoted in Spanish chronicles as saying the custom "was given to our ancestors by the gods." As shown in the Codexes Borgia and Borbonicus, the Maya also venerated an Anubis-like dog figure, which, like the Guanche's sacred dogs, conveyed human souls to the Underworld.

But perhaps the deity who most revealed similarities among cultures of the Old World and New World was Maat. She was central to Egyptian spirituality as the essence of the universal order. Indeed, her very name was synonymous with a profound principle of well-regulated, purposeful existence and embodied cosmic harmony. As the supreme moral power, she held sway over all the gods, even Ra himself. She was the personification of the physical and metaphysical laws governing all creation. After the forty-two judges heard the Negative Confession, a renunciation of evil recited by the spirit of the deceased, she weighed her feather in the balance against his or her heart. The feather was her emblem. Alone and poised upright, it stood for correctness, truth, harmony, balance between the opposing forces of cosmic creativity and stability. It signified equipoise, the sacred still point. In a wall painting from the tomb of Huy the viceroy of Napata (Nubia) presents the feathered Maat scepter to his pharaoh, the young Tutankhamun. Variations of her name are Maet, Maht—and Maya.

The American Maya called themselves after the city of Mayapán. Did the city and its people receive their names from the Atlantean goddess? They did indeed understand the same principle of Maat, although they referred to it instead as Chu-el, a word for the underside of natural phenomena, which the Maya believed were organized into harmonious action by a universally governing intelligence. Proof of its existence was found in the observable balance between nature, with the regular rotation of the seasons and all their attendant plant, animal, and metrological interactivity, and the predictable rotation of the heavens above. Everything the Maya saw evidenced the synchronized cooperation of function and motion among all living and nonliving matter. The purpose of civilization was to put humankind in accord with Chu-el (Maat).

Atlanto-Egyptian themes are evident in Mesoamerican architecture as well. Many stone figures with European features can be found in supporting or "upholding" positions, mostly in the form of caryatids, at Tula, a Mexican city named after the Toltec Red and Black Land. On the sides of the pyramid at Tenayuca two large coiled snakes face the setting sun on days of the summer solstice. They recall the Egyptian Apep, a monstrous serpent of the night that battled the sun god, Ra, during his long Underworld journey through the darkness of death to the dawn of a new life. The Tenayuca pyramid and Apep share the same solar concept. Like Egypt's Great Pyramid, with its architectural representation of the days in a solar year, the temple at El Tajin features 365 niches. Chichén Itzá's El Castillo features 365 steps signifying the number of days in a calendar year.

The Calixtlahuaca Temple of Tlaloc (the Aztec Atlas) was built of red and black volcanic stone, the same materials Plato's Atlanteans used to construct their public buildings. The temple also recalls the Toltec description of Atlantis so evocatively described as "the red and black land" because of its abundant volcanic rock. Like the Egyptian pyramids, astronomical alignments were incorporated into Olmec, Mayan, and Aztec pyramids, which were identically oriented to the four cardinal directions. In both Egyptian and Mesoamerican civilizations temple murals were laid out in a 19-square grid system, a narrow comparison that opponents of cultural diffusion are unable to explain away.

Comparing the step pyramids of Mexico's Cholula with the Egyptian Saqqara, Mulhall concluded: "Alike in orientation, in structure, and even in their internal galleries and chambers, these mysterious monuments of the east and west stand as witnesses to some common source whence their builders drew their plan" (Mulhall 1911, 96). And like the earliest tombs of the Nile Valley, Aztec pyramids contained a small ceremonial mound, usually a little hill of conically formed mud covered by a stone cast, symbolizing the Primal Mound that arose from the waters of creation during the First Time.

The Mesoamerican ceremonial center at Tzuntzuntzan comprised five circular pyramids, each with ten layers separated by six banks, highly suggestive of the sunken capital. Plato said that the sacred numerals 5 and 6 were incorporated in Atlantean astronomy, ritual architecture, and city planning. Mexico's Palace of Tetitla had fifty-six rooms, and the principal pyramid at Tula, with its colossal Atlantean statues, is built of five complete levels, as is the Great Vestibule. El Tajin features six altars along the length of its ceremonial stairway, and six receding platforms. While the sacred numerals or their multiples are not part of every Mesoamerican structure, their repetition at many if not most of the memorializing temples and pyramids is sufficient to establish their Atlantean implications.

Among the Mayan high priests, 5 was honored as Cajalom, Father of Life, the same meaning it held in Pythagorean mysticism. Menninger writes, "The ancient Mexicans possessed a number sequence clearly based on ranks of twenty along with—and this was its amazing feature—a sequence of units ordered on the number Five" (Menninger 1949, 62). The Aztec Calendar Stone at Mexico City's National Museum of Anthropology is a circle of pentagrams grouped in an arc of ten, while the lotus petals composing the second ring are likewise grouped in tens. Quetzalcoatl appeared during the Fifth Sun, or fifth epoch; his alter ego, Tezcatlipoca, celebrated his festival on the fifth month of the sun. The young man selected as Quetzalcoatl's impersonator assumed

Quetzalcoatl's divinity on the fifth day before the feast of the Feathered Serpent. Clearly, the number 5 assumed spiritual significance for both pre-Columbian Americans and ancient Atlanteans.

The Maya commemorated a Greater Arrival, the first of two massive waves of foreign immigration from across the Sunrise Sea following a world-class cataclysm. The newcomers transformed Middle America from a backward wilderness into a flourishing civilization that would cyclically wax, wane, and revive itself for the next forty-five centuries. The identity of those culture bearers is unmistakably revealed in the art, myths, histories, and the very architecture of every Mesoamerican culture, from Olmec to Aztec. In pre-Columbian America, the geologically unstable kingdom from which they came was known by many names—Aztlan, the Red and Black Land, Mani, Valum, Old Tula, Tollan, Tlapallan. But they all belonged to an oceanic capital more famously remembered as Atlantis.

16

THE LESSER ARRIVAL
OF SURVIVORS

*Tollan's towers are burned. Quetzalcoatl and his family
are arrived here after the death of his homeland.*

FROM THE TOLTEC *SONG OF THE FEATHERED SERPENT*

O f all the intriguing comparisons between Mesoamerica and ancient Egypt, a common commemorative day they shared seems to
have memorialized the final destruction of Atlantis. The repercussions of
that midocean event sent tens of thousands of survivors streaming
toward the Valley of Mexico in the east and the Nile Valley in the west.
Peoples in both areas of the world set down what had happened in script
and stone. Every November 2 the Aztecs sprinkled flowers on the graves
of loved ones in honor of Resurrection Day, the same rite conducted on
the same date known in Roman times as the Ausares Hilaria, a resurrection day celebrated by the cult followers of Osiris, the hero who over-
came death. Not coincidentally, research into comparative traditions
around the world indicates that Resurrection Day and the Ausares
Hilaria fell at the same time Atlantis suffered its ultimate cataclysm, in
the first days of November 1198 B.C.E. (Joseph 2002, 156).

But the single most persuasive physical artifact of Mayan civilization on behalf of Atlanteans in Mesoamerica once decorated a city
building lost in the jungles of Guatemala. The sculpted image depicted
a ceremoniously dressed man (obviously intended to portray a royal

personage) rowing his ornamented boat away from an erupting volcanic island. In the background between the man and a stone temple collapsing into the sea, a male figure with closed eyes and one hand raised appeared to be drowning, his long, light-colored hair floating on the water. Skeptics are hard-pressed to interpret this scene as anything other than the death and escape of leaders from the destruction of Atlantis.

The stone relief was originally part of a very long frieze extending perhaps as much as several hundred feet in a broad band entirely around the upper exterior of the so-called Central Acropolis. This structure lies at the center of the Maya's greatest ceremonial city, the jungle metropolis of Tikal in Guatemala. The frieze itself was a series of sculpted illustrations obviously representing highlights in the history of the Maya from their beginnings to the abandonment of Tikal sometime in the late tenth century C.E. The first panel, beginning in the east (appropriately enough), featured the Atlantis scene.

Tikal was first professionally explored and documented by the early-twentieth-century photographer Teobert Maler. A conventional scholar with no patience for tales of sunken civilizations, he was so struck by his discovery of the frieze that he completely abandoned his academic skepticism and became convinced that the panel did indeed portray the last moments of Atlantis. Its appearance in Tikal, prominently positioned by the Maya, could mean only that members of their aristocracy were survivors of the catastrophe. Henceforward, Maler regarded the Mayan and, in fact, all Mesoamerican civilization as the product of interactions between native peoples and Atlantean culture bearers.

After making accurate and detailed drawings and photographs of the frieze, Maler had it removed from the Acropolis and shipped to Austria. Its display at the Voelkerkunde Museum caused a sensation and was among its greatest treasures until 1945. In that fateful year the Tikal stonework disappeared when Soviet troops looted Vienna. At least Maler's copies, including those made of the Atlantean scene, are preserved at the University of Pennsylvania.

The Tikal frieze graphically depicted not merely a migration, as described in earlier Mayan traditions of the Greater Arrival, but the final destruction of Atlantis in 1198 B.C.E., which forced the appearance of a second and final major wave of newcomers who formed the Lesser Arrival. The coming of these culture-bearing survivors in the early twelfth century B.C.E. is validated by an important event in Mexican prehistory. So sudden and large-scale was the upsurge in population and accelerated development that scholars originally believed Mesoamerican civilization actually began at this time. The final Atlantean catastrophe, the Maya's Lesser Arrival, and current archaeological evidence combine to confirm that all three elements were part of a crucial social impact made on Mesoamerica by foreigners landing on the shores of the Yucatán after escaping a natural catastrophe in the Atlantic Ocean around 1200 B.C.E. To the Maya's chronological way of thinking, *lesser* did not mean this arrival was any less important in terms of numbers or cultural significance, but referred instead to the lesser amount of time that had passed, relative to the earlier Greater Arrival. To the Maya, *lesser* meant "more recent."

The members of this Lesser Arrival were abundantly described throughout Mesoamerican art and literature as a people physically distinct from the native population. Wall paintings at Cacaxtla in Mexico City show their leader, the Feathered Serpent, with facial features that that are not Amerindian. He is portrayed emerging from a conch shell, symbolic of his oceanic origins. An Olmec stone relief at La Venta shows the head of a man with flowing beard and a typically European countenance. Bearded faces are in evidence on a funeral urn at Copán, Chichén Itzá's Temple of Kukulcan, throughout Tepatlaxco in Veracruz, on numerous objects at the important Olmec site of Monte Albán, and across the temple walls of Tula. There are many more examples at other ceremonial centers in Mexico and Central America.

The native Indians of the region were and are a dark-skinned, beardless, smallish people with the epicanthic fold (eyes upturned at the corners) and zygomatic arches (high cheekbones) of their Mongolian ancestors, who crossed over the frozen Bering Straits from Asia thirty thousand years ago. In contrast, most skeletal remains of individuals belonging to the Pilli, the Mayan ruling class, show that they were markedly taller than the masses of laboring peasants, known as the Mayeques. During the late sixteenth century Mexican traveler Gaspar Antonio Chimosa, in his *Historical Recollections,* reported that "the natives say that those who built the said edifices [at Itzmal] were men of greater stature than those of this time." When Hernán Cortés met Montezuma II face to face, he remarked on the Aztec emperor's beard, relatively fair complexion, and tall stature, none of which were reflected in the physical appearance of his subjects.

Andres de Avendane y Loyola, a Spanish trader in the early seventeenth century, described the pitifully few surviving Itzas—another Mayan ruling elite who had been neither exterminated nor assimilated by the European conquerors—as "well-featured and, like mestizos, nearly all of a light complexion and of very perfect stature and natural gifts." A similar description was provided by Juan de Villagntierre, who personally participated in the subjugation of Mexico during the mid-1500s. Even today isolated Indian groups in the southeastern Yucatán and northern Belize (former British Honduras), where many of the aristocratic Pilli (see fig. 16.1) or Itzas took refuge after the Conquest, show a frequency of lighter skin color that is remarkable given that evidence of their intermarriage with modern Europeans is lacking. Such racial anomalies must be a genetic remnant carried over from the old ruling-class strain.

Fig. 16.1. This Mayan sculpture, circa 400 A.D., found during an excavation of the ceremonial center of Labna, is a stone portrait of a well-fed aristocrat belonging to the Pilli, or upper class, which was said to have been directly descended from fair, light-haired followers of Kukulcan. The European facial features of this man sharply contrast with those of native Mexicans. (St. Louis Art Museum)

The Maya city of Mutul was founded by Zacmutul, whose name means, literally, "White Man." A fresco from Chichén Itzá's Temple of the Warriors depicts nobles with light yellow faces, while supplicating prisoners are shown as dark brown. A vase from Quirigua, at the St. Louis Art Museum, features the bust of a man with a red beard, blue eyes, creamy complexion, and a bull neck. These examples are by no means unique. There are hundreds more from Olmec beginnings to the Aztecs. Harvard's Ernest Hooten, who published his in-depth examination of Canary Islands skeletal remains, pointed out the "Armenioid racial type" (Hooten 1904, 304) recurrent among the Mayan elite. Seconding Hooten's observation was anthropologist M. Wells Jakeman, who described the Itzá's orthognathic faces and narrow, high-bridged noses as typically Armenioid-Caucasian. Their receding foreheads, full, curved lips, and firm chins deepened this impression, he wrote in his important *The Origin and History of the Mayas* (1957).

The Maya's physical anthropology was underscored by the Mayan language itself, which alone of the more than seven hundred native languages of Mesoamerica shows marked similarities to Indo-European speech in its shared use of monosyllables and homophones (words that are pronounced the same but have different meanings, such as *two* and *too*). More to the point, Mayan was agglutinative in that it employed prefixes and suffixes for declension (the inflection of nouns), as opposed to inflectional languages, where changes are internal. Even arch-skeptics of Atlantis, such as the well-known author L. Sprague de Camp, admit that Mayan resembles the Ural-Altaic or Finno-Urgic languages spoken in western Turkey.

These linguistic parallels with Caucasian speech simultaneously support the Maya elite's Caucasoid identity and suggest that the Atlantean tongue must have been similarly Armenian-like (Ural-Altaic). It was therefore related, perhaps closely, to the Etruscan and Trojan languages, both Finno-Urgic. Indeed, Etruria, according to Plato, belonged to the Atlantean empire, and Troy was a blood-related, commercially important ally of Atlantis. Over the course of time, Mayan resemblances to its Caucasian roots broke down considerably in the details so that surviving cognates (words that show a parent relationship between two or more languages) are less frequent, but the few that may still be found are revealing. For example, the Mayan word for "master builder" or "skilled craftsman" is *menyah,* and *menyan* is a Trojan term meaning "race of builders or measurers," "city surveyors" (Nuttall 1900, 532, 533). Other examples appear among some important Mesoamerican place names, as demonstrated by a comparison of Armenian cities known as late as classical times and Mayan ceremonial centers:

ARMENIAN CITIES	MAYAN CEREMONIAL CENTERS
Colima	Cholima
Colua	Cholula
Zalissa	Xalisco
Zuivan	Zuivana

This intriguing parallel was first brought to light by the nineteenth-century father of Atlantology, Ignatius Donnelly, who found the Armenian cities listed in Ptolemy's *Geography of Asia Minor.* Of course, the most cogent, inescapable comparison can be seen in the Aztec Aztlan and Plato's Atlantis.

Mesoamerican parallels with the sunken civilization go far beyond cognates, however. That zodiacs were developed in both Mesoamerica and preclassical Europe is remarkable enough, but that these two zodiacs should be so alike as to feature the same astrological signs invalidates the possibility of a mere cultural coincidence.

A manifestation of the Feathered Serpent was Ehecatl, represented in Aztec sacred art (the Vienna Codex) as a bent figure supporting the heavens, precisely like Atlas, the Atlantean founder of astrology. Forman writes of Ehecatl, "He was an astrological deity" (Forman 1968, 46), so his identification with Atlas in both form and function is clear. Ehecatl, the Atlas-like Egyptian Shu, and the Sumerian Enlil each bore the title God of the Wind.

Ehecatl's temples represented the most recognizably Atlantean structures in Mesoamerica, as indeed they should, given his identification with Atlas. All are circular and consist of five or six layers of concentric platforms stacked to make a step pyramid. The numerals incorporated in these temples were the same sacred numbers that, according to Plato, the Atlanteans incorporated into architecture and city planning.

Monuments to Ehecatl reflect as nowhere else in the world (except among some of the megalithic ruins of Britain and the Canary Islands) the building style and layout of Atlantis. The best-preserved examples are found at Tula (El Corral), Calixtlahuaca, Zempoala, and Cuicuilco, as well as in a subterranean concentric pyramid excavated during construction of the Mexico City subway, where it is still on public display.

Ehecatl's chief temple, which exhibited numerous Atlantean features, was demolished to make way for a Catholic cathedral in the old Aztec capital. But Spanish chroniclers made a detailed description of it before the new religion transformed Tenochtitlán into the Mexican capital. Similarities extended beyond the repetition of the sacred numerals throughout its construction, however; Ehecatl's 50-foot-high pyramid was painted red, white, and black, the building colors that Plato tells us were favored by the architects of Atlantis. Moreover, the circular structure was positioned at the precise midpoint—the very hub, in fact—of the central ceremonial complex of Tenochtitlán. This great city was itself deliberately patterned after the Atlantean original. Built as an island in the middle of an artificial lake, its outline was configured to resemble a scorpion, the zodiacal sign that corresponds to Atlas (Gleadow 1961, 99). The Aztec constellation was identical to the Old World Scorpio (Forman 1968, 201). As McNice observed, "It is surprising to find a scorpion, usually encountered in hot, dry countries, established as a watery sign" (McNice 1955, 95).

The single Mesoamerican structure that most closely follows Plato's description of Atlantean sacred architecture is found at Cuicuilco, on the southern outskirts of Mexico City. Circular in design, it is made up of five rings or levels and is surrounded by an encircling moat once filled with water to represent the sea. Hunter writes, "Pre-classic pottery from the Guerrreo region of western Mexico depicts circular towers or pyramids having many platforms that we can assume typify temples or shrines (1978, 18)."

A fluted, circular pyramid at La Venta, on the Gulf coastal plain, was being used by the Olmecs in the Middle Classic period (1500 to 600 B.C.E.). Campbell explains that Cuicuilco, perhaps the oldest pyramid in Mexico, was actually modeled after a volcanic island, situated as it was in the center of a ceremonial lake (Campbell 1961, 104). Atlantean symbolism here is apparent.

Although construction at Cuicuilco was still going on as late as 400 B.C.E., its origins (in the form of a mud-brick structure beneath) date from the Middle Preclassic period—in other words, from the same epoch (circa 1200 B.C.E.) in which Atlantis was destroyed. Its self-evidently Atlantean architectural design, incorporation of Plato's sacred numerals, time of construction, and identification with Ehecatl, the Aztec Atlas, clearly define Cuicuilco as the product of Atlantean builders in Mesoamerica following the obliteration of their faraway homeland. Ironically, Cuicuilco was itself overwhelmed by a similar fate in the third century B.C.E., when a nearby volcanic eruption of major proportions buried the pyramid under 25 feet of lava.

During excavations more than two thousand years later diggers recovered the small stone portrait of a man with decidedly European facial features, sporting conical headgear such as the Trojans wore and wearing a pointed beard. A similar head, fashioned in jade, with fuller, curly facial hair (now at Chicago's Field Museum of Natural History) was recovered from Tenochtitlán near the former location of Ehecatl's great tricolor pyramid. Its discovery here, decidedly foreign cast of features, and execution in jade argue strongly on behalf of its identity as a genuine Atlantean artifact. It is at least a post-Deluge piece representing a true-life Atlantean figure.

Hardly less significant or suggestive than Cuicuilco was the practice of Aztec city planners to build their most important ceremonial centers in the middle of artificial lakes, like their capital, Tenochtitlán. In his *Historia verdadera de la Conquista* Bernal Diaz, an eyewitness to the Spanish Conquest, described "towns and villages on the surface of the water. Everywhere, great towers, temples and pyramids rose out of the water."

Mexico's major pyramids were believed to stand over the primeval abyss of waters from which the gods and first humans arose. When Cortés attacked the pyramid at Cholula, the Aztec priests tore out openings in its sides, convinced that by doing so a devastating flood would be unloosed to drown the Spaniards.

Herodotus reports in his *Histories* that Khufu's Great Pyramid on the Giza Plateau was built over a subterranean lake with an artificial mound in the center, commemorating the island of Atum, homeland of gods and humans before the Flood. Every Egyptian temple had its own sacred lake, usually in a horseshoe shape modeled after the antediluvian waters, where priests bathed themselves at dawn before undertaking their ritual activities. So too the Aztec priests of Tlaloc took ceremonial ablutions at his palace in Tetitla. The ziggurat of Ur was also said to have capped the Abzu, the primeval waste of waters.

As though these examples were not obvious enough, their Atlantean implications are made even clearer by Lucian in his *De Dea Syria*. He describes a shrine to the native version of Juno, the queen of heaven, second in power only to her husband, Jove. Lucian writes that her sacred structure at Hierapolis was built by none other than Deucalion, the Deluge hero, culture bearer, and survivor from Atlantis in Greek tradition. The shrine was raised over a chasm into which the waters of the Great Flood were said to have drained. Hierapolis, the Holy City—today's Manbi Membij—lies about 50 miles northeast of Aleppo in Syria and was already a religious center in the early fourth millennium B.C.E., when the first Atlanteans were making their way into the eastern Mediterranean.

The Juno Lucian mentions was in his time worshipped as Atargatis, who echoed Atlantean origins, especially in her earlier known name, Atar. According to Imel, "Out of respect for her, her worshippers abstained from eating fish," because she came from across the sea. In her shrine Atargatis was represented as a mermaid who was the daughter of a drowned woman, a reference perhaps to sunken Atlantis.

Thor Heyerdahl wrote in his *Ra Expeditions* that features of Hittite civilization were particularly apparent among Olmec and Mayan cultures. He noted as a significant point of comparison the deep, oval depressions for eyes in life-sized statuary from both parts of the world. The Hittites and Olmecs preferred to work in stone relief, often portraying important personages in close, face-to-face conversations, an approach found nowhere else in either the Old World or the New. In execution and theme, a Hittite stele now in the Aleppo Museum is little different from an Olmec stele at La Venta, in the Villahermosa Archaeological Park. Both represent a bearded man with Armenioid facial structure (a long, thin nose and narrow skull) fighting a snake. The very fact that both cultures made use of stelae, certainly not common among most other ancient peoples, suggests a connection of some kind.

Anatolian-Mesoamerican parallels can be seen in less magnificent but no less revealing artifacts. Panpipes were so typical of civilizations in Asia Minor that they were used to argue on behalf of Anatolian origins for the Etruscans, who embraced them as a national instrument. The pipes were likewise a fixture of Mayan ceremonial life. The Mayan version is identical to its Anatolian counterpart, even to the same pitches and tone. An item similarly associated with Asia Minor and the Etruscans was the pointy, upturned shoes worn by the Olmecs. Sandals depicted on a Chacmool statue at Chichén Itzá are the same as Guanche sandals in the Canary Islands. Olmec wheeled animal toys (remarkable for a people conventional scholars insist were ignorant of the wheel) at Tres Zapotes are little different from Hittite examples.

None of this is to suggest that the Hittites, a landlocked people who established their imperial grip on Asia Minor and much of the Middle East when the Atlantean empire arose in the Distant West, ever traveled to pre-Columbian America. Rather, they were themselves a Caucasoid people not unlike the Atlanteans, who *did* sail to the Opposite Continent and colonized parts of it. Those features in Mesoamerica that appear Hittite or Anatolian are the same Atlantean themes that influenced all Bronze Age civilizations, particularly those allied or related to Atlantis. The Hittite cosmological myth of Ullikummi, an Anatolian version of Atlas, and Troy's perceived direct descent from Electra, an Atlantis, told of Atlantean origins for the leading powers of Asia Minor in preclassical times. Even here the Maya's Popol Vuh describes a giant, Zipacnu, who defies the gods by growing like a mountain, upward from the middle of the sea toward the sky. The Hittite version differs only in the giant's name, and both renditions locate him in the Atlantic Ocean.

The most surprising Mayan parallel of its kind was a retelling of the Trojan War. The natives of the Yucatán recounted for their Spanish conquerors how a prince from Chichén Itzá steals the bride of the king of Izmal. Hunac Ceel, the ruler of Mayapán and ally of Izmal, takes vengeance on the abductor and his people, who had given sanctuary to their prince and his kidnap victim, by attacking Chichén Itzá and eventually burning it to the ground after a ten-year siege during which there were many heroes and losses on both sides. Surviving Itzas sailed away from the destroyed city to an island, their new home, which they called Tayasal. It sat in the middle of a great "lake" they named after themselves.

The Aztec version is even closer to the Trojan original: A young prince, Yappan, is tempted by three goddesses. He chooses Xochiquetzal, the spring goddess of love and beauty, and as a consequence of his choice is killed (Brundage 1960, 162). This close parallel with the tale of Paris can mean only that it was imported from the Old World before the arrival of the Spanish Christians, who deemed all European myths no less worthy of damnation than those encountered in the New World.

The story of Troy was repeated by the Toltecs, who identified the lord of Chichén Itzá as Topiltzin, yet another name for the Atlantean Feathered Serpent. After losing a major war and escaping to Tollan, an island nation across the eastern sea, he sails to Toltec shores with some veterans of the defeat. (See fig. 16.2.) The same version is preserved in

Fig. 16.2. An artist's reconstruction of a damaged Toltec pottery vessel is remarkably similar to those found in Egyptian illustrations at Medinet Habu of sea battles with invading Sea People. In both instances warriors wearing rayed-crown helmets struggle in the water. The Toltec story of Tollan is a Mesoamerican version of the Atlanto-Trojan War. (Photo courtesy of the National Museum of Anthropology and Archaeology, Mexico City)

the Mayan *Book of Chilam Chumayel*. The more familiar Chichén Itzá, Mayapán, and Izmal stand in for Ilios and the cities of Mycenaean Greece. Chichén Itzá, for example, is never razed to the ground.

Virgil has the Trojan prince, Ilioneus, say:

How fearful was the hurricane which streamed from merciless Mycenae and swept over Ida's plains, and how destiny impelled the continents of Europe and Asia to meet together in shock, all men have heard, even they who dwell far distant from us at the world's end where the river of Ocean circles back, and those too who live remote in the zone stretching, central to the fire, beneath a pitiless sun (*Aeneid,* Book VII, 221–27).

His remote zone "beneath a pitiless sun" appears to be referring to the tropical Yucatán, nearer the equator—that is, more "central to the fire."

There are other Mesoamerican comparisons with Trojan myth, such as the Olmec legend of Chibchan Cogi, the twelve-year-old prince abducted for his beauty by the shaman-king Yanacana, in the guise of a "winged jaguar." The story also belongs to Ganymede, prince of Troy. Zeus, in the form of an eagle, kidnaps him and flies off with his prize to Mount Olympus, where Ganymede serves as the god's cup bearer and catamite.

The Trojan epic made an indelible impact on all Mesoamerican peoples because it was part of the Atlantean foundation story; their Feathered Serpent ancestors fled to Mexico not only from a natural catastrophe, but from the military disaster that preceded it. Troy's Atlantean allies likewise retreated from the fall of Ilios to their oceanic homeland before it was destroyed. The Toltec version of Topiltzin and the Mayas' *Book of Chilam Chumayel* actually connect the Trojan War with the flight of its defeated veterans to Atlantis (Tollan and Tayasal), from whose annihilation they escaped to the shores of the Yucatán.

That final destruction, which generated the Lesser Arrival of Atlantean refugees to Mesoamerica, was dramatically preserved in the most sacred records of the ancient Mexicans. The *Anales de Quahtitlan* describe the ancestral cataclysm in a straightforward manner: "And this year was that of the *Ce-calli* [Great Water], and on the first day all was lost. The mountain itself was submerged in the water." This account is reminiscent of Plato's *Timaeus,* which told how Atlantis was obliterated "in a single day and a night." Even though the *Anales de Quahtitlan* predates the Spanish Conquest, it displays some intriguing resemblances to flood traditions in other parts of the ancient world.

The name of the Toltec Deluge hero is Nata, an apparent Tenoche version of the biblical Noah. He and his wife, Nena, were told of the coming disaster by Tezcatlipoca, just as the Sumerian Ziusudra was forewarned by the sea god Enki, and the Babylonian Xiusthros by Kronos, ruler of the Atlantic Ocean. In the Hindu *Matsya Purana,* the god Vishnu, in the guise of a fish, predicts the coming of a catastrophic flood, then tells Manu, "The Earth shall become like ashes, the very air too shall be scorched with heat." Oppenheimer observes that "the details suggest a grand disaster, such as may follow a meteorite strike" (Oppenheimer 1999, 241).

The disaster-migration theme is repeated in the Maya's Popol Vuh, cited earlier. It tells of an ancestral race arriving by sea after the Hun yecil (the Aztec Hun-Esil, or Drowning of the Trees), a catastrophic deluge and earthquake, to build a temple at the Huehuhuetan River in memory of their escape. Known as the House of Darkness for its subterranean caverns, the temple was used as a depository for written records carried from the drowned homeland. In 1691 just such an underground temple was found near the city of Saconusco; its precious library was burned on orders of church officials as the incomprehensible works of Satan.

The Popol Vuh goes on to recount that the gods, jealous of the growing power of humans over nature, clouded their wisdom, and the Mayan monarchs "had to return the keys of civilization" to the great kingdom across the Sunrise Sea. A middle class, the Macehual, grew from elements of both the Pilli aristocrats and Mayeques proletariat. A few Mayeques were allowed into the ruling class by demonstrating extraordinary individual abilities, such as the capture of four or more of the enemy. In time this "upward mobility" began to swamp the ruling upper class. The Mayeques had an inveterate addiction to human sacrifice, a practice relied on with increasing frequency by the diluted Pilli to terrorize the native masses into submission. Even so, as late as the Conquest, the old Feathered Serpent blood had not entirely died out, as physical descriptions of Montezuma indicate. Aware of the racial disparities between his own people and the Spaniards, the emperor deliberately chose a taller, fair-skinned, lightly bearded member of his royal entourage as his personal envoy to Cortés.

Controversy still surrounds the disappearance of previous Mesoamerican civilizations, particularly those of the Olmec and Maya. It seems probable, however, that the gap between the aloof, all-powerful Pilli and the lowly, laboring Mayeques narrowed through intermarriage by way of ambitious middle-class commoners, the Machuals. The aristocrats had preserved as their legacy the arts and sciences handed down to them by their Atlantean ancestors. Inevitably this diminished, and the decrepit elite shrank to so small a size it could no longer effectively exert its absolute authority over the broad masses of native peoples. They simply deserted the feebly administered ceremonial cities and melted back into the preliterate jungle lifestyle they had known for tens of thousands of years before the coming of all the various Feathered Serpents. Translations of the Mayan stelae relate that their civilization finally collapsed amid incessant warfare between rival cities.

Remnants of the aristocracy moved on to restart high culture elsewhere throughout Mesoamerica, although they never surpassed Mayan achievements in the subsequent Mixtec, Toltec, and, finally, Aztec states. By the time Cortés set foot on the east coast of Montezuma's empire, Mesoamerican civilization was again turning on its cycle of decline. Before the close of the sixteenth century the generations of elite survivors, descendants of the Greater and Lesser Arrivals from Atlantis, had all but died out.

17

ATLANTEAN SONS OF THE SUN

> *Machu Picchu may well have marked the mountain about*
> *sixty leagues from Cuzco where the Children of the Sun*
> *were said to have been created, or alternatively the moun-*
> *tain on which they alone escaped the waters of the flood.*

PIERRE GRIMAL, *LAROUSSE WORLD MYTHOLOGY*

When the first Spanish sailors approached the shores of Peru, they beheld, while still out at sea some distance, what they took for a colossal white crucifix laid out alone on the otherwise bare, sloping shore. It seemed to point significantly toward the undiscovered interior. To the Christian conquistadors, its appearance was a sign from heaven confirming the righteousness and inevitable triumph of their mission in the New World.

Instead, the "crucifix" turned out to be one of the mysterious geoglyphs the Spaniards called the Candelabra. Some 200 feet long and visible for more than 12 miles out to sea from the Paracas coast, it actually represents a mounted jimson weed, revered by the ancient Peruvians for its hallucinogenic qualities. The Candelabra of the Andes was only the first of many wonders the sixteenth-century Europeans were to encounter in what the natives referred to as their Tawantisuyu. This was an enormous, highly disciplined empire that ran from the Andean border in Ecuador to the Maule River in Chile, roughly the same distance from New York to Panama, all of it connected by more than 9,500 miles of superb roads. The coastal highway alone ran for 2,500 miles.

Nor was this extensive road system a mere series of crudely forged pathways, but a paved network that traversed jungles and swamps, deserts and moutains. Way stations with stores, shade trees, and watering facilites were regularly spaced along every route. The roads themselves were impeccably maintained and were regularly swept by teams of broom men. These highways were so wide that Spanish cavalry rode over them, eight horses abreast. The roads were used mostly by the *casquis*, runners who carried news from every corner of the empire. As one *casqui* approached his way station, he blew his conch shell to alert his successor. Then as he came into shouting distance of this next runner, and without breaking stride, he yelled out his bit of news. Before he reached his station, the other runner was on his way with the information. In this manner, they could and did cover 2,200 miles in five days' time. Because hundreds of *casqui*s were in constant use, the emperor knew even the most trivial details in the day-to-day life of his Tawantisuyu.

The achievements of his engineers in bridge building were no less spectacular. One suspension bridge over the Apurímac River, built during the mid-fifteenth century, was still in use until the turn of the twentieth century. It was so huge and expertly constructed that Francisco Pizarro's entire cavalry rode across it in safety. Andean feats of irrigation rivaled the best Roman waterworks. The Ascope aqueduct still conducts water to sea level from 4,000 feet and over more than a mile after some 1,200 years of continuous use. Chan-Chan's massive reservoir, built before 900 C.E., held two million cubic gallons of water. The pre-Inca walls of Sacsahuaman, outside the Inca capital at Cuzco, stand 22 feet high and comprise hundreds of perfectly positioned blocks, some weighing in excess of 200 tons.

In 1932 chance aerial discovery was made of a stone wall beginning near Puente, not far from the Peruvian coast and running along the northern banks of the Rio Santo to Lima. Researchers for the American Geographical Society estimated that in their original state the ramparts were about 15 feet thick at the base, tapering upward to an average height of 12 feet. Only 40 miles of the wall were still visible, but it undoubtedly connected at one time with the Pacific coast, and its opposite end was lost in the thick jungle cover. It may have been built by the Chimu, noted for their outsized structures, as a bulwark against Inca aggression during the late fourteenth century, but the wall's real age and origins are unknown. Who could have achieved such a monumental feat of civilized splendor?

The renowned world explorer and author David Hatcher Childress wondered,

> While Bolivian archaeologists insist that ancestors of the local Aymara Indians built both Tiahuanaco and Puma Punku [massive ceremonial centers], it would seem that their culture has certainly taken a slide back, as they now can barely make a subsistence living on the high, barren plateau. Neither they nor the Spanish government of impoverished Bolivia are capable of duplicating the engineering feats of Tiahuanaco or Puma Punku (1986, 138).

The Spaniards, however, were far more impressed by the Inca emperor's stunning collection of gold and silver. Precious metals of the whole empire belonged exclusively to the ruling class, and the brilliant produce of every mine was funneled to palaces and temples. Approximately 130 million sundried bricks went into the construction of the two thousand-year-old Huaca del Sol outside Trujillo in northern Peru. Suspecting it contained treasure, the Spanish connected this "pyramid of the sun" to an improvised canal leading from the nearby river and flushed out literally tons of gold and silver artifacts from the 750-foot-long, 450-foot-wide structure. Originally, the walls and ceiling of its interior temple were entirely sheeted with beaten gold and contained twelve life-sized statues of solid gold. The nearby Pyramid of the Moon was almost identically decorated and stocked with silver. At Cuzco, the Inca capital, the grounds of the Coricancha, or Enclosure of the Sun, glimmered with hundreds of lifelike birds, butterflies, llamas, and flowers, all executed in gold. The Coricancha itself enshrined a 9-foot-wide gold disc representing the sun god, together with numerous statues executed in solid gold.

Obsessed as they were with plunder, the conquistadors were unconcerned with the origins, technology, or politics of Andean civilization. Their priests, however, were particularly interested in the Indians' religion, and immediately set about to replace it with Christianity. Like the Aztecs, the Incas were utterly subdued and their culture virtually blotted out within a century after the calamitous European arrival.

Mesoamerican and Andean civilizations grew up independently, and they appear to have made little contact. Some scholars conclude that they were unaware of each other's existence, yet Aztec imperialists held sway over Mexico at the same time the Inca empire dominated South America from Ecuador to Chile.

It is upon this point of similar but separate development that pre-Conquest South America's alien origins begin to unfold. For societies supposedly evolving in mutual ignorance of the outside world, dates for Mesoamerican and Andean civilizations show a striking parallel. Both suddenly emerged around 3000 B.C.E. on the seacoast and experienced two subsequent cultural surges at the same time—1600 and 1200 B.C.E., respectively. Conventional archaeologists used to believe that the earliest conceivable level for organized society in South America was a pre–Ceramic Age beginning in the mid-third millennium B.C.E. That early chronology had to be discarded in spring 2001, when improved dating techniques of the remains of a Peruvian city revealed that it had been built in 2627 B.C.E.

Located about 120 miles north of Lima and 14 miles from the Pacific Ocean in the Supe River Valley, Caral was an urban center dominated by six pyramids, the largest 60 feet high, measuring 450 by 500 feet at its base, and built from quarried stone. The city also featured a trio of sunken plazas, blocks of apartment buildings, modest homes, and grander residences. Researchers speculate that thirty thousand or more persons resided at the site. Caral is not unique, however. Another seventeen cities, all dating to the same period or earlier, lie in the immediate vicinity. The existence of these complex metropolitan areas, with their monumental architecture and large populations, means that Andean beginnings around 3000 B.C.E. (less than four centuries before Caral was built) are almost certain.

Indeed, even before the discovery of Caral's provenance—the early-third millennium B.C.E.—archaeologists knew that a ziggurat-like structure with its geometric forecourt, the Huaca de los Sacrificios, dated to 2857 B.C.E. The site is doubtless even older because radiocarbon assays were limited to the final phases of its use. As Moseley observes, "Basal dates would certainly be earlier, and construction of this huaca probably began and ended earlier than at other mounds" (1994, 116). Despite its age, the Huaca de los Sacrificios is not a primitive edifice but features walls built of massive basalt blocks, instead of rounded boulders, connected to an elegant stairway.

Most South American archaeologists long ago concluded that their continent's earliest civilization began on Peru's northern coast around the turn of the fourth millennium B.C.E. in a period they define as the Salavarry. Its outstanding features were massive stone and dried-brick temple platforms with walled forecourts, very much resembling Sumerian ziggurats built in Mesopotamia at the same time. From its beginning, Andean civilization, wherever and whenever it is observed, burst all at once upon the native Indians, who had maintained a subsistence-level existence for tens of thousands of years. Pyramid construction, medicine, mummification, irrigation, organized agriculture, city planning, labor management, social stratification, centralized administration, and the growth of cities and ceremonial centers were present from the start. As in Mexico, civilization showed no signs of previous development but appeared in the Andes full-blown.

Popular imagination equates pre-Conquest Peru with the Inca empire. The Incas were only the final manifestation of Andean civilization, however. They emerged during the Late Intermediate period, around 1300 C.E., after subduing the most recent of at least five major cultures that preceded them. The Sechin-Chavin was particularly important because it spread civilization up and down the Pacific coast beginning after 1200 B.C.E. When the Sechin-Chavin collapsed about a thousand years later, the Nazca people became extraordinary irrigationists in the south, while the Moches built the fabulous Huaca del Sol in the north. Before 600 C.E. these cultures too were on the wane, and their places were eventually taken by the Chimus, whose imperialist ambitions and cyclopean wall building at Chan-Chan, the capital of more than one hundred thousand inhabitants, were in turn absorbed by the even more ambitious Incas before the first half of the fifteenth century.

While each of these cultures made its own imprint on Andean civilization, like the Mesoamerican cultures, they were all related and were actually more variations on a common theme than fundamentally distinct and separate societies. Features inaugurated during the Salavarry period, which are evident at Caral, were perpetuated in various forms until the Spanish Conquest. Just as in Mexican prehistory, the Andean paralleled four major cultural surges generated by the sudden immigration of foreign culture bearers in large numbers. The first, around the turn of the fourth millennium B.C.E., when South American civilization began in north-coastal Peru, coincides with the Maya's foundation year of 3113, the birth of dynastic Egypt, and the earliest seismic upheavals on the island of Atlantis, which prompted many of its inhabitants to seek safer residence in other parts of the world.

Another flood account from the Tiahuanaco period tells of the sea god Thonapa who drowned the people of Yamquisapa, an island kingdom, for their self-centered luxury and adoration of the statue of a woman atop a hill called Cachapucara. Thonapa destroyed the idolatrous statue and hill by sinking both of them, along with most of their worshippers, into the ocean. This version is particularly cogent for its apparent reference to Kleito's shrine (Cachapucara?) on the central hill of Atlantis, as described by Plato. He tells how the place where she lay with the sea god, Poseidon, to beget the semidivine lineage of Atlantean kings was revered thereafter as a sacred precinct. The migration of Thonapa's chosen survivors corresponds to the cataclysm of 2200 B.C.E.

A third wave of Atlantean migration around 1600 B.C.E. was reflected both in what conventional investigators have regarded as the sudden beginning of Olmec civilization and in the abrupt introduction of pottery in the Titicaca Basin, which is indicative of newcomers who may have built the ceremonial city of Tiahuanaco (see fig. 17.1) at this time. Three hundred years later the flight of survivors from the final destruction of Atlantis caused a sudden bulge in Olmec culture, while a major horizon in Peruvian prehistory, the Sechin-Chavin culture, came into being.

These three fundamental levels in the archaeological record also appear in native Andean tradition. The original inhabitants were known as the Ayar-uyssus (Husbandmen), whose residence in South America was so venerable that it was believed to have sprung from the ground at the dawn of creation.

Untold generations later an entirely different people arrived from over the sea to the northern shores of Peru. These were the Ayar-mancotopas, exceedingly wise bands of men and women who built the earliest cities, raised the first pyramids and other monumental structures, understood applied mathematics, cured illnesses with medicines, and instituted all the cultural features for which Andean civilization came to

Fig. 17.1. The dramatic entrance to Bolivia's Tiahuanaco. The Spanish chronicler Cieza de Leon recorded a local Indian legend: "Tiahuanaco was built in a single night by unknown giants after the Flood."

be known. In the Chimu version, they were led by King Naymlap, who landed with his followers in "a fleet of big canoes."

Long after the Ayar-manco-topas established themselves, the Ayar-chakis suddenly appeared as Wanderers, refugees from earthquakes and floods that made impossible continued residency at their distant homeland. Their leader was Manco Capac and his wife, Mama Occlo. They established the Flowering Age when master craftsmen built Tiahuanaco about 3,500 years ago. Indeed, radiocarbon testing at the ceremonial center yielded an early construction date of around 1600 B.C.E. (Childress 1986, 139).

Considered today a reliable authority on Inca history, Friar Blas Valera, the son of a conquistador and an Indian woman, composed a manuscript (now in the La Paz Jesuit Monastery) that provides some details of Manco Capac's story. He and his sister-bride left their birthplace, the Isle of the Sun, after the kingdom grew decadent during a time known as Pur-Un-Runa, the Era of Savages. Their sinful homeland was destroyed in a flood sent as punishment from the gods, who spared Manco Capac and his large, virtuous family.

The last wave of foreign immigration was made up of the Ayar-auccas, also refugees, but from a more terrible natural catastrophe—the sudden obliteration of their once-mighty kingdom in fire and flood. Appropriately remembered as the Warlike People, they were almost certainly veterans of the failed Atlantean wars in the eastern Mediterranean and survivors of the final destruction of Atlantis, in 1198 B.C.E. Their Atlantean identity is confirmed by the Incas themselves: They described the Ayar-auccas as four twin giants who held up the sky but who eventually grew tired of their exertions on behalf of an ungrateful humanity and let the sky fall into the sea, creating a worldwide deluge that destroyed most of humankind. One of the Ayar-auccas arrived in Cuzco, where he transformed himself into a *huaca,* or sacred stone, but not before mating with a local woman to sire the first Inca of royal blood. Henceforward Cuzco, known as the Navel of the World, was the capital of the Inca empire.

Blas Valera's version refers to these Deluge survivors as Micmacs, or colonists. Later the story was transferred to Lake Titicaca and its small island, named Isla del Sol after Manco Capac's oceanic homeland. In compiling a list of all the Inca and pre-Inca kings, Valera arrived at a specific year for the beginning of their royal dynasties: 1220 B.C.E. This date, determined nearly five centuries ago, entirely through the genealogy of Bolivia's pre-Conquest monarchs, coincides almost perfectly with the final destruction of Atlantis in 1198 B.C.E.

The story of the Ayar-auccas is a self-evident Peruvian rendering of the Atlantis catastrophe incorporated into the Incas' imperial foundation myth. But not only the Incas knew about the Ayar-auccas. The Anti Indians of Bolivia; the Arawak Macusis of the Guinanas, in Colombia; and Brazil's Tamanacs believed most of the Ayar-auccas perished during a fiery catastrophe followed by an annihilating deluge. The Tupi-Guarni-speaking Indians said that Monan, the creator god, became vexed with the sins of men and women destroyed the City of Shining Roofs with a terrible flame from the heavens. But Irin Mage, a sorcerer, extinguished the conflagration with a deluge, inadvertently drowning most of humankind.

A linguistic theme highlighting the foreign character of the City of Shining Roofs is *mage,* an archaic western European word likewise signifying "magician." Only the Tupi Flood hero Tamandare and his extended family, who had been warned beforehand, survived and sailed to South America. Today, the northern shores of Brazil are known as the Tamandare Coast, in memory of the Atlantean survivor.

The creation myth of Bolivia's Munduku claimed that the creator sun god, Ra-imi, made the earth by forming it into the shape of a flat stone on the head of a lesser deity, who could not indefinitely support his burden and eventually dropped the world into the sea. Ra-imi recalls the Egyptian Ra, who likewise had his own flood myth, but the unnamed deity who held up the world and was responsible for its descent into the ocean is clearly a reference to Atlas, the Upholder. The Inca Inti-Ra-imi was the annual Festival of the Sun. In addition to its connection to the Egyptian Ra, Inti was a common Old Kingdom name, particularly among Egyptian noblemen. In February 2001, a Sixth Dynasty *mastaba* (a single-story brick-adobe monument) was excavated at Abu Sir, southwest of Cairo, where a judge named Inti had been interred 4,300 years ago.

The Inca's chief deity was Inti, a sky god and sun god represented in sacred art by a man's face in a solar disc. Such a deity was the Egyptian Horus, whose name was derived from the root *hor,* "face," used for the word *sky* or *heaven (hort)*. In fact, the hieroglyph for *sky* is a man's face. As described in chapter 4, "Atlanteans into Egypt," the Smsu-Hor, Followers of Horus, were part of an early Atlantean migration that brought civilization to the Nile Delta during the late fourth millennium B.C.E. Horus, like Inti, was the personification of kingship, and both pharaoh and Inca were accepted as living incarnations of the sun god. In his cult center of Hicrakonopolis at the Upper Nile, Horus took the form of a solar disc with wings. As such he appeared over the doorway of every temple entrance to protect against evil. A winged sun also appears over the doorway of the Inca temple at Ocosingo.

The Orinoco Indian Deluge, known as the Time of the Catena-ma-Noa (Water of Noa), names the flood hero in Genesis. Patagonia's Zeu-kha is no less close to the Sumerian Ziusudra. In 1629 Fernando Montesinos, who traded extensively in Peru as the viceroy's secretary, wrote in his *Memorias Antiguas Historiales del Peru* that native high priests told him of their ancestors who were led to South America by a great-grandson of Noah, or, at any rate, an Inca version of the biblical Deluge figure. Noa's capital was the Gilded One, which the Orinoco said had been "lost." The gold-crazed Spaniards took this to mean that the city was concealed somewhere in the jungle, and so began their fruitless search for El Dorado, when, in fact, folk tradition recounted that the Gilded One had been lost in the Deluge.

Natives in the Lima region told the first Spaniards about "a race of giants" who countless generations before had arrived "in big canoes." After exhausting local supplies of fish and game, the giants sailed north along the Pacific coast to Chan-Chan, where they erected the great mud-brick walls of that vast urban complex.

The "warlike" Ayar-auccas were led by the peaceful At-ach-u-chu. The premier founding father of Andean civilization, he was revered from deeply prehistoric times to the Spanish Conquest of the sixteenth century. He was consistently described as the great culture bearer from a distant land in the east who arrived on the shores of Lake Titicaca after surviving a cataclysmic deluge—the Unu-Pachacuti, or World Overturned by Water.

Like that of Manco Capac before him, his story was later transferred inland to the Bolivian Andes. The Peruvian natives called him the Teacher of All Things, a man who established in South America the arts of civilization, including agriculture, religion, astronomy, weights and measures, social organization, and government. Although Tiahuanaco was already built by the time he arrived, he was said to have constructed the nearby Akapana Pyramid. A related Aymara version recounts that "Tiahuanaco was built in a single night, after the Flood, by unknown giants" (Readers' Digest editors 1986, 39).

At-ach-u-chu was said to have moved on after a few years, disappearing into the west, but subsequent generations of those he left behind always expected his eventual return. All the features of this supremely important figure in Andean tradition, starting with the At- at the beginning of his name, clearly define him as the leader of survivors from the final destruction of Atlantis, who reestablished themselves by creating a hybrid civilization, a mix of local cultures with Atlantean technology, in Peru and Bolivia.

Parallels between Mesoamerica's Feathered Serpent and South America's Teacher of All Things are apparent. At-ach-u-chu even dressed much the same as Quetzalcoatl. "The analogy is more remarkable," Prescott wrote, "as there is no trace of any communication with, or even knowledge of, each other to be found in the two nations" (1952, 232). At-ach-u-chu's resemblance to similar culture bearers appearing after a great natural disaster in the Atlantic Ocean is a common theme recognized throughout the Americas, from the Menominee Indians' Marine Man of Michigan's Upper Peninsula to the Patagonian Zeu-kha at Tierra del Fuego. These related founding heroes from over the sea apparently represent the impact native peoples experienced from the large-scale arrival of Atlantis refugees in four major waves of immigration over nearly two thousand years. It is not surprising, then, that at least the folkish memory of these arrivals should have been preserved in the valued oral traditions of every native people whose revered ancestors knew and interacted with the Atlanteans.

These traditions consistently describe At-ach-u-chu as the tall, bearded, red-haired, fair-skinned elder of five brothers, known collectively as Viracochas (White Men). Before his statue was destroyed by Christian zealots, it is said, the "hair, complexion, features, raiment and sandals" reminded the conquistadors of the apostle Saint Bartholomew as depicted in popular holy cards of the time. The statue's description matches a painting known as the Inca Viracocha at Madrid's Museo de America. Colonial portraits at the Copacabana Monastery of Manco Capac and Mama Occlo also represent their subjects with facial features that are unlike those of the native Indian population.

Today, At-ach-u-chu is better remembered by his title, Kon-Tiki-Viracocha, or White Man of the Sea Foam—in other words, a foreigner who arrived by ship, "sea foam" being a poetic description of its bow wave. Pre-Inca Moche pottery shows what must be Viracocha, his sandals made of foam, bringing the sun (i.e., solar worship) across the sea from the east. Other Moche examples depicting a similar scene feature quartets of bearded men in square helmets clinging to rafts. As Cieze de Leon, a Spanish historian who studied the Incas firsthand, related, "When the Indians of the district were asked who made that ancient monument [Tiahuanaco's ceremonial center, the Kalasaya], they reply that they were made by other peoples, bearded and white like ourselves, who came to that region and settled there many ages before the reign of the Incas." In time the leader of the local Aymara Indians "entered the larger of the two islands in Lake Titicaca and found there a race of white people with beards, and fought them until he had killed them all." Due to these calamities Manco Capac relocated his throne to Cuzco, the new capital.

Aymara Indian tradition described each of the three waves of foreign immigration—the Ayar-manco-topas, -chakis, and -auccas—as having been composed of white-skinned, fair-haired people. The Incas themselves selected the fairest girls from the ruling class to serve as "white virgins" at the altars of the sun god, Inti. Some idea of the cleavage between the Inca rulers and their subjects may be gleaned from Emperor Tupac Inca Yupanqui's explanation that "science was not intended for the people, but for those of generous blood." Titu Cusi, the penultimate Inca at Vilacambamba, told Don Diego Rodriguez that his ancestors did not belong to "the wild Indians."

As throughout Mesoamerican civilization, two divergent, unrelated groups made up Andean society. Amerindians comprised the broad masses of the working class, while a numerically tiny, lighter-skinned elite with European features made up the priestly and ruling elite. With the decline of this elite a mixed group arose to form an intermediary or ancillary aristocracy, and by the time of the Spanish arrival, to occupy even the royal house. In fact, the preliterate Guarani Indians spoke of the Incas as the "white kings." The emperors claimed descent from these light-skinned culture bearers, and a definite physical cleft did indeed exist between the Indian proletariat and the Inca aristocracy. A portrait in Lima's Copacabana Monastery of Huayna Capac, the great Inca emperor who consolidated the conquests of his forebears during the early sixteenth century, represents a man with thoroughly European facial features. A profile in Antonio de Herrera's chronicle of the Spanish Conquest, *Historia* (in Madrid's Biblioteca Nacional), likewise shows Huascar with a non-Indian countenance.

A contemporary painting of Huayna Capac's other son, Atahualpa, the last Inca emperor, reveals someone of mixed parentage, suggesting he and Huascar were only half-brothers. Their father doubtless had many wives, and the brothers clearly did not have the same mother. Their mixed ancestry may have been at the root of the deadly enmity that broke out between the brothers after the death of their father, Huayna Capac. Until then, both ruled together in a shared regency. Commissioned during the early eighteenth century, a painting at Cuzco of Cornilla Inca, the last surviving member of the royal line, portrays a tall man with regular features, light eyes, straight auburn hair, and a long, narrow nose. On-location illustrations sketched by Fray Martin de Murina at the beginning of the seventeenth century clearly show the physical differences that divided the Andean classes. Contrast between the light-skinned aristocracy and the dark-skinned masses, in stature as well as physiognomy, is so pronounced that the impression given by de Murina's drawings is that of an entirely alien people superimposed on a larger native population.

The European characteristics seen in these portrayals of the Incas are borne out by their few surviving physical remains, most particularly at the Atacama cemetery. There mummies of the pre-Conquest royal families still evidence a fine, wavy, light-auburn hair. Mummies of the Paracas peninsula dated to at least the fourth century B.C.E. (the Late Chavin period), show a rusty reddish-brown hair color. Trujillo's underground museum features an unborn Chimu fetus with fine blond hair. By far the most impressive examples are on public display in the Mummy Room at Lima's Herrera Museum. Remarkably preserved in vacuum-sealed glass cases are the mummified bundles of Inca royalty. Of the dozen or so specimens, four have light-brown hair and three are blond with traces of red. Hair color and texture do not change or deteriorate after death, and the Andean mummification process did not affect the hair of the deceased. Moreover, the Paracas mummies are men who were much taller than the natives and who had narrower skulls.

Pedro Pizarro, son of the man who conquered the Inca empire, wrote:

[T]he ruling class of the Kingdom of Peru was fair-skinned with fair hair about the color of ripe wheat. Most of the great lords and ladies looked white like Spaniards. In that country I met an Indian woman with her child, both so fair-skinned that they were hardly distinguishable from fair, white people. Their fellow countrymen called them "children of the gods."

Thor Heyerdahl could not help wondering at the contrast between a people who once raised stupendous pyramids and temples, and modern Peru's indigenous population, whose culture and way of life do not seem to have descended from the same cultural tradition. In fact, the

Indians of Peru do not claim descent from the Incas, who, in their own tradition, arrived long after the ancestors of the native peoples were established in Peru. The subdued and exterminated master craftsmen of Andean civilization's Flowering Age are enigmatic pieces in the puzzle of pre-Conquest South America. "Whence this remarkable race came," William Prescott wrote, "and what was its early history are among those mysteries that meet us so frequently in the annals of the New World, and which time and the antiquary has as yet done little to explain" (Prescott 1952, 158).

When a young Inca prince became the neophyte emperor, he was crowned with a blond wig and told to benefit humankind, as did his great ancestors (Prescott 1952, 312). Like every Egyptian pharaoh, he was then presented with a false chin-beard, the *sonkhasapa*—a word still in use among the beardless Indians. The *sonkhasapa* is by no means the only such item with an apparent counterpart in the Nile Valley civilization. The Inca empire itself—the Tawantisuyu—seems like an inflection of Tawy, a name by which Egypt was commonly known to its own people. Tawy means crossroads, which, in view of the road-building Incas, is especially appropriate. The name recurs in an Atlantean context as far away as the Great Lakes region of North America, among the Huron Indians. Tawiscara was their flood hero, who "guided the torrents into smooth seas and lakes" after the catastrophe from which the Hurons' ancestors fled. Another linguistic comparison occurs in the ancient Peruvian Yaro, a paradisiacal land of the dead resplendent for its vast and rich fields. In Egyptian tomb art, the deceased were often portrayed plowing the bountiful fields of the afterlife, known as Iaro.

Maru was the sunken land from which Manco Capac and his Believers, the Ayar-manco-topas, arrived in Peru. Sekhet-*Aaru* was an inundated island in the Distant West from which the first humans and gods escaped to the Nile Delta. The name Maru/Yaro/Aaru/Iaro is a worldwide title for Atlantis and means Field of Reeds, or Place of Great Wisdom, because reeds were writing utensils symbolizing learning. Variations appear as far away as India, where the Manu were the Inca-like Sons of the Sun, survivors of the Great Flood, who brought early civilization to the subcontinent. Indeed, the Andean culture hero At-ach-u-chu bears a striking resemblance to Atcha, remembered by the ancient Egyptians as a far-off, opulent but vanished city echoing lost Atlantis. Here At-ach-u-chu may mean Man from Atcha (Atlantis).

In Peru, as in Mesoamerica, pyramids were less like the smooth-sided Great Pyramid standing on the Giza Plateau than the Early Dynastic step pyramids, such as Zoser's at Saqqara, or the Sumerian ziggurat of Ur. That the construction of these pyramids on either side of the world were contemporary with each other bespeaks their common inspiration. A well-preserved typical example is a step pyramid in the Chicana Valley. Its close resemblance to an Old World ziggurat or Zoser-like pyramid is underlined by its walled and partitioned fore-court, identical to Egyptian counterparts. (See fig. 17.2.)

The ceremonial center at Vilcashuaman is certainly more ziggurat than pyramid, although the Huaca del Sol, or Pyramid of the Sun, out-side Trujillo features a forecourt very similar to Egyptian layouts. The hourglass-shaped building clamps used to hold massive stone blocks in

Fig. 17.2. Like its counterparts in Mesoptamia, Egypt, and Mexico, this stone model of a step pyramid represents the original sacred mountain from which the founders of Andean civilization arrived after a terrible deluge. It was originally a centerpiece in the Inca's holy of holies, the Coricancha, the Enclosure of God. (Cuzco Museum of Art and Archaeology, Peru)

place at Medinet Habu are indeed identical to those employed in the building of Tiahuanaco for the same purpose. Medinet Habu, incidentally, is the victory temple in West Thebes where Ramses III enshrined his triumph over the Sea People from Atlantis.

Many Andean pyramids, such as the Moche Huaca del Sol, were consecrated to the sun god, just as their Egyptian counterparts were commonly known as Mountains of Ra; Ra being the chief solar deity. Peru's Pyramid of the Sun and Egypt's Great Pyramid share the same base length—758 feet. Especially pertinent to our investigation, this was the same dimension, according to Plato, of the Citadel, the Holy of Holies, at the very center of Atlantis.

Chavin de Huantar was a seminal Peruvian urban site, featuring an eastward-facing pyramid as its primary temple. There is an emphasis throughout on human figures with animal heads, particularly those of eagles and hawks—all highly suggestive of Egyptian religious motifs. Prescott went so far as to conclude that Andean resemblances "to early dynastic Egypt go beyond architectural similarities to include numerous cultural parallels" (Prescott 1952, 182). Those parallels extend beyond Egypt to other Old World cultures on which Atlantean refugees had an impact. In the Minoan Linear B written language, for example, the word for gold is *kuruso;* in Quechua, the Inca tongue, it is *kuri.* The Minoan word for ship, *cara-mequera,* is the same name by which the Tupi-Guarnis, with their legend of the Atlantis-like City of Shining Roofs, identify themselves. Even the pre-Inca city Tiahuanaco has Minoan correspondences. The name is derived from *tiawanaca,* or "this from the god," meaning "king"; *wanaca* in Minoan Linear B is "monarch." "Rain" in Quechua is *pluvia,* precisely the same term in Latin, from which the English word *pluvial* is derived.

In Trojan (Patumnilli) and other Anatolian languages, particularly Luvian and Hittite, *tepe* signifies a hill or mountain. For example, Kuel-Tepe is the site of an important city with temples and palaces built around a large ceremonial mound, about 500 miles east of Troy. Kuel-Tepe was a major trading center for metals and textiles from at least the nineteenth century B.C.E. Excavations at pre-Assyrian levels uncovered a *megaron,* or large rectangular room, a basic unit in later Greek architecture, with antecedents in Early Bronze Age Ilios. Wai-Tepu, Mountain of the Sun, was the Brazilian version of Manco Capac, that

Son of the Sun. Tepe-Quem is an extinct volcano in the Lower Amazon once mined for its diamonds. Interestingly, the same name in Mayan likewise refers to a mountain, meaning Great Stone. In Zapotec, one of the two principal language groups in Oaxaca, Mexico, the Anatolian word for hill, *tepe,* is still current.

Hiram Bingham, the discoverer of "the lost city of the Incas," Machu Picchu (fig. 17.3), wrote that "some of the two-handled jars are almost identical with one found in ancient Troy" (Bingham 1939, 20). He noted that the roofs of the houses in Machu Picchu were bound by thatch to stone gables, the same construction feature employed in the smaller buildings at the Trojan capital, Ilios. Homet, who explored the Lower Amazon in the early twentieth century, likewise discovered biconical urns covered with herringbone patterns, swastikas, spirals, and zigzag lines typical of pottery decoration found at Troy. He concluded that the Amazon finds were debased Trojan work. The same

Fig. 17.3. The holy mountain-city of Machu Picchu was home of the Inca's Accla Cuna, a college of chosen women who orally preserved the high wisdom of Kon-Tiki Viracocha, the founder of Andean civilization who came from over the sea.

swastikas and spirals were incised on the Pedra Pintada, a large stone also located in the Lower Amazon, where warships fresh from defeat at Troy and the final destruction of Atlantis may have entered South America. The American researcher and author Harold T. Wilkins, who spent years investigating Atlantean influences in South America during the mid-twentieth century, learned from the Muyscas Indians of Colombia their word for sun—*sua*. *Suastika* in Old World Sanskrit means "sun wheel."

Like the Atlantean kings described by Plato, Inca emperors wore full-length robes of imperial purple. Their mantles were stained with tinctures distilled from insect and mollusk dyes, a process otherwise without parallel beyond the provinces of Troy until the post–Bronze Age florescence of the Phoenicians. The Aztec emperor Montezuma II wore an azure robe when he received the Spaniards. Some of the finest surviving examples of the Inca's royal robes were found among the 429 mummies at the Paracas necropolis.

Andean mummification has already been mentioned in connection with the fair hair—rare among Indians—of its preserved dead. Moseley points out that mummification was known in Peru "about the time ancient Egyptians began using embalming processes for similar ends" (1994, 93). In between Egypt in the east and Peru in the west, mummification was practiced by the Guanche inhabitants of the Canary Islands.

In *Ancient Man in Michigan*, Henry Gilman observed that "the mound-builders and Peruvians of America and the Neolithic people of France and the Canary Islands had alike an extraordinary custom of boring a circular hole in the top of the skulls of their dead, so that the soul might easily pass in and out" (Gilman 1898, 111). Inca priests suspended around the neck of the deceased a Vase of Justification containing holy water in memory of the Great Flood, from which heroes and gods arrived in the Andes. The same funeral rite was identically practiced by the Maya and Egyptians.

These various correspondences in Andean civilization from Egypt, Troy, Minoan Crete, and the Canary Islands were interconnected by the Atlantean phenomenon that influenced them all. The very name Opposite Continent was first mentioned by Plato in his description of the sunken capital.

When, in the early sixteenth century, they first walked ashore at what has since become Colombia, the Spaniards were informed by their Indian hosts that they had arrived in the Land of Amuraca. Bearing the royal title Serpent (Amuraca), they said, was a bearded white man who was not unlike the conquistadors themselves. He had long ago arrived following a terrible flood, which had forced him and his followers to seek refuge. He afterward taught the natives the benefits of agriculture, medicine, and religion, then built the first of several stone cities.

Amuraca's resemblance to the Feathered Serpent can mean only that the same set of Old World culture bearers arrived throughout the Americas. It suggests, too, that the name given to the New World was not derived from that of a contemporary Italian mapmaker. The Europeans did not use native descriptions for lands they conquered; they sought to lend greater legitimacy to their New World holdings by rechristening them with Old World names. Thus, the Atlanto-Colombian Amuraca was changed to the America of Amerigo Vespucci for political reasons.

It does indeed seem strange that the New World would have been christened after a Genoese mapmaker who was generally unknown until five years before his death, when Martin Waldseemüller's *Cosmographiae introductio* was published in 1507. The indigenous provenance of the name America is supported by the fact that Columbus himself, on his third voyage to the New World, met Indian natives who introduced themselves as Americos. The same tribe was identified by Alonso de Ojeda on his second voyage to Hispaniola. Moreover, the "land of perpetual wind," a reference to a mountain range in the province of Chantoles between Juigalpa and Liberdad, in Nicaragua, was known to the Maya as Amerisque and was so recorded in the sailing logs of Columbus, as well as in the writings of Vespucci.

Even here, a linguistic connection with the ancient world appears in the name of the island kingdom from which Amuraca sailed to Colombia: Amurru. The same name in Akkadian, the language of the Semitic conquerors of Sumer at the close of the third millennium B.C.E., coincidental with the third Atlantean catastrophe, in 2290 B.C.E., means "western lands."

In Quechua the seven visible stars in the constellation of the Pleiades were known as the Aclla Cuna—the Chosen Women or Little

Mothers. The Pleiades were associated with the Great Deluge from which Kon-Tiki-Viracocha fled to South America. Aclla Cuna was also the name of the Inca's most sacred mystery cult, which was composed exclusively of the most beautiful, virtuous, and intelligent women, who orally preserved the high wisdom and ancestral traditions of the Ayar-manco-topas. The Chosen Women were identified with the Pleiades, or the Atlantises, as they were known in Greek myth.

Dressed in Atlantean colors (red, white, and black), the Little Mothers were provided with magnificent estates at Cuzco, the capital of the Inca empire, and the mountain citadel of Machu Picchu. For reasons still unknown, they vanished from their high-altitude convent, where rare red orchids grow from cracks in the massive blocks of beautifully cut stone. These flowers, according to local Aymara legend, are reincarnated souls of the Aclla Cuna, come back to adorn the remote holy city of Machu Picchu.

All this brings to mind an obscure medieval chronicle from the other side of the world, the Frisians' *Oera Linda Bok*. In recounting the cataclysm that struck Atland, its anonymous author tells how the leader of a group of survivors led them across the sea. They followed his blue banner into the west and were never heard from again.

The admiral's name was Inka.

18

AFTERMATH

To those who had an eye to see, the depth of their degeneracy was obvious enough. To the majority, whose judgement was distracted by superficial appearances, however, they appeared, in the pursuit of unbridled self-indulgence and power, to be at the height of their good fortune. But Zeus, the god of gods, who reigns by law, and whose eye can see such things, when he perceived the deplorable condition of this formerly admirable people, decided to punish them and reduce them through his stern justice.

PLATO, *CRITIAS*

Readers of *Survivors of Atlantis* might easily succumb to the effects of information overload. Yet how else might we approach a worldwide drama spanning 2,800 years, without citing the latest scientific conclusions and a wealth of folk material from either side of the Atlantic Ocean? In the end, however, what matters is not the retention of facts, but the overall impression they leave in the mind. For some that impression amounts to rekindling the racial memory of an event that traumatized much of humankind. It is beginning to surface in our collective consciousness only now, after so many thousands of years, because science is retrieving the pieces of a seminal image fragmented and suppressed by a long-ago dark age.

But why stir it up all over again? Why not let the past rest forgotten on the ocean floor? If nothing else, we may thereby appreciate the fragility of our own civilization. Doubtless the Atlanteans, at the zenith of their magnificence, imagined they would go on forever. After more than three thousand years of continued existence and in control of a global empire stretching from the Americas to the Mediterranean, who or what was to stop them? Fully conscious of their economic and military superiority, they assumed the rest of humanity would be better off under an Atlantean warlord. It was this kind of arrogance in which many other superpowers have since indulged themselves prior to their demise. History is littered with the wreckage of broken civilizations whose people believed their particular way of life should be forced on others for their own good, regardless of whether anyone approved of such high-handed imposition.

Atlantis began as a collection of Stone Age agriculturists, coalesced into loosely confederated tribes, matured into a Bronze Age kingdom, fattened as a seaborne empire, and perished during a natural catastrophe. The pattern has been repeated often enough; only the final means of death vary. The Hittites, Maya, Inca, Easter Islanders, Persians, Romans, Hapsburgs, Soviets—all imagined themselves exempt from the cycles of history. America began as a collection of religious communities, became a republic, and now wants to be the very thing it rebelled against: an empire. The real tragedy of it all is that once a society goes into decline, its inhabitants are either too arrogant or powerless to learn from the past or apply its lessons in time to avoid collapse.

An undeniable theme running throughout worldwide traditions of the Atlantean calamity emphasizes that it was not entirely an accident of nature, nor were its victims wholly innocent. Rather, they had become so corrupt and devoid of the virtues for which they were previously long renowned that their fate fell on them as a divine judgment. It is remarkable to encounter this moral interpretation from Plato's dialogues to the oral accounts of North America's Mandan Indians; from the Ge-speaking tribes of Brazil to Vikings in Scandinavia. Egyptians, Sumerians, Babylonians, Canary Islanders, Irish, Welsh, Berbers, Gauls, Etruscans, Iberians—all claimed the Atlanteans were somehow answerable for their own destruction. Wars were fought for goals other than self-preservation, self-gratification took precedence over the general welfare, and greed replaced ideals. These were the conditions deemed characteristic of a society in disarray. In them the ancients perceived a very real relationship between social and cosmic harmony: One was but an expression of the other. To allow any serious imbalance in human affairs was to tempt heaven. Hence the Atlanteans were considered morally responsible for the catastrophe that deprived them of their greatness.

Let their story be a cautionary tale for our time. Otherwise, someone may someday write a book called *Survivors of the Twenty-first Century.*

BIBLIOGRAPHY

Introduction: A Million Tons of Copper

Benedict, C. Henry. *Red Metal.* Ann Arbor, Mich.: University of Michigan Press, 1958.

Brendt, George. "Great Lakes Geology." *North American Geological Symposium* (1983): 33.

Brown, Charles E. *The Wisconsin Archaeologist*, no. 5 (September 1926).

Coles, J. M., and A. F. Harding. *The Bronze Age in Europe.* London: Thames and Hudson, 1979.

Drier, Roy W. "Prehistoric Mining in the Copper Country." In Octave DuTemple, ed. *Ancient Copper Mines of Upper Michigan.* Calumet, Mich.: Marlin, 1962.

DuTemple, Octave, ed. *Ancient Copper Mines of Upper Michigan.* Calumet, Mich.: Marlin, 1962.

Ferguson, William P. F. "Michigan's Most Ancient Industry: The Prehistoric Mines and Miners of Isle Royale." In Octave DuTemple, ed. *Ancient Copper Mines of Upper Michigan.* Calumet, Mich.: Marlin, 1962.

Fisher, James. "Historical Sketch of the Lake Superior Copper District." *Mining Gazette* 7 (September 1929).

Fox, George R. "The Ancient Copper Workings on Isle Royale." *Wisconsin Archaeologist*, no. 10 (1915): 74.

Holmes, W. H. "Aboriginal Copper Mines of Isle Royale, Lake Superior." *American Anthropologist*, no. 3 (1901): 137.

Houghton, Jacob. "The Ancient Copper Mines of Lake Superior." In Octave DuTemple, ed. *Ancient Copper Mines of Upper Michigan.* Calumet, Mich.: Marlin, 1962.

Joseph, Frank. *Atlantis in Wisconsin.* St. Paul, Minn.: Galde, 1995.

Murock, Angus. *Boom Copper.* New York: Macmillan, 1943.

Parker, Jack. "The First Copper Miners." *Compressed Air* (January 1975): 8.

Plato. *The Dialogues.* Translated by William Taylor. London: University of London Press, 1902.

Roeder, Patrick. *Indians of the Upper Great Lakes.* New York: Harper, 1922.

Savage, Dean James. "Dug for Copper in Prehistoric Days." *Sunday Mining Gazette* 7 (May 1911).

Scott, William P. "Reminiscences of Isle Royale." *Michigan History Magazine*, no. 9 (1933): 38.

Whittlesey, Charles. "The Ancient Miners of Lake Superior." *Annals of Science*, no. 1 (August 1852).

Winchell, N. H. "Ancient Copper of Isle Royale." *The Engineering and Mining Journal* (December 1881): 102.

Chapter 1: Atlantis at War

Anderson, R. C. *Oared Fighting Ships*. New York: Percival Marshall, 1962.

Blegen, C. W. *Troy and the Trojans*. New York: Praeger, 1963.

———. *Troy: The Excavations Conducted by the University of Cincinnati, 1932 to 1938*. 4 vols. Princeton, N.J.: Princeton University Press, 1958.

Brestead, James. *A History of Egypt*. New York: Scribner's, 1964.

Burma: Asiatic Researches, vol. 6. In Harold T. Wilkins, *Mysteries of Ancient South America*. Kempton, Ill.: Adventures Unlimited, 2000.

Casson, Lionel "New Light on Ancient Rigging and Boat-building." *American Neptune*, vol. 1, no. 14 (1964).

———. *Ships and Seamanship of the Ancient World*. London: Gollancz, 1971.

Coles, J. M., and A. F. Harding. *The Bronze Age in Europe*. London: Thames and Hudson, 1979.

Deuel, Leo. *Memoirs of Heinrich Schliemann*. New York: Harper and Row, 1977.

Doria, Charles, and Harris Lenowitz. *Origins: Creation Texts from the Ancient Mediterranean*. New York: Doubleday, 1976.

Graves, Robert. *The Greek Myths*. New York: Brazilier, 1960.

Gurney, O. R. *The Hittites*. New York: Malcoms, 1952.

Hutchinson, R. W. *Prehistoric Crete*. Baltimore: Penguin, 1968.

MacKenzie, Donald A. *Crete and Pre-Hellenic Myths and Legends*. London: Senate Press, 1912.

MacQueen, J. G. *The Hittites and Their Contemporaries in Asia Minor*. London: Richter, 1975.

Mylonas, G. E. *Mycenae and the Mycenaean Age*. Princeton, N.J.: Princeton Publishers, 1966.

Ovid, *Metamorphoses*. Translated by R. J. Littlejohn. London: Beckwith, 1959.

Page, D. *History and the Homeric Iliad*. Berkeley, Calif.: Berkeley, 1959.

Schliemann, Heinrich. *Ilios*. New York: Arno, 1976.

Simpson, R. H. *Mycenaean Greece*. Park Ridge N.J.: Noyes, 1981.

Steinhoff, George, and Kenneth Seele. *When Egypt Ruled the East*. Chicago: University of Chicago Press, 1957.

Virgil. *The Aeneid*. Translated by W. F. Jackson Knight. London: Penguin, 1956.

Chapter 2: The Penalty of Empire

Bass, George Cape. *Gelidonya: A Bronze Age Shipwreck*. New York: American Philosophical Society, 1967.

Brestead, James. *Ancient Records of Egypt: The Historical Documents*, vol. 4. Chicago: Oriental Institute Press, 1906.

Casson, Lionel. *Ships and Seamanship of the Ancient World*. London: Gollancz, 1971.

Edey, Maitland A. *The Sea Traders*. New York: Time-Life Books, 1974.

Edgerton W. F., and J. Wilson. *Historical Records of Ramses III: The Text of Medinet Habu*. Chicago: University of Chicago Press, 1964.

Homer. *The Iliad*. Translated by W. Schmidt. London: Standford House, 1960.

Homer. *The Odyssey*. Translated by Dennis Lindzwerg. Chicago: Regnerey, 1963.

Lehmann, Johannes. *The Hittites: People of a Thousand Gods*. New York: Viking, 1977.

Morrison, D. J. *The Empire Builders*. New York: Time-Life Books, 1980.

Murname, W. F. *United with Eternity: A Concise Guide to the Monuments of Medinet Habu*. Chicago: University of Chicago Press, 1980.

Page, D. *History of the Homeric Iliad*. Berkeley, Calif.: Berkeley, 1959.

Qunitus of Smyrna. *The Little Iliad*. Translated by Westbrook Murphy. New York: Macmillan, 1960.

Roebuck, Carl. *The World of Ancient Times*. New York: Scribner's, 1966.

Ryan, Walter. *Bronze Age Troy*. London: MacVey, 1959.

Sanders, N. K. *The Sea Peoples, Warriors of the Ancient Mediterranean*. London: Thames and Hudson, 1973.

Taylour, William. *The Mycenaeans*. New York: Praeger, 1958.

Thompson, George. *The Prehistoric Aegean*. New York: Lawrence and Wishart, 1954.

Virgil. *The Aeneid*. Translated by W. F. Jackson Knight. London: Penguin, 1956.

Wilkins, Harold T. *Mysteries of Ancient South America*. Kempton, Ill.: Adventures Unlimited, 2000.

Wyse, Elizabeth, ed. *Past Worlds: The Times Atlas of Archaeology*. New York: Crescent, 1995.

Chapter 3: The Four Cataclysms

Abbot, Patrick L. *Natural Disasters*. Boston: McGraw-Hill, 2004.

Caroli, Kenneth. Personal correspondence with the author, summer 2003.

Chang, Kwang-chih. *Shang Civilization*. New York: Macmillan, 1980.

Childress, David Hatcher. *Lost Cities of China, Central Asia and India*. Kempton, Ill.: Adventures Unlimited, 1985.

Corliss, William R. *Ancient Structures*. Glen Arm, Md.: Sourcebook Project, 2001.

Drews, Robert. *The End of the Bronze Age*. Princeton, N.J.: Princeton University Press, 1993.

Fong, Wen, ed. *The Great Bronze Age of China*. New York: Macmillan, 1980.

Godwin, David. *Godwin's Cabbalistic Encyclopedia*. St. Paul, Minn.: Llewellyn, 1991.

Goldsmith, Donald. *Nemesis, the Death-Star and Other Theories of Mass-Extinction*. New York: Walker, 1985.

Hewitt, R. *From Earthquake, Fire, and Flood*. London: Scientific Book Club, 1958.

Joseph, Frank. *The Destruction of Atlantis*. Rochester, Vt.: Bear and Company, 2002.

Knight, Christopher, and Robert Lomas. *Uriel's Machine*, Rockport, Mass.: Fair Winds, 1999.

Mifsud, Anton. *Malta: Echoes of Plato's Island*. Valleta, Malta: A. C. Aquilina, 2001.

The Oera Linda Bok. Translated by Howard Schnell. London: Truebner, 1876.

Oppenheimer, Robert. *Eden of the East*. New York: Orion, 1999.

Palmer, Trevor, and Mark E. Bailey, eds. *Natural Catastrophes During Bronze Age Civilizations: Archaeological, Geological, Astronomical, and Cultural Perspectives*. Oxford: Archaeo Press, 1988.

Plato. *The Dialogues*. Translated by William Taylor. London: University of London Press, 1902.

Rosi, Mauro. *Volcanoes*. Ontario: Firefly, 2003.

Schoch, Robert M. *Voices of the Rocks*. New York: Harmony Books, 1999.

Scrutton, Robert J. *The Other Atlantis*. London: Daniel, 1977.

Wright, Karen. "Empires in the Dust: Collapse of Bronze Age Cultures in 2000 B.C.E.," *Discover*, vol. 12, no. 59 (March 1998).

Xu, H. Mike. *Origin of the Olmec Civilization*. Edmond, Okla.: University of Central Oklahoma Press, 1996.

Chapter 4: Atlanteans into Egypt

Aldred, Cyril. *The Egyptians*. New York: Praeger, 1962.

Baines, John, and Jaromir Malek. *Atlas of Ancient Egypt*. Oxford: Oxford University Press, 1980.

Barrett, Clive. *The Egyptian Gods and Goddesses*. London: Aquarian Press, 1992.

Bernal, Martin. *Black Athena*. New Brunswick, N.J.: Rutgers University Press, 1987.

Boylan, Patrick. *Thoth, the Hermes of Egypt*. Oxford: Oxford University Press, 1922.

Brestead, James. *A History of Egypt*. New York: Scribner's, 1909.

Budge, E. A. Wallis. *Ancient Egyptian Amulets and Talismans*. New York: University Books, 1968.

Clark, R. T. Rundle. *Myth and Symbol in Ancient Egypt*. London: Thames and Hudson, 1959.

Emery, Walter B. *Archaic Egypt: Culture and Civilization in Egypt Five Thousand Years Ago*. London: Penguin, 1961.

Heyerdahl, Thor. *Prehistoric Man across the Ocean*. New York: Doubleday, 1971.

Imel, Martha Ann, and Dorothy Myers. *Goddesses in World Mythology: A Biographical Dictionary*. London: Oxford University Press, 1993.

Ions, Veronica. *Egyptian Mythology*. London: Hamlyn, 1968.

Joseph, Frank. *The Destruction of Atlantis*. Rochester, Vt.: Bear and Company, 2002.

Kronkheit, C. A. *A Dictionary of Ancient Egyptian Terms*. Chicago: University of Chicago Press, 1929.

Lauton, Ian, and Chris Ogilvie-Herald. *Giza: The Truth*. Montpelier, Vt.: Invisible Cities, 2001.

Leonard, R. Cedric. *The Quest for Atlantis*. New York: Manor, 1979.

Leonard, R. *Library of History*. London: Ratcliff, 1904.

Mercatante, Anthony S. *Who's Who in Egyptian Mythology*. New York: Clarkson N. Potter, 1978.

Mercer, A. B. Samuel. *Horus, the Royal God of Egypt*. Cambridge, Mass.: Society of Oriental Research, 1960.

Petrie, W. M. Flinders. *A History of Egypt*. Vol. 3, *The IX and XX Dynasties*. London: Methuen, 1896.

Plato. *The Dialogues*. Translated by William Taylor. London: University of London Press, 1902.

Steinhoff, George, and Kenneth Seele. *When Egypt Ruled the East*. Chicago: University of Chicago Press, 1957.

West, John Anthony. *The Serpent in the Sky*. New York: Harper and Row, 1979.

Chapter 5: Noah Was Atlantean

Campbell, Joseph. *The Masks of God*. New York: Macmillan, 1961.

Emery, W. B. *Archaic Egypt*. London: Pelican, 1961.

The Epic of Gilgamesh. Translated by N.K. Sandars. Harmondsworth, Middlesex, U.K.: Penguin, 1970.

Filby, F. A. *The Flood Reconsidered*. London: Pickering, 1970.

Gaster, Theodore H. *Myth, Legend and Custom in the Old Testament*. New York: Harper and Row, 1969.

Graves, Robert, and Raphael Patai. *Hebrew Myths: The Book of Genesis*. New York: Greenwich House, 1964.

Heidel, A. *The Babylonian Genesis*. Chicago: University of Chicago Press, 1938.

Hooke, S. H. *Babylonian and Assyrian Religion*. New York: Hutchinson's University Library, 1953.

Imel, Martha Ann, and Dorothy Myers Imel. *Goddesses in World Mythology: A Biographical Dictionary*. Oxford: Oxford University Press, 1993.

Keller, Werner. *The Bible as History*. London: Hodder and Stoughton, 1970.

King, Leonard. *Legends of Babylon and Egypt in Relation to Hebrew Tradition*. London: Oxford University Press, 1918.

Kramer, Noah. *The Sumerians*. Chicago: University of Chicago Press, 1969.

MacKenzie, Donald A. *Mythology of the Babylonian People*. London: Bracken, 1996.

Mallowan, M. E. L. *Early Mesopotamia and Iran*. New York: McGraw Hill, 1965.

McKerrell, H. "Seafaring Merchants of Ur?" *Antiquity* 51, no. 21 (1977).

Renfrew, Alfred M. *The Flood*. St. Louis, Mo.: Concordia, 1951.

Sanderson, Stuart. *Babylon*. New York: Praeger, 1958.

Spence, Lewis. *Myths and Legends of Babylon and Assyria*. London: George G. Harrap, 1916.

Chapter 6: The Greeks Knew It All

Apollonius Rhodius. *The Argonautica*. Translated by R. C. Seaton. London: Heinemann, 1955.

Graves, Robert. *The Greek Myths,* vol. 2. New York: Brazilier, 1961.

Hesiod. *The Complete Hesiod*. Translated by Westbrook Murphy. New York: Macmillan, 1958.

Imel, Martha Ann, and Dorothy Myers Imel. *Goddesses in World Mythology: A Biographical Dictionary*. Oxford: Oxford University Press, 1993.

Kerényi, C. *The Gods of the Greeks*. Translated by Norman Cameron. New York: Grove, 1960.

Markale, Jean. *The Templar Treasure at Gisors*. Rochester, Vt.: Inner Traditions, 2003.

McEvedy, Colin. *The Penguin Atlas of Ancient History*. New York: Penguin, 1980.

Morford, Mark P. O., and Robert J. Lenardon. *Classical Mythology*. New York: Longman, 1971.

Taylor, Frank. *The World of the Greeks and Romans*. New York: Doubleday, 1959.

Taylour, William. *The Mycenaeans*. New York: Praeger, 1958.

Zangerer, Eberhard. *The Flood from Heaven*. New York: William Morrow and Company, 1992.

Chapter 7: Atlanteans across the Sahara

Briggs, Cabot. *The Stone Age Races of Northwest Africa*. London: Oxford University Press, 1973.

Daniel, Glyn. *The Illustrated Encyclopedia of Archaeology*. New York: Crowell, 1977.

de Prorok, Byron. *In Quest of Lost Worlds*. Kempton, Ill.: Adventures Unlimited, 2001.

Fitzgerald, L. J. *The Great Migration*. London: Skeffington, 1933.

Hope, Murray. *Atlantis*. New York: Western Tradition Books, 1970.

Plato. *The Dialogues*. Translated by William Taylor. London: University of London Press, 1902.

Porch, Douglas. *The Conquest of the Sahara*. New York: Knopf, 1984.

Renfrew, Colin, ed. *Past Worlds: The Times Atlas of Archaeology*. Avenel, N.J.: Crescent, 1995.

Spence, Lewis. *The History of Atlantis*. New York: Bell, 1968.

Zimmerman, J. E. *Dictionary of Classical Mythology*. New York: Bantam, 1971.

Chapter 8: Amazons versus Atlantis

Bord, Colin, and Janet Bord. *Mysterious Britain*. St. Albans, U.K.: Granada, 1975.

Conrad, J. R. *The Horn and the Sword: The History of the Bull as a Symbol of Power and Fertility*. New York: Dutton, 1957.

Davies, Nigel. *The Ancient Kingdoms of Mexico*. London: Penguin, 1982.

de Acuna, Cristovel. *Expeditions into the Valley of the Amazons*. Translated by C. R. Markham. London: Hakluyt Society, 1859.

de Prorok, Byron. *In Quest of Lost Worlds*. Kempton, Ill.: Adventures Unlimited, 2001.

Diodorus, Siculus. *The Geography*. Translated by C. H. Oldfather. London: Heinemann, 1968.

Doria, Charles, and Harris Lenowitz. *Origins: Creation Texts from the Ancient Mediterranean*. New York: Doubleday, 1976.

Emery, W. B. *Archaic Egypt.* London: Pelican, 1961.

Graves, Robert. *The White Goddess.* New York: Creative Age, 1948.

Herodotus. *The Histories.* Translated by Aubrey de Selincourt. Baltimore: Penguin, 1954.

Hood, Sinclair. *The Minoans, Crete in the Bronze Age.* London: Thames and Hudson, 1971.

Howey, M. O. *The Horse in Myth and Magic.* London: Ashington, 1972.

Imel, Martha Ann, and Dorothy Myers Imel. *Goddesses in World Mythology: A Biographical Dictionary.* Oxford: Oxford University Press, 1993.

Petrie, Flinders. "The Hill Figures of England." Paper presented to the Royal Institute, London, 1930.

Rothery, G. C. *The Amazons in Antiquity and Modern Times.* London: Griffiths, 1910.

Spence, Lewis. *The Occult Sciences in Atlantis.* London: Rider and Company, 1942.

Willets, R. F. *Cretan Cults and Festivals.* London: Routledge and Keagan Paul, 1962.

Chapter 9: Gone to Hades

Aelian. *The Nature of Animals.* Translated by A. Graubart. Lawrence, Kans.: University of Kansas Press, 1971.

Espinosa, Alonsode. *The Guanches of Tenerife.* Translated by Sir Clements Markham. London: Longmans, 1891.

Gambier, J. D. "People of the Canary Islands." *Smithsonian Institution Report* 31, no. 4 (June 1903): 111.

Gambier, J. W. *The History of the Discovery and Conquest of the Canary Islands.* London: Antiquary, 1894.

Hooten, Ernest. *The Ancient Inhabitants of the Canary Islands.* Cambridge, Mass.: Harvard University Press, 1915.

Howey, M. O. *The Cults of the Dog.* London: Ashington, 1972.

Mercer, John. *Fuerteventura of the Canary Islands.* Mechanicsburg, Pa.: Stackpole, 1973.

Myhill, Henry. *The Canary Islands.* London: Faber and Faber, 1968.

Reid, Howard. *In Search of the Immortals.* New York: St. Martin's, 1999.

Roessler, Otto. *Die Weltsaeule in Glauben und Gebrauch der Kanarier.* Leipzig: Hermann Huehne Verlag, 1941.

Woelfel, Dietrich. *Die Kanarischen Inseln: Die Westafrikanische Hochkulturen und das Mittelmeer.* Bamberg, Germany: West-Rheinlichen Verlag, 1950.

Yeoward, Eileen. *The Canary Islands.* London: Stockwell, 1975.

Chapter 10: Children of Atlantis

Arribas, A. *The Iberians.* New York: Praeger, 1958.

Bloch, Raymond. *The Ancient Civilization of the Etruscans.* Geneva, Switzerland: Nagel, 1969.

————. *The Etruscans.* New York: Praeger, 1961.

Caroli, Kenneth. Personal correspondence with the author. Summer 2003.

Hencken, Hugh. *Tarquinia and Etruscan Origins.* New York: Praeger, 1967.

MacKendrick, Paul. *The Iberian Stones Speak.* New York: Funk and Wagnalls, 1969.

Massa, Aldo. *The World of the Etruscans.* Geneva: Editions Minerva, 1973.

Ogilvie, R. M. *Early Rome and the Estruscans.* New York: Humanities Press, 1976.

Pallottino, M. *The Etruscans.* New York: Harper and Row, 1978.

Pardo, A. *The World of Ancient Spain.* Geneva: Minerva, 1976.

Plato. *The Dialogues.* Translated by William Taylor. London: University of London Press, 1902.

Savory, H. N. *Spain and Portugal.* New York: Praeger, 1968.

Whishaw, Elena Maria. *Atlantis in Spain.* Kempton, Ill.: Adventures Unlimited, 1994.

Chapter 11: Atlantean Kings for Ireland and Wales

Bonwick, James. *Irish Druids and the Old Irish Religions.* London: Dorset, 1986.

Darah, John. *The Real Camelot.* London: Thames and Hudson, 1981.

de Jubainville, Arbois. *Irish Myth.* Dublin: Haversock House, 1902.

Fox, Aileen. *Southwest England.* New York: Praeger, 1962.

Geoffrey of Monmouth. *The History of the Kings of Britain.* Translated by Lewis Thorpe. London: Penguin, 1969.

Howard, Robert E. "The Thing in the Crypt." In *The Collected Short Stories of Robert E. Howard.* New York: Anderson House, 1962.

Hoyle, Fred. *On Stonehenge.* London: Heinemann, 1977.

Imel, Martha Ann, and Dorothy Myers Imel. *Goddesses in World Mythology: A Biographical Dictionary.* Oxford: Oxford University Press, 1993.

MacCana, Prosinas. *Celtic Mythology.* London: Hamlyn, 1970.

O'Brien, Henry. *The Round Towers of Atlantis.* Kempton, Ill.: Adventures Unlimited, 2002.

O'Kelly, Claire. *New Grange.* Cork: Houston Printers, 1973.

Palmer, Trevor, and Mark E. Bailey, eds. *Natural Catastrophes During Bronze Age Civilizations: Archaeological, Geological, Astronomical, and Cultural Perspectives.* Oxford: Archaeo Press, 1998.

Piggott, Stuart. *The Druids.* New York: Praeger, 1968.

Powell, T. G. E. *The Celts.* New York: Praeger, 1959.

Roberts, Anthony. *Atlantean Traditions in Ancient Britain.* London: Rider, 1975.

Sharkey, John. *Celtic Mysteries: The Ancient Religion.* London: Thames and Hudson, 1970.

Spence, Lewis. *The History and Origin of Druidism.* Yorkshire, U.K.: E. P. Publishers, 1976.

————. *The Problem of Atlantis.* New York: University, 1965.

Tolstoy, Matthew. *The Quest for Merlin.* London: Glendower, 1985.

Chapter 12: How the Bad Days Came

Allardice, Pamela. *Myths, Gods and Fantasy: A Sourcebook*. New York: Avery, 1991.

Blachette, Walther. *Das Buch der Deutscher Sinnzeichen*. Munich: Fritz Ehler Verlag, 1941.

Brogger, A. E. *The Viking World*. New York: Grosset and Dunlap, 1959.

Colum, Padraic. *Nordic Gods and Heroes*. New York: Dover, 1996.

Crossley-Holland, Kevin. *The Norse Myths*. New York: Pantheon, 1980.

Davidson, Ellis H. R. *Gods and Myths of Northern Europe*. New York: Penguin, 1982.

————. *Pagan Scandinavia*. New York: Praeger, 1963.

————. *Scandinavian Mythology*. New York: Bedricks, 1988.

DuChalliu, Paul B. *The Viking Age: The Early History, Manners and Customs of the Ancestors of the English-Speaking Nations*. London: Murray, 1889.

Gimbutas, Marija. *The Civilization of the Goddess: The World of Old Europe*. San Francisco: HarperSanFrancisco, 1991.

————. *The Language of the Goddess*. San Francisco: HarperSanFrancisco, 1989.

————. *The Living Goddesses*. Berkeley, Calif.: University of California Press, 1999.

Green, Roger Lancelyn. *Myths of the Norsemen*. New York: Penguin, 1984.

Grimm, Jacob. *Teutonic Mythology*. 4 vols. Translated by Steven Stallybrass. New York: Dover, 1966.

Imel, Martha Ann, and Dorothy Myers Imel. *Goddesses in World Mythology: A Biographical Dictionary*. Oxford: Oxford University Press, 1993.

Jones, Gwyn. *A History of the Vikings*. New York: Oxford University Press, 1984.

Kehoe, Alice B. "Vestiges of the Natural History of Archaelolgy." In *Across Before Columbus?* Edgecomb, Maine: NEARA, 1998.

Leach, Maria, Editor. *Funk and Wagnalls Dictionary of Folklore, Mythology and Legend*. New York: HarperCollins, 1984.

The Oera Linda Bok. Translated by Howard Schnell. London: Truebner, 1876.

Scrutton, Robert J. *The Other Atlantis*. London: Daniel, 1977.

Spence, Lewis. *The History of Atlantis*. New York: Bell, 1958.

Spengler, Oswald. *The Decline of the West*. New York: Random House, 1962.

Sturlusson, Snorri. *The Prose Edda*. Translated by Jean I. Young. Berkeley, Calif.: University of California Press, 1954.

Walker, Barbara G. *The Woman's Encyclopedia of Myths and Secrets*. San Francisco: HarperSanFrancisco, 1983.

Chapter 13: Native Americans Remember Atlantis

Armstrong, R. A. *The Mythology of All Races*. New York: Cooper Square, 1964.

Beckwith, Hiram W. *The Illinois and Indiana Indians*. Chicago: Fergus Printing, 1884.

Blackett, W. S. *The Lost History of America*. London: Truebner, 1883.

Catlin, George. *Illustrations of the Manners, Customs, and Conditions of the North American Indians*. New York: Dover, 1970.

Childress, David Hatcher. *Lost Cities of North and Central America*. Kempton, Ill.: Adventures Unlimited, 1992.

Ford, James, and Clarence Webb. *Anthropological Papers of the American Museum of Natural History* 46, 1956.

Hennes, D. *The American Aborigines: Their Origins and Antiquity*. New York: Cooper Square, 1963.

Hodge, F. W. *The Handbook of the American Indians North of Mexico*. 30 volumes. Washington, D.C.: Bulletins of the Bureau of American Ethnology, 1907.

Marriott, Alice, and Carol K. Rachlin. *American Indian Mythology*. New York: New American Library, 1968.

Peithmar, Irwin M. *Echoes of the Red Man*. New York: Expectation Press, 1955.

Spence, Lewis. *Atlantis in America*. New York: Bell, 1975.

Tyler, H. A. *Pueblo Gods and Myths*. Norman Okla.: University of Oklahoma Press, 1964.

van Over, R. *Sun Songs: Creation Myths from around the World*. New York: New American Library, 1980.

Waters, Frank. *The Book of the Hopi*. New York: Viking, 1963.

Chapter 14: Feathered Serpents from Sunken Cities

Brundage, Henry. *Aztec Myth and Symbol*. New York: Doubleday, 1960.

Burland, C. A., and Werner Forman. *Feathered Serpent and Smoking Mirror*. New York: Putnam, 1975.

Burland, C. A. *The Fifth Sun: Aztec Gods, Aztec World*. Austin: University of Texas Press, 1983.

———. *The Gods of Mexico*. London: Eyre and Spottiswoode, 1970.

Boswick, Walter. *Scottish Lore*. London: Strath-Gordon, 1924.

Coryn, J. H., trans. *The Prophet*. Lima, Ohio: Antioch Press, 1931.

Forman, Werner. *Aztec Gods and Goddesses*. London: Thames and Hudson, 1968.

Frazer, J. G. *The Golden Bough*. London: Macmillan, 1922.

Hendrick. *Quetzalcoatl*. Carbondale, Ill.: Southern Illinois University Press, 1967.

Irwin, Constance. *Fair Gods and Stone Faces*. New York: St. Martin's, 1963.

Nutall, Zelia. *The Fundamental Principles of Old and New World Civilizations*. Cambridge, Mass.: Peabody Museum, Harvard University, 1900.

Savoy, Gene. *On the Trail of the Feathered Serpent*. New York: Bobbs-Merrill, 1974.

Spence, Lewis. *Atlantis in America*. New York: Bell, 1975.

Spinden, Henry. *Mesoamerican Myth*. New York: Roundtree, 1947.

van Over, R. *Sun Songs: Creation Myths from around the World*. New York: New American Library, 1980.

Chapter 15: The Greater Arrival from Atlantis

Borges, Jorge Luis. *Atlas of the Mountain*. New York: Praeger, 1980.

Budge, E. A. Wallis. *The Egyptian Book of the Dead*. New York: Harcourt, 1907.

Burland, C. A. *The Gods of Mexico*. London: Eyre and Spottiswoode, 1970.

Coe, Michael D. *Mexico*. New York: Praeger, 1966.

Corliss, William R. *Ancient Structures*. Glen Arm, Md.: Sourcebook Project, 2001.

Davies, Nigel. *The Ancient Kingdoms of Mexico*. London: Penguin, 1982.

de Landa, Friar Diego. *Yucatán before and after the Conquest* (Relacion de las Cosas de Yucatán). New York: Dover, 1977.

del Castillo, Bernal Diaz. *The True History of the Conquest of New Spain*. Translated by Alfred P. Maudslay. London: Hakluyt Society, 1910.

Donnelly, Ignatius. *Atlantis: The Antediluvian World*. New York: Harpers, 1882.

Gallenkamp, Charles. *Maya*. London: Muller, 1960.

Jairazbhoy, R. A. *Ramses III, Father of America*. London: Karnak, 1992.

Jakeman, M. Wells. *The Origin and History of the Mayas*. Los Angeles: Research Publishing, 1945.

Lindsay, Richard. *The Zodiac*. London: Twelve Trees Press, 1969.

Morley, Sylvanus. *The Ancient Maya*. California: Stanford University Press, 1946.

The Popol Vuh. Translated by Dennis Tedlock. New York: Simon and Schuster, 1985.

Sahagun. *Florentine Codex: General History of the Things of New Spain*. Translated by A. J. O. Anderson and C. E. Dibble. New Mexico: Worther, 1963.

Thompson, Gunnar. *American Discovery*. Seattle, Wash.: Argonauts Misty Isles Press, 1994.

Vaillant, George C. *Aztecs of Mexico*. New York: Doubleday, 1962.

Xu, H. Mike. *Origin of the Olmec Civilization*. Edmond, Okla.: University of Central Oklahoma Press, 1996.

Chapter 16: The Lesser Arrival of Survivors

Banincourt, Michael. *Five Letters of Cortez to the Emperor*. New York: Norton, 1962.

Brundage, Henry. *Aztec Myth and Symbol*. New York: Doubleday, 1960.

Campbell, Joseph. *The Masks of God*. New York: Macmillan, 1961.

Cavendish, Richard, and Brian Innes. *Man, Myth and Magic: The Illustrated Encyclopedia of Mythology, Religion, and the Unknown*. New York: M. Cavendish, 1997.

Childress, David Hatcher. *Lost Cities and Ancient Civilizations of North and Central America*. Kempton, Ill.: Adventures Unlimited, 1992.

DeCamp, L. Sprague. *Lost Civilizations*. New York: Dover, 1970.

Donnelly, Ignatius. *Atlantis, the Antedilluvian World*. New York: Harper, 1882.

Duran, Fray Diego. *Book of the Gods and the Rites of the Ancient Calendar*. Translated by Fernando Horcasitas and Doris Heyden. Norman, Okla.: University of Oklahoma Press, 1971.

Forman, Werner. *Aztec Gods and Goddesses*. London: Thames and Hudson, 1968.

Gleadow, William. *Roots of Astrology*. London: Carmichael, 1961.

Heyerdahl, Thor. *The Ra Expeditions*. New York: Doubleday, 1972.

Hooten, Ernest. *The Ancient Inhabitants of the Canary Islands*. Cambridge, Mass.: Harvard University Press, 1904.

Hunter, Bruce C. *A Guide to Ancient Mexican Ruins*. Norman, Okla.: University of Oklahoma Press, 1978.

Irwin, Constance. *Fair Gods and Stone Faces*. New York: St. Martin's, 1963.

Jairazbhoy, R. A. *Ramses III, Father of America*. London: Karnak, 1992.

Jakeman, M. Wells. *The Origin and History of the Mayas*. Los Angeles: Research Publishing, 1957.

Joseph, Frank. *Destruction of Atlantis*. Rochester, Vt.: Bear and Company, 2002.

McNice, Alice. *Astrology*. New York: Macmillan, 1955.

Menninger, Ralph. *Numbers in Myth and Magic*. New York: Holloway House, 1949.

Moreley, S. *The Ancient Maya*. Stanford, Calif.: Stanford University Press, 1946.

Mulhall, Marion M. *Beginnings or Glimpses of Vanished Civilizations*. New York: Longmans and Green, 1911.

Nicholson, I. *Mexican and Central American Mythology*. London: Hamlyn, 1967.

Nutall, Zelia. *Fundamental Principles of Old and New World Civilizations*. Cambridge, Mass.: Peabody Museum, Harvard University, 1900.

Oppenheimer, Stephen. *Eden of the East*. New York: Orion, 1999.

Prescott, William. *The Conquest of Mexico*. New York: Julian Messner, 1950.

Rowe, J. H. *Diffusion and Archaeology*. New York: Asherwood, 1966.

Stacy-Judd, Robert B. *Atlantis, Mother of Empires*. Kempton, Ill.: Adventures Unlimited, 1999.

Thompson, Gunnar. *American Discovery: The Real Story*. Seattle: Argonauts Misty Isles Press, 1994.

Thompson, J. Eric. *The Rise and Fall of Maya Civilization*. Norman, Okla.: University of Oklahoma Press, 1954.

Tompkins, Peter. *Secrets of the Mexican Pyramids*. New York: Harper and Row, 1970.

Tozzer, Alfred M. *A Maya Grammar*. New York: Dover, 1978.

von Hagen, Victor. *Ancient Sun Kingdoms of the Americas*. London: Panther, 1967.

Wicke, R. *Olmec*. Tucson: University of Arizona Press, 1971.

Chapter 17: Atlantean Sons of the Sun

Bingham, Hiram. *Lost City of the Incas*. New York: Scribner's, 1939.

Bushnell, G. H. S. *Peru*. New York: Praeger, 1967.

Childress, David Hatcher. *Lost Cities and Ancient Mysteries of South America*. Kempton, Ill.: Adventures Unlimited, 1986.

de Onis, Harriet, trans. *The Incas of Pedro de Cieza de Leon*. Norman, Okla.: University of Oklahoma Press, 1959.

Engl, Lieselotte, and Theo Engl. *Twilight of Ancient Peru*. New York: McGraw-Hill, 1969.

Furgeson, James. *Rude Stone Monuments*. London: Rudder, 1872.

Gilman, Henry. *Ancient Man in Michigan*. Chicago: Regnery, 1898.

Grimal, Pierre. *Larousse World Mythology*. New York: Putnam, 1958.

Heyerdahl, Thor. *The Ra Expeditions*. New York: Doubleday, 1972.

Homet, William. *Mysteries of the Amazon*. New York: Ryder, 1961.

Lanning, Edward P. *Peru before the Incas*. New Jersey: Prentice-Hall, 1967.

Leicht, Hermann. *Pre-Inca Art and Culture*. New York: Orion, 1960.

Metraux, Alfred. *The History of the Incas*. New York: Penteon, 1969.

Moseley, Michael E. *The Incas and Their Ancestors*. London: Thames and Hudson, 1994.

Osborne, Harold. *South American Mythology*. London: Hamlyn, 1970.

Prescott, William. *The Conquest of Peru*. New York: Meissner, 1952.

Editors of *Readers' Digest*. *Mysteries of the Ancient Americans*. New York: Readers Digest, 1986.

Spence, Lewis. *Atlantis in America*. New York: Bell, 1975.

Wilkins, Hariold T. *Ancient Mysteries of South America*. Kempton, Ill.: Adventures Unlimited Press, 2000.

Chapter 18: Aftermath

Plato. *The Dialogues*. Translated by William Taylor. London: University of London Press, 1902.

BOOKS OF RELATED INTEREST

The Destruction of Atlantis
Compelling Evidence of the Sudden Fall of the Legendary Civilization
by Frank Joseph

Atlantis and the Ten Plagues of Egypt
The Secret History Hidden in the Valley of the Kings
by Graham Phillips

The Genesis Race
Our Extraterrestrial DNA and the True Origins of the Species
by Will Hart

The 12th Planet
by Zecharia Sitchin

From the Ashes of Angels
The Forbidden Legacy of a Fallen Race
by Andrew Collins

Maya Cosmogenesis 2012
The True Meaning of the Maya Calendar End-Date
by John Major Jenkins

Genesis of the Cosmos
The Ancient Science of Continuous Creation
by Paul A. LaViolette, Ph.D.

Voyage to Atlantis
The Discovery of a Legendary Land
by James W. Mavor, Jr.

Inner Traditions • Bear & Company
P.O. Box 388
Rochester, VT 05767
1-800-246-8648
www.InnerTraditions.com

Or contact your local bookseller